LYNCHED

Christine Carroll

TJ Press

First published in paperback by
True Jeopardy Press (London, UK) in 2020

authorccarroll@yahoo.com

ISBN 9781838024802

A CIP record for this publication
may be found with the British Library

For my father, RIP

Chapter One

It was the fifth day of June 1996 when the world, which had previously been full of light and hope, turned irrevocably black and bleak. It was a day, indelibly etched on my brain, when I not only could have lost my life but was also left with a lifelong, seemingly insurmountable struggle and challenge; an enduring protracted grind and labour I would never have thought would have befallen me. It was a time when I had to draw upon all my life's positive experiences and those intermittent adverse predicaments I overcame to wilfully see me through. With whatever will power was bestowed on me I fought with all my might for life, not just life in itself, but one that would be tolerable and would still give me some enjoyment. I wished for contentment and the ability to continue to experience episodes of achievement that so far marked a highly varied and exciting existence.

They say adversity makes one stronger but I would gladly turn back the clock to when I turned forty years of age and was at the peak of my career when all my education, experiences and achievements had culminated in a life I thought could not possibly get any better. I was looking forward to personal happiness, a continuing fulfilling career and the chance to reap the rewards I had always strived for. However, in one fell swoop my well-laid aspirations were permanently usurped. I did not realise then that everything I had learned, the situations that had given me confidence and the ability to handle complex situations, would all have to be drawn upon to overcome a horrid and unnatural casualty.

I often wondered whether there is such a thing as fate. Although I always snatched up opportunities and made things happen I, nevertheless, frequently predicted events and normally always relied on my gut instincts. I even made business decisions throughout my career based on premonition, all else being equal, and the choices I made usually panned out well. But the one time when I went completely against the grain my decision sealed my fate.

Like in a twisted fairy-tale, the seed was sown on the morning of the 18th of April 1996, when my eyes flickered open to stillness in my bedroom at 7 a.m. I grimaced as I felt an ache in my right shoulder and thought I had caught a draught from a fly window I had left open overnight. Regardless of the discomfort, it was time to shake off the integument of sleep and prepare myself for another hectic day of gruelling meetings and decision-making that ran the gamut of all my responsibilities at work. After emitting a few querulous groans, I perked up.

At the time, I was thirty-nine years old working as a senior executive manager in the provision of healthcare to adults and children with intellectual difficulties and mental health issues, since 1991, a position that involved longs hours and very few breaks. Although it was extremely busy and highly pressurised, I thoroughly enjoyed my work. During my career, I had been employed by American global companies and was selected to set up a new division in St. James's Park in London for a subsidiary of 3M Corporation, while living in South Kensington. I also had very rewarding employment with United International Pictures PLC.

After living in Minnesota in the US for six years, I became corporate director of a large ambulatory surgery centre in Nashville, where I established fledgeling on-line satellite clinics across Tennessee. However, I felt that strong pull towards returning to Ireland and my family. At this particular stage in my life, I felt tremendous satisfaction and fulfilment in making some positive differences, albeit indirectly, to those less fortunate. However, even in the corporate sector I found my work very challenging and ultimately satisfying and rewarding. I had always been very comfortable in leadership roles.

On that particular morning, the 18th of April, there was no room for giving more than a cursory acknowledgement to my shoulder when so much had to be accomplished. Off I went to work without much ado, as I had a very busy agenda that day.

I felt a weary and exhaustive tiredness on retiring to bed that night and as dawn broke several hours later I roused feeling dreadfully breathless. Each time I inhaled and exhaled, I experienced a sharp, stabbing pain in the front and back of my chest; the severity of the ache I had experienced the previous morning had increased tenfold. I was rarely ill but that day I felt totally drained and my face appeared very pale and pasty. Thankfully, and unusually, I had planned a half day off from work and I dragged myself into the shower trying at the same time to keep my focus from how I was feeling.

After a morning of intensive meetings with all the staff in one of the clinics in Blackrock, County Dublin, I went into the village to meet a friend for a pre-planned lunch. When I arrived at the restaurant she was already seated and I languorously plopped myself down in the chair opposite her, seizing a breath to explain, 'Anne, I really feel terribly unwell.' I had no appetite and when we left, I noticed there was a walk-in clinic nearby. Dr John Duignan of the Stillorgan Medical Centre, who had been my general practitioner since 1991 and was only a short drive away, would not yet have commenced his afternoon practice. Instead, I succumbed and tentatively entered the clinic.

I thought the doctor on duty, after she gave me a thorough examination, was going to inform me I had come down with a nasty dose of influenza. She administered an antibiotic and firmly told me that it was imperative I go immediately to the nearest medical centre where I could get a chest x-ray taken and that was the Blackrock Clinic, a short distance away.

Having had the x-ray taken I was asked to remain in the changing cubicle. I expected the radiologist to return and tell me to get dressed and leave. Then rather taken aback, she called me for a repeat but being the ultimate optimist, I thought the first one had come out blurred.

I waited again in painful anticipation when suddenly and unexpectedly she reappeared. She urgently announced that she had been trying to contact a thoracic surgeon but to no avail, being a Friday afternoon. Staring at her confused and alarmed and with a questioning look, she informed me I had a spontaneous pneumothorax and must go immediately to the nearest accident and emergency department. Not comprehending I responded, 'Pardon? What on earth is a spontaneous pneumothorax?' She informed me that my right lung had collapsed. I was to say, at the very least, bewildered, and with ponderous equanimity I thought, *Hmm, no wonder I am feeling so ill.*

When I exited the clinic, I delayed under the front door canopy with the x-ray in one hand and my car keys in the other, contemplating my next move. I needed a familiar and reassuring face and someone who could understand my physical distress. Before I contacted one of my closest friends, I decided I would go to see my general practitioner since it was by now mid-afternoon.

Unfortunately, Dr Duignan was not on duty but a locum general practitioner steered me into a treatment room and eased me onto an examination table to rest. I gave her the x-ray and brief report and she briskly went into an adjacent room to contact St. Vincent's University Hospital, also within minutes' driving distance. By then my feeling of trepidation began to abate and I tried to calm my bouts of breathlessness. She hurriedly returned and informed me that the Accident & Emergency department doctors were expecting me.

Once I arrived at the hospital, I was summoned through and a kind-tempered nurse telephoned one of my closest friends who duly hurried to the hospital to give me support. I did not want my partner and family worried and I insisted they not be contacted until I was on a treatment regime. I had willed a sense of calmness around me and I understood once my lung was reinflated the sharp breathless pain would subside. Another set of x-rays was taken and a decision was made by the doctor on duty to insert a tube into my right side and manoeuvre it up through my ribs to my lung so that it would drain overnight into a glass bottle and reinflate.

He told me he would give me a local injection at the insertion point of the tube and proceeded, in rather a nervous and inexperienced manner I thought, to push and feed it up to my lung. Although it was not pleasant, it was by no means a great ordeal. In addition, because I was lying in a supine position, thankfully I could not see what he was doing. When the procedure was completed, I was transferred to the main hospital and by then it was approaching 9:30 p.m.

I was asked upon admission for my private health insurance details and I gave them my Voluntary Health Insurance Company (VHI) membership number. A consultant physician, Dr John Hegarty, assumed responsibility for my care. Finally, the nurses settled me for the night and I expected to wake up with the pain having at least lost its edge and my breathing easier. However, during the night, nothing drained into the stout and ugly-looking bottle and I felt no better.

Dr Hegarty came to see me first thing in the morning and he immediately ordered an x-ray. With efficient speed, I was taken to the radiology department and it was confirmed that my lung was still collapsed. Without delay, a doctor on John Hegarty's team informed me that he believed the existing tube had not been pushed up far enough. He said he would have to insert another one to try to get it right up to the top of the lung. He appeared to be very competent with a reassuring manner and when he asked me if a few trainee doctors could observe the procedure, I unhesitatingly agreed.

As I turned to assume a supine position again, a very young Asian trainee doctor stood directly facing me and as the existing tube was being forcefully pulled out, I saw she was cringing and grimacing. She grasped and held my hand while the replacement was inserted and fed upwards and I was amused because I think it was more for her benefit than for mine. It probably looked far more gruesome than it actually felt. The procedure was performed quickly and with confidence and as the trainees left my bedside, they graciously thanked me.

Over the next couple of days my lung drained and gradually reinflated. When another x-ray confirmed it on the 23rd of April, off home I went and it was wonderful to be able to breathe properly and without pain. I spent a short time recuperating, returned to work at my usual hectic pace and resumed my social activities. As I attended to the productive busyness of my life, I thought my lung collapsing was just a slight blip in the scheme of things. However, I was terribly, terribly wrong and while I was getting on with life, I was completely unaware that fate had not done with me.

Chapter Two

From the moment I left the hospital on the 23rd of April, I was impervious to my health as I am not a natural worrier. I had an additional major project coming up at work on the 30th of May on top of my normal responsibilities. It certainly diluted my time to think.

On the morning of the 30th, I met with my project team to finalise plans for the day, leaving nothing to chance. Immediately afterwards, as I was rushing up a flight of stairs to give an important document to my assistant, I was suddenly struck down as if someone had come up stealthily behind me and forcefully stabbed me in my right upper back. I grabbed onto the curved, ornate bannisters and collapsed onto the stairs and gasped, 'Oh no, my lung has gone again.' I remained there for a while, immobile and splayed out, trying to breathe and hoping the pain would ease.

After some time had passed and still holding on to the bannisters, I gradually made my way, step by slow step, back down to my office, plonked myself down in my chair and rang my assistant who hurried down with water to revive me. Not only was the breathlessness and pain severe but I thought what terrible timing. When I felt a little revived, and instead of going directly to A&E, I was downright foolish enough to continue working until I saw the project successfully through. With the assistance of a number of very dedicated and competent employees who could see I was very traumatised, I managed to somehow keep going until approximately 7 p.m. when I was taken to St. Vincent's Hospital again.

As I lay on a trolley in one of the cubicles in the A&E department after a set of x-rays had been taken, I just hoped I was wrong about my lung collapsing again. I knew, and despaired that there was no other reason for the pain and breathlessness. And, finally, I overheard doctors discussing the results and then that dreaded word: 'pneumothorax'. I silently moaned, Déjà vu, here we go again, another tube up into my lung.

One of the doctors advised me he was going to contact a cardiothoracic surgeon, Mr Vincent Lynch. After an interminably long wait, he returned and explained to me that since my lung had now collapsed a second time, Mr Lynch instructed him to put me on his surgical list for the following day for surgery to seal the lung and I was to fast from midnight. As it was, I had been too busy that day to eat and I was parched and famished. Mr Lynch also told the registrar that since he was going to perform surgery there was no necessity to insert a tube. I was finally given an injection to relieve the pain and transferred to the main public hospital at around midnight. My hunger pangs and thirst continued unabated.

Since the admission's office already had my insurance details, I signed the form authorising Mr Lynch to become my private consultant and he assumed responsibility for my care. My mother arrived the following morning as Edward, my partner of two years, was away until the Sunday. My closest friends and my employer were contacted as well.

The following day, time ticked away and no one gave me any information about my surgery. My mother was as apprehensive as I was. Finally, I approached the nurses but I got the distinct sense that they were not too eager to contact Mr Lynch to find out what the position was in the theatre. I felt there was great hesitancy on their part. By 5 p.m., when I still had no idea what was transpiring, I again asked one of the nurses to check with Mr Lynch about the situation as I was starved and parched by this stage. That was all I asked, a perfectly reasonable and rational question, in my opinion.

Shortly after I had spoken to the nurse, this small white-haired man, who looked around sixty years of age and dressed in green surgical gear, stormed into the ward with a foul look on his face. He loomed over me and began to absolutely bellow at and lambaste me, in what I thought to be a Northern Irish accent, for allegedly calling him up to see me. He spouted out that there were much more serious patients than me, and I just gaped at him he was in such a vitriolic temper. I could not believe what I was being subjected to. He was fuming such that I could see the veins pronounced at his temples. My mother was rendered speechless by his attitude and behaviour.

Even though I am not an aggressive person, I am far from timid and though I was lying there ill and vulnerable I finally decided I had taken quite enough abuse from him. After the initial shock dissipated, I managed to muster up the courage and retorted, 'Now you just hold on a minute, Mr Lynch. Firstly, I did not ask for you to come up here and secondly, I can quite understand that if there are patients with more serious injuries than I have, they obviously have to be treated first.

'All I wanted to know was whether I was going to have surgery or not and if not I could have some tea and toast.' I had not realised then that when one is admitted to hospital the admission's nurse notes one's emotional state and mine read, 'calm and pleasant', but now Mr Lynch had me tormented.

He was quite taken aback and seemed astounded that I had the audacity to stand up to him and I should have retorted my thoughts out loud but not being able to take any further harassment I silently said, *How dare you or anyone else treat a patient in such a horrendous and callous manner. Is there not a charter in this hospital to prevent this sort of barrage of abuse being hurled at a patient?* I understood then that if this was the manner in which he normally treated his patients then I could quite understand why I felt the reluctance on the nurses' part to contact him. All I asked for was information and I had an eerie and terrible feeling that people were afraid of him.

I had attended other surgeons on occasion during my lifetime and had never, even remotely, heard the likes of Mr Lynch or witnessed such rage in a member of the medical profession. Obviously, either he had not received any training in how to relate to patients in a proper and respectful manner or he thought he could behave in whatever intimidating fashion he thought fit. I worried that perhaps he had been getting away with this sort of behaviour for a protracted length of time.

As with all bullies, when they are faced down and stood up to they back off. When he realised I was not going to take any further abominable verbal attacks he calmed himself somewhat. He told me that the theatre was now closed and he would put me on his list for the following Wednesday, the 5th of June, his next scheduled theatre day. That seemed a tediously long time to have to wait with a collapsed lung and I told him, 'Well, if I have to wait and all you are doing is administering medication for the pain, I can just as easily stay in my parents' home and come back in on the following Wednesday morning.' But, of course, I would not have returned; I would have gone to a different surgeon. That was what was going through my mind. Then he told me, 'You can't, you have pneumonia.'

I had been in that hospital since approximately half past seven the previous evening when I arrived in A&E. Absolutely no one had given me this information and I doubt if Mr Lynch would have either until I said I would discharge myself. No wonder I had felt so unwell along with the pain and breathlessness. My gut was screaming at me to get out of that hospital, away from that man but I was just too ill and afraid. Now that I had found out about the pneumonia, it was vital I was administered antibiotics. I thought, what a nightmare, I was now really under Mr Lynch's power and control. I needed care, so what could I do but remain? It turned out to be the only disastrous decision I had ever made in my life. Totally and utterly, it was to turn my life on its head into a continuing realm of pain, suffering and loss.

Mr Lynch told me he would perform keyhole surgery on my lung and he gave instructions to the nurse, in my presence, to administer injections to keep the pain at bay while I waited for the surgery. When he left the ward, I was then not only ill but also traumatised and it took me some time to recover from his onslaught.

While I waited the several days for the video-assisted thoracic surgery (VATS), I had ample time to ponder and try to determine the cause of my lung collapsing. I had never previously had a problem with the functioning of a major organ. It seemed incongruously out of step with my heretofore, physical stamina. The only possibility I could relate it to was a virus I contracted when I returned to Ireland from the US in 1991. Even though my lungs were scanned at the time and proved normal, perhaps a weakness remained. I had the innate feeling, however, that while a collapsed lung was not nice, I had no disease. Throughout my life, I had always kept active, fit, and healthy with a consistently nourishing diet and regular exercise.

I reminisced to when I was growing up in the country, an only girl, sandwiched between two brothers until a much younger one expanded our circle when I was twelve. I learned to take knocks and dust myself off. I had always been very active in athletics, swimming and playing tennis and afterwards came to develop a steady love of playing squash. For many years, I water-skied on the lakes in the US after work and at weekends, most of the time somersaulting over the skis. I was more ardent, I believe, than adept. I also learned to play golf when I returned to Ireland, more for the fresh air than the game and as far back as I can remember I took regular walks and had a gym membership that I actively availed of. In the world of corporate business, stamina was, in my mind, the key to continued success.

Even when I was growing up in Ireland I was either studying, practising and playing the piano, working or volunteering many hours as pianist for the Enniscorthy Musical Society in County Wexford, along with my father who had a trained and sonorous baritone voice. We spent many querulous hours sparring with each other in comical amusement. At Easter, when we were involved in putting on a show and my spare time was consequently diluted, I usually, in jest, charged him if he wanted a solo score transcribed. I believe I inherited whatever musical talent I had from his mother who taught music in Munich, Germany, an accomplished woman who mastered five languages. She passed away when I was only three years old and consequently I always felt cheated out of knowing her. Unfortunately, my ancestors' genes completely bypassed me when it came to my vocals and people would protest at my frantic attempts to join in a chorus.

I was the sole student of music in the year of my Leaving Certificate and, therefore, my parents had to fund private studies. As it transpired, my last teacher, who had a unique talent, had actually been tutored by my grandmother which was very poignant and meaningful.

My life's passion has always been classical music and my parents almost had to wrench me away from the piano. My main ambition, which I prematurely sought, was to pursue a music degree. However, after major consideration and reflection, even when I achieved very high marks in the honour's paper in the Leaving Certificate, I came to the realisation that, in those days, with limited opportunities for women, I would end up teaching when all I really wanted to do was perform. As they say, 'timing is everything' and in the end I read business studies to post-graduate level. I retained my passion without having to depend on it for financial support and kept it as my dearest companion. Therefore, like my father, who inherited land and, therefore, had to forego a professional singing career, we both held on to our natural inclination towards the performing arts.

I had always wondered why I had an appetite and aptitude for mathematics, especially calculus, and also leaned towards classical piano and capturing its essence. One of my university professors told me it made perfect sense. The technical side of classical piano, he explained, compares in a significant and profound way to the logic of mathematics. The artistic component, I discovered, was of great benefit in moulding a creative flair in the business world. Therefore, each subject reciprocated benefits to the other.

My interest in business and economics filtered, I assume, down through my father's maternal side of the family as well, since his grandfather was evidently a very successful entrepreneur. There was an article published some years back in the *Enniscorthy Echo*, a weekly newspaper, which gave an account of his business acumen and endeavours headlined with the accolade of 'Entrepreneur of the 19th Century'. Even though it was only provincial recognition, I always held a high admiration for his vision and business successes in those days.

Unfortunately, my maternal grandparents both died at young ages so I know very little about them. However, the family is the most handsome I have ever known. My mother herself, was endowed with beauty that no one failed to notice and remark upon, and a photograph of my maternal grandmother proves the link to the subsequent attractiveness of her children. When growing up, I always wished some of those genes would eventually project themselves in me, even in minute amounts.

My godmother, who I adored, had the stoical determination of a career-oriented and sound businessperson. I attribute my early training and practical knowledge of running a business to her. She was widowed at twenty-one years of age and treated me like the only child and daughter she never had the opportunity to have. I loved being in her company. She had the habit of admonishing and praising me at the same time and she would jestingly give me the slightest inkling of a dig in the ribs as if to assure me that she was close at hand.

A strong-willed woman who made no pretension of being financially generous, she made me earn every cent. Along with a weekly allowance from my parents, for chores well done, I had enough money to develop an interest and keep abreast of fashion. It gave me a grounding in 'dressing for success' for the business world but in a feminine way.

I always loved the world of academia and its related necessity to study. It is a propensity that accompanied me all my life through university and beyond and only aspiring to passing an examination was never an option for me. It was not because I always wanted to achieve an 'A' in every subject I studied, it was the quest to learn as much as possible about a subject that spurred me on. From the time I was a child, I have always been an avid reader of various genres of books and I was never without a dictionary, thesaurus and general reference guides.

My first taste for long-haul travel and experiencing another culture was at the age of eighteen when I took several planes to reach Acapulco in Mexico, quite a journey in those days. That was the beginning of a life of adventure and by the time I was forty, I had been to forty-one countries in five continents and to many of them several times. Moreover, because my health was never an issue, I was always equally at home in reclusive hinterland as I was in several star-pampered luxury resorts; it did not matter.

Since my parents had decided to send me to the Sisters of Mercy in Enniscorthy, nine miles away, and my siblings to the Christian Brothers, rather than to local schools, all my friends lived in and around Enniscorthy so I was rather sheltered and reliant on my parents or godmother for lifts. When I was out of their sight, they knew exactly where I was. And while, up to the age of forty, I had achieved as much of a stimulating and varied life as I had set out to do, I always had security. I certainly was no angel but I never took risks that landed me in trouble.

Thank goodness I had never succumbed to procrastination and had so many opportunities to pursue a full life because that old adage, 'Do not put off what you can do today' for me always rang true. One often hears of people on their deathbeds tell their mourners of their regrets or they deferred their dreams until they retired. They often believed that time would be kind to them and nothing untoward would happen to crush their dreams. When I was very young, I never realised that life does pass us by so quickly, or thought of being old or that life could be snatched from us like the snuffing out of a candle.

Many of the positive things that happened to me up to the age of forty were not because they fell into my lap. I strived with sustained effort and perseverance, sometimes in the face of adversity, and put my heart and soul into everything I did. It was not perfectionism that drove me but a non-foreboding acceptance of a life that does not stretch to infinity. I never let my thoughts become rancid. I moved on and tried not to feel sorry for myself; self-pity for more than a brief indulgence I always felt was a road to nowhere. Years ago, I remember when the concept, 'The art of positive thinking,' became a buzzing cliché. I never gave much credence to it until tragedy struck me down. I realised much later in life that one can actually 'trick' the brain into thinking in a more optimistic and enlightened manner. It does take practice, however.

There are many people, due to circumstances beyond their own control, who can do nothing to change their situation. Even if they can, often an indolent mood may thwart a brain's positive responses. And, of course, because of human nature, it is often routinely easier to do nothing after calamity strikes. But while my healthy heart continued to pump away without effort, I always believed it was far better to constantly strive for some quality of life rather than just wait for the moment of life's quittance.

Early on the morning of Tuesday the 4th of June, Mr Lynch suddenly appeared at my bedside and, contrary to his previous behaviour, this time he was extremely unctuous. He told me he had placed me on his list for the following morning and would perform keyhole surgery to excise the blisters on the top part of my lung. He would then use tiny staples to seal it. He said that I would only have a few tiny scars, that he had performed two hundred of these procedures and the operation would be a 'cinch'. He overwhelmed me by insisting I had nothing to worry about and did not prepare me for any untoward consequences or possible side effects. He had that attitude, I believe, that patients did not need to know and he left the ward as suddenly and as quickly as he had appeared. I had no time to question him.

To my detriment, I mistook acute arrogance for competence. I believed that I had nothing to fear as I was in such capable and experienced hands, according to him. One would have had to meet Mr Lynch to really grasp the absolute God-like opinion he had of himself. I have to say I was really taken in and he did not offer any suggestion as to why my lung had blisters on it and never asked me about my medical history. He spent no more than five minutes at my bedside.

Because I had keyhole surgery in the US in the early eighties for a condition called endometriosis, where the surgeon placed a video camera and laser in through my navel and burned out all the disease, I knew and greatly appreciated the benefits of keyhole surgery. On leaving the hospital that time, the surgeon gave me a videotape of the entire operation. He was quite a brilliant surgeon and post-operatively I was a little sore as one can imagine but I was out of hospital that same day, back to work three days later and have never had a problem since. Because he was so competent in his specialty, I erroneously thought that Mr Lynch had the same level of skill and expertise.

After he dashed off, I was not in the least bit apprehensive and it never once dawned on me that he was incapable of doing what he lauded himself he would deliver. He had assured me that I would be out of hospital in a few days or less and I believed I would be back to work with my life intact; it was just another insignificant glitch in my life.

I was not to know that morning that the risk of removing myself from that hospital with a collapsed lung and even with pneumonia turned out to be very, very minor compared to the risk of remaining.

Chapter Three

On the morning of June the 5th, I awoke thankfully prepared to have the VATS and get my life back on track again. I was brought down to a theatre anteroom and found myself placed near a man who was also awaiting surgery. Since I was not in the least bit anxious, we both ended up laughing and joking about nonsense. I was then received in the theatre at approximately ten thirty, prepped for the surgery and the anaesthetist sent me off into oblivion without incident.

Then, at approximately 12:40 p.m., I began to slowly come around into the most hellish ordeal I could never have imagined. I started screaming and screaming, whether out loud or in my head I do not know. All I remember was asking God to take me, away from the pain that was so unbelievably and vastly unbearable. It was absolute sheer torture, as if scorching acid had been poured into my chest. My mind could not register or grasp anything except the ferocious pain. I was unaware of where I was and above all, I could not take in or even imagine what could have happened to me. I tried but failed to open my eyelids and kept begging for relief but the unimaginable and unthinkable agony continued for a long, long while.

The only reason for my existence at that point was to plead for relief or gladly die there and then. Nothing else mattered; nothing else was on my mind. When, in the end, my pleading won out and I stopped screaming, I knew what paradise was. The medication was finally successful in taking the unbearable edge off the pain. I never ever thought that I would experience such powerful and overwhelming agony. That feeling of sheer acidic-like torture comes back to haunt me when I least expect it.

Once I managed to open my eyes in a flutter for a second, all I could see flashing in front of me was the colour red and I thought I was hallucinating. What I was yet to discover was that I was covered and saturated in my own blood. My entire chest was padded up and a large, thick and ugly-looking rubber tube protruded from my right side into a large glass bottle on the floor. In addition, tubes were coming out of my arm and hand. I was so disoriented and the pain still so severe I could not even form a word; I could only groan. My body felt as if it had been savaged. I had to wait almost eight years before I was to receive a probable explanation as to why I was put into such hell. And I remember hearing an old saying once by a wise old woman that 'if you believe in the devil, he will appear', but I ask, in what macabre form?

After the nurses and doctors succeeded in easing the damnable edge of the violent pain, I was moved and my mother was waiting for me in a frantic and distraught state. She did not know why I was so long down in theatre and could not get any explanation from the staff. When she saw me covered in blood and in so much distress, she nearly collapsed from shock. I could hear her voice but I could not understand what she was saying. I just caught the word 'breast' and in my mind, I thought she had meant to say 'chest'. Mr Lynch had already been up to see and bombard her with excuses, leaving her in a traumatic state of confusion and fear. She could not comprehend him and she was so distraught she had actually thought, she told me later, that he had said he had to 'remove part of my breast'. Because I was inert, I lay there as if comatose and while I could not see what he had done to me, I certainly felt it.

Sometime later, when my mind began to function, I heard the great man himself arrive at my bedside. All I could hear were the words, endlessly repeated, 'I am sorry for hitting your artery but it was in the wrong place.' Hit my artery? Was that why I had seen red? He kept badgering me with his excuses and I just wanted to be left in peace. I was still unable to look at him or ask any questions at that point.

Time passed before he reappeared and harangued me, saying that as soon as he entered my breast he hit my mammary artery (now called the thoracic artery). He said he had to perform emergency open surgery to stop the bleeding. So, he had told my mother 'breast' after all. He blamed the entire butchery on my anatomy, swearing that it was way out towards my right side when it should have been close to my sternum. It was obviously all my fault and I felt I was being reproved for it.

I wanted him to be removed from my bedside and leave me alone. His tone was completely devoid of remorse, concern or compassion for the suffering I had endured and would have to endure. He continued to badger me while I lay there scared witless, disoriented and confused. To add insult to injury he lauded himself by saying he had saved my life. I have no words to describe how I felt about that despicable man. He put me in a terribly risky situation, butchered my body with his own hands and then I should be grateful to him for not dying. And how ironic it was that I had actually wanted to be taken and I was not to know at the time that, eventually, it would have been a Godsend to me personally if I had actually died. I was to suffer constant and almost unbearable agony over many years in the aftermath of that surgery. Death would have been kinder.

Nothing he said ever rang true to me and I had this powerful, persistent and overwhelming feeling he was immediately trying to cover up what he had done. He kept trying to convince me to accept his explanation of why the surgery had gone so horribly wrong. But I never did and I saw that he knew. For the first time in my life I felt like a victim to such an extent that I thought a crime had been committed against my person; it was simple brutality.

My partner, Edward, arrived at the hospital early that evening not knowing or expecting what he was going to encounter. My mother was so relieved to see him. He was totally and utterly shocked beyond comprehension when he saw me in such morbid condition. Of course, I knew nothing at the time of Edward's conversation with my mother, nor when she left. I learned some days afterwards that she was so very, very tired and distressed that he convinced her to go home, get some rest and that he would look after me. She reluctantly left. I was aware Edward was there and whenever I managed to slightly open my eyes, all I could see was his face almost touching mine; he never let go of my hand.

Edward informed me afterwards that he did not once leave my bedside as he was constantly listening for my breath and monitoring my pulse, he was so worried. Being a veterinary surgeon, he knew what distress signs to look for and he genuinely thought I was not going to pull through. Apparently, he remained in that position until he was exhausted himself and sleep had finally given me some comfort.

When I roused the following morning and tried to move, the sheer agony of it prevented me, but I was more alert and could slightly open my eyes. I discovered that a tube that had been placed in my left hand had become dislodged and I did not know what it was for. I asked a nurse for pain relief and she informed me that the tube had been connected to a morphine pump. However, when she went to reconnect it to my hand I asked her not to as I had enough tubes going in and out of my body; she gave me an injection instead.

My mother arrived again that morning and by this time family, friends and colleagues knew what ill fate had befallen me. I slightly raised my head and realised the extent of the blood that had dried and was caked all over me. Dear God, what had Mr Lynch done to me? One minute I was laughing going into theatre and the next I was nearly dead. Edward told me for a long time after that, for years in fact, I looked corpse-like, I was so pale and gaunt looking.

I hated the morbid feeling of that blood so my mother asked a nurse if she would wash some of it off. She had rather a struggle trying to remove my gown since I could not bear to move but somehow she managed. Then, with a bowl of tepid water, she very gently sponged off much of what was caked on the front of my body. However, when she and my mother tried to lift me to wash the blood from my back it was excruciating. I yelped and groaned profusely and it had to be abandoned. At least, I could no longer see bright red.

Mr Lynch arrived again at my bedside that day and kept repeating the same old story: he was sorry but it was not his fault. On no occasion did he ask me how I was actually feeling nor did he attempt to put my mind at ease. I was baffled and could not understand what on earth he had thought he was doing going through my breast to perform VATS or how he could have severed my artery. I remember thinking, *who do you think I am that you believe I am that naïve? Just because I do not rant and rave and cause trouble does not mean I am also stupid and a fool. I am listening very attentively and taking everything you say in, you can count on that.* And it emerged a long time afterwards that I had absolutely no pathological obstructions or adhesions that would have prevented the keyhole surgery from being successfully completed if Mr Lynch had competently performed the procedure.

Many years later, other thoracic surgeons gave their opinions that he had performed the VATS neglecting to conform to safe, acceptable and standard practice. Instead of putting his instruments in through my side, called the triangle of safety under my armpit, working towards my back torso, he instead shoved an instrument through a major part of my breast, severing my mammary artery. It spouted blood so fast that he violently spliced open my chest wall and forcibly spread open my rib cage with a surgical metal rib spreader. He held it apart with a surgical vice which, of necessity, involved severe trauma to my adjacent muscles, ribs and nerves that were crushed and damaged as a result. In addition, my breast was two to three times its normal size and there was also a scar just under my right shoulder blade where he had inserted another instrument.

Eventually, a very empathetic nurse, when I was able to tolerate it, changed the padding around my chest and for the first time I was able to see the extent of the damage. It made my stomach churn. I do not use the word 'butchery' easily or lightly but that was what my body looked like. That day all the staff in my place of work poured in good wishes and sent copious flowers. Everyone I knew was shocked.

For the first week, I was totally bedridden and unable to move. In all that time, Mr Lynch not once showed any compassion. He never provided me with any explanation as to why he had performed VATS in the way he had. I am certain he never looked into the cause of why I had blisters on my lung. His entire focus, as far as I could determine, was to just keep the pain at bay with painkillers and have me removed from the hospital as quickly as possible. In other words, in my opinion, dump me.

The chest drain was finally and forcefully pulled out on the twelfth day. With sheer endurance and determination, I tried to drag myself around and with each lurching and treacherous step, I gained a little confidence. I had absolutely no complaints about the front line hospital staff members who were at all times kind and courteous but I did want to know one thing. Why did the CEO of that hospital employ a consultant like Mr Lynch who could do such damage to a patient and in addition, harass and bully her? Much later on, I discovered I was not the only one Mr Lynch had destroyed.

It was all very disturbing in the ward I was finally ensconced in. Opposite me to my right, a young woman with beautiful long, thick and silky black hair was lying in bed paralysed. There was a note above her head saying that to communicate she would give one blink for 'yes' and two for 'no' or vice versa. Obviously, it was none of my business to ask the nurses what had happened to her. When Mr Lynch came to see me one day, I watched as he went over to the end of her bed and checked her chart, startling me, *Oh dear God no, is she another patient of his,* I fearfully wondered? Her husband came in to sit at her bedside every single day. I never heard he and Mr Lynch ever exchange a word or even nod to each other. I did not witness any other consultant attend her and my suspicions about him cast themselves in stone.

I felt so unbelievably sorry for that couple and one day, I believe it was a Sunday, her husband brought their daughter to the hospital. She looked about five years of age and remarkably cute in an adorable summer dress. She was such a jolly little girl, skipping around the ward. She came over to me and said, 'My mammy is sleeping.' I almost burst into tears with the sadness of it all and my heart was wrenched listening to her. During two weeks in hospital you get to know people and the woman's husband and I always exchanged greetings but neither of us asked each other the obvious questions.

Then on one particular day while I was still bedridden, a woman who was accompanied by her daughter arrived in the ward. She undressed and got into the bed next to me on my right side, directly opposite the young, paralysed woman. She told me she was admitted to have one of her lungs removed and I thought by her facial skin that she might have been a heavy smoker. She looked older than me because of the effect of the smoke on her skin, but she was actually ten years younger. Her daughter left the ward for a while and her mother sat up in bed and asked me what had happened to the young woman opposite. It was an extremely awkward question to deal with because really all I knew was that she had locked-in syndrome. I was in a real dilemma because I did not want to frighten her nor did I wish to speculate so I said I did not know, which was the truth.

Then, suddenly, Mr Lynch barged into the ward with a number of trainee doctors scurrying behind him. Without pulling the screen around the woman to talk to her in private, he demanded, in his arrogant, bellowing voice, 'Get up out of bed and go home.' He then turned on his heel and brusquely left the ward with the trainees trying to keep pace with him. She turned her head to me in shock and her eyes locked with mine. I wanted so much to help her bring that terrible man back to give her an explanation but I was bedbound and incapable of moving. She did not know whether he decided this because there was no hope for her or the operation was deferred; nothing.

We just stared at each other and I felt her anguish and a huge pang of pity. I could tell she just did not have the courage or wherewithal to demand that Mr Lynch return and explain why she was to go home. I thought, well, if that is the modern way of training young people in patient care, rights and compassion, it certainly did not bode well for the future care of patients or the reputation of the medical profession.

I began finally to mobilise around the corridors as much as I could tolerate, holding onto the walls but my entire chest wall was inflamed and I had a constant, sharp pain in the thoracic area. Mr Lynch, as usual, would not give me any possible explanation for this intractable pain. His remedy, as always, was to keep administering painkillers and he continued with his opinion that everything would settle down. I got to know those corridors as well as my own hallway.

On the morning of the 14th of June, a nurse slowly and efficiently removed the copious large black stitches from the myriad of scars that had been inflicted on my person. I was due to be discharged from hospital that afternoon. Although I was glad to leave, I was in no fit state to be out of hospital. My father and my brother picked me up to bring me home to County Wexford to recuperate. As I had arrived at the hospital attired in a business suit, it was very strange and awkward being assisted back into it. I had forgotten to ask them to bring in casual clothing.

While I was sitting on the bed waiting for the discharge papers, I still had that constant nerve pain along with the acute post-operative pain. I was bent over, not able to hold myself up and a nurse called one of the doctors. He told me he did not know what was causing this neuropathic pain and just reiterated what Mr Lynch kept saying. *Well, I thought, forgive me if I have absolutely no faith in either Mr Lynch's competence or his judgement.* I wondered repeatedly how it could be possible to seek treatment in one of Ireland's major teaching hospitals, and for a rather routine and well-established procedure to go so badly out of control and to end up with me leaving in a wheelchair.

As I was brought down to the exit doors of St. Vincent's, I gravely worried how I was going to get through even the next month, being so totally dependent. How long was it going to take to put all my structures and tissues back to their rightful positions? How could I find out what had happened to me when all I had were some blisters on the top of my lung? I did not have cancer, I had no pathological obstructions and I had been in otherwise perfect health. How was I to rationalise it? I had no answers.

Before my father and brother helped me into the car, I eventually and suddenly broke down and leaned my head on my brother's shoulder. I sobbed and sobbed my heart out with gut wrenching force until I was completely drained of emotion and had no tears left. It was like the horridness of the previous two weeks hit me like a thunderbolt.

My brother had padded up the back seat of the car and I lay down for the journey, grateful to get away from Mr Lynch and leave my mental and physical revulsion of him behind me. However, when my brother began to drive, every movement jerked me and I was just too raw and in too much pain to travel the distance. Instead he brought me to my apartment in Dublin. Edward came to stay and assist me until I could make the journey home, as I needed serious after-care and support. All I could do was lay flat on my back after that brief trip from the hospital and I was unable to even turn on the mattress. I felt dreadfully vulnerable and terribly afraid, wondering what was going to happen to me. I was still in terrible shock.

Chapter Four

It was a very strange experience being physically dependent on my family as I was always independent and did whatever I could for them. They were in great distress when they saw the extent of my injuries and even more so seeing me extremely traumatised and struggling.

Thank goodness it was a dry, warm and sunny June while I was trying to recuperate and every day I was assisted out to the garden to rest rather than being bed and housebound. As my parents lived in the country, there was great peace around and all I could hear was the myriad of birds chirping away, a cacophony of sounds almost in competition and the soothing sound of the stream at the base of the rolling lawn. The garden was secluded with tall, varied oak, chestnut trees and evergreens. It was the ideal place in which to try to heal and breathe in fresh air after the stifling and cloying atmosphere of the hospital. Since the house is on a cliff, I managed, after a few weeks, to meander down the gradually sloping laneways and stroll around the banks of the river Slaney, which our family land bordered. I had to use a walking stick to support the right side of my body. It was essential to build up my stamina because with the responsibilities I had in my position at work, I had to focus on returning to it as soon as possible.

Another major consequence of the surgery was that I found I had absolutely no ability to write as I could not control my right hand; I could not even manage to hold a pen. However, worst of all, every time I passed my piano I felt a huge sadness engulf me. In addition, whenever I got a particularly bad flare-up in my chest wall, my hand would literally cramp and gnarl up. I thought then that it was only a temporary symptom but this was wishful thinking and another misguided perception on my part. There was no sign of the constant nerve pain dissipating but I kept struggling along until I saw Mr Lynch for a follow-up visit.

One day before this date, I developed terribly severe abdominal cramps throughout the course of twelve hours. My mother called out our family doctor who gave me an injection to ease the pain. This was something entirely new and I could not understand why they were so acute. I kept bending over on the bed trying to ease them, consequently placing dreadful stress on my raw chest. I wondered at the time if these were what labour pains were like; they were completely abnormal. The cramps finally subsided and never returned but at the back of my mind I was puzzled because something was definitely amiss. I decided to ask Mr Lynch if he had any ideas about them.

When I attended him, again I told him that I was very unwell, between the awful nerve pain, muscle and rib damage, loss of the control in my hand and of course, my breast was 'on fire'. Before I had the opportunity to tell him about the cramps he interjected and asked me if I knew why my breast was so large. I told him that I presumed it was due to the surgical instrument he shoved through it. Then he provided me with an extraordinary revelation. It can happen that when one tampers with the breast, hormones are triggered and the brain recognises them as pregnancy symptoms. In effect, I had a phantom pregnancy.

Then the reason for those cramps became perfectly lucid. I was probably spot on in thinking I had been in labour. There is a medical term for this condition Mr Lynch informed me but it eludes me now. Then, as if this was not enough, his next statement absolutely appalled me when he said, in a dreadfully flippant way, 'At least you are not lactating.' I looked at him aghast and with disgust wondering if he was insane. I could only imagine that he went into medicine for the lucrative lifestyle he could lead. After my experience of him, it certainly did not appear to me to be out of compassion or any humanitarian consideration. What did not make any sense whatsoever was that since he knew about this phenomenon, why did he tamper with my breast? He then asked me if I would like him to put me on hormone treatment to reverse the symptoms and I refused. I did not want any more medication and since he had destroyed me in his role as a thoracic surgeon, I certainly was not going to allow him to treat me as my gynaecologist as well.

I asked him to refer me for physiotherapy, which was my main priority. I badly needed to rebuild my physiology and strength but he just dismissed my request and said, again, I would get better in time and to keep taking the medication. I knew myself that I urgently required rehabilitation but because I was afraid of doing anything that might lead to a further collapse of my lung, I was too afraid to risk it. Therefore, I felt again I had no choice but to listen to him. I was amazed really at the control he had over me, which he only got because I was ill and highly vulnerable. But why was he so reluctant to refer me? Did he not want the results of his aborted VATS known?

One might wonder why I did not go to another thoracic surgeon but Ireland is such a closed society in terms of second opinions that colleagues are very reluctant to take over the care of another surgeon's patient, especially when the operation had been disastrous. In hindsight, I wish I had ignored Mr Lynch, taken the risk and independently gone to a physiotherapist before all my structures and tissues had set in unnatural positions. He just took his fee, that had reached quite a sum at this stage, and sent me on my way with a follow-up visit for July the 29th. Because he refused to refer me for physiotherapy, it is my belief that he was absolutely negligent in neglecting to provide me with proper aftercare. It seemed to me that he was totally over-reliant and dependent on medication as his fix for his fallout.

***

Before I returned to see Mr Lynch, Edward brought me to his own home for two weeks to spend valuable time alone together and it provided me with a change of environment. Before he ventured off to work every morning to attend to his diverse business interests, he always brought me a light breakfast. Once he was gone, I relaxed and spent long hours reading books of various genres. The peace and tranquillity of those days were irreplaceable, knowing I was totally protected and safe and my nightmares eased. He always made it a point of returning home early, laden with foodstuffs so that I would become well nourished. I was still very pale, weak, extremely thin and in severe pain. However, anything I needed he provided, so I was very content in the knowledge that I was being cared for.

Once I acquired a little stamina after eating, he would drive us to a canal lock in a very picturesque part of County Kildare where many bright colourful barges were moored. To build up my energy levels, we would stroll along a wide pathway with the canal on one side and a large ditch with overgrown shrubs, hedging and wild flowers on the other. It helped gladden my heart to smell the different scents. Edward always walked at the water's edge just in case I became weak, tumbled over into the dark depths of the water, and contracted pneumonia. This became our constant routine every warm, early evening for the duration of my stay with him.

It was with great regret that I had to return to Dublin and I tried to walk as much as possible. I was due to return to see Mr Lynch on the 29th of July. I repeated the same symptoms to him. I could barely cope with the muscle, ribs and breast problems but the constant nerve pain was dastardly and the loss of control of my right hand made everything very difficult. I wished I could have put my hand into my tautened chest and pulled out all the nerves.

While pain medication helped the other symptoms, it could not provide me with any relief from the intractable nerve pain. I pleaded to Mr Lynch again for physiotherapy or to see a neurologist but I was dismissed with the same old repetitive answer and medication. All he did was give me another follow-up date for August the 26th and, again, took my money and I did not see any point in these visits except to line his pockets.

Even though I was still physically weak and in pain, I returned to work on the 6th of August, part-time for the first week. It was really, really incredibly tough going and much of the time I actually had to manually hold my chest wall up to get some balance and ease the pressure. My whole focus was on keeping my career going and my days were extremely difficult. Every day after work, I would collapse onto my couch in pain, exhausted and physically distressed. I had to constantly try to hide my illness from the staff so that they would continue to retain confidence in my decisions. However, a number of the middle managers knew by looking at the pain lines in my face alone that I was in agony and they were all very supportive. That was the extent of my life for many years.

When I returned to work, the clinicians were flabbergasted that Mr Lynch had gone through my breast to perform VATS and many comments were made that I should litigate. At the time I said that it took every ounce of energy just trying to keep going and that I could not even think about a lawsuit. All I consistently wished for was the intractable pain to subside. I did obviously care about all the ugly scars I was left with, but they would never have been enough to even remotely think about leaning towards litigation. Of course, that was provided that I recovered my life pain free and would not be driven demented. Because I was responsible for not only head office but also for clinics in other parts of Dublin and Wicklow, most times I had to be driven to business meetings.

My next encounter with Mr Lynch on the 26th went from bad to worse. While I was waiting to see him in his open plan office, I suddenly heard a raised and very angry voice. There was a young married couple sitting in front of his desk that I could see through a glass partition and the woman's husband stood up and was extremely irate with Mr Lynch because he kept telling him his wife would get better when, in fact, she was deteriorating. He was so livid he was shouting. I do not know what was said after that since he lowered his voice. I could totally understand his reaction and frustration as I was in the same sorry position myself.

When it came to my turn, as I sat down in front of Mr Lynch's desk, I noticed that his right wrist was in a cast and he was writing with his left hand. I asked him what had happened and the last thing I expected him to say was, 'I fell out of a tree at home.' I immediately told myself, 'Christine, do not go there', and I asked no further questions. I thought with sardonic amusement that perhaps he was a tree surgeon as well. All I could feel was genuine pity for the next patient he was going to operate on and I reiterated that I was not improving.

I then asked him if there were any consequences in relation to my mammary artery having been sealed off and one would think I would have got used to his unacceptable language and manner by then but he thought he was being hilarious by saying, 'Well not unless you are eighty and need a bypass.' This man I believed was becoming more sick every occasion I met him and I was further disgusted hearing this totally inconsiderate flippancy again. Just because one is eighty years of age does not mean it is time to die. Valuable time could be lost if emergency staff do not know that the mammary artery is sealed off and the surgeon has to try another blood supply. I thought, not for the first time, that Mr Lynch was a horrible man. As usual, he sent me off with a prescription, nothing else, and told me to come back again in February 1997. It felt like he was just trying to be rid of me. If only I had received physiotherapy intervention at that time, perhaps it would have changed the course of my life.

During the period September 1996 to the end of January 1997 I often almost passed out in my office with the pain and weakness and my assistant would always be alert and prepared when I would buzz her. She would come down the stairs with a sugary drink and chocolate to revive me and boost my energy levels. The only thing I could do physically was walk. I had to relinquish everything else and I could not sit for any length of time. My hand still would not function properly nor could I play my precious piano. My closest friends were such a help, however, and got me through some very difficult times with performing physical chores for me and being very supportive. That cliché, 'You know who your real friends are when you are in trouble,' came true for me because of the unbelievable amount of assistance they gave me on a day-to-day basis. Even to this day, I am amazed at how kind many people are.

If it had been true that I had helped people in the past in various ways, it came back to me tenfold. I did not want my parents and Edward to be worried about me but with good friends there is not such pressure. As in life, we all get our ups and downs so there is give and take and I was never at a loss for help. It was so vital because my family and Edward lived a significant distance from me. My friends never made me feel under any obligation so on a day-to-day basis I relied on them. They had all known me for a very long time when I was healthy, vibrant and energetic and now they were greatly saddened and worried about the extent of my injuries and debilitation. I did not seek anyone's sympathy but it came to me nevertheless. Of course, as well as being with me every weekend, if I did need Edward he would come to Dublin immediately.

I became constantly worried all the time, contrary to my nature, about what would become of me in the future. I kept willing and pushing myself to get better, always believing that I would completely overcome my disabilities. However, I was in complete denial and far too optimistic.

Chapter Five

It was only a matter of time, I knew, before I finally and totally collapsed and my prediction unfortunately came through on the 27th of January 1997. I was in a crucial meeting at work that morning and, after a weekend of no relief whatsoever, my body was totally spent. I felt a fainting spell coming on and everything became hazy and began to turn black. I knew to put my head down between my knees and my assistant took charge. She immediately telephoned Mr Lynch who instructed her to bring me to his rooms immediately. When we reached the Blackrock Clinic, I was helped into a wheelchair and brought in to be examined by him. He saw that I was in great pain and distress, told me I was very ill and would have to be admitted to hospital immediately. While I was there, I asked him again if he ever found out or tried to find out what had caused the blisters to develop at the top of my lung and he said he had not.

Then, for the first time, over six months since the surgery, he asked me if I ever had any prior medical conditions. I told him what had been written in my hospital records under the medical history section in June 1996, that I had had endometriosis in my uterus removed by keyhole surgery in the early eighties, but that I had never had a problem with it since. It had been totally cured and I only had a few other minor ailments over the years. He did not think it important and I got no further with him but I was not to know then that years later he would use this piece of medical information to help cover-up his alleged negligence. He admitted me to St. Vincent's Private Hospital immediately, and the nurses had to wrap me in a duvet for about three hours to improve my circulation.

I assumed that since all the pain was in my chest wall that Mr Lynch would immediately call in a neurologist or orthopaedic consultant to examine me, but no, he just put me on morphine injections. He then advised me that he was going to do a series of tests to determine what was causing my symptoms. This was completely out of order. I reminded him I was a very healthy person and the pain was entirely in my thoracic area, all due to his surgery. He tried to persuade me that he was being thorough, but I knew better. My instincts told me he was going to try to discover something in my anatomy, other than in my chest wall, to blame so he could enhance his cover-up of the surgery. There was absolutely no need whatsoever for a myriad of tests to be performed and leave me waiting for treatment.

During the following seemingly endless two weeks I was put through a battery of tests for my heart, abdomen, kidneys, respiration, and an MRI scan and each time a test was clear he would barge into the ward and in his usual bellowing voice would say, 'There is nothing wrong with you,' for the other patients to hear. He must have been extremely disappointed, however, when all the tests proved negative and that he was unable to come up with any other plausible reason to relate the pain to. I felt, because I kept questioning him, he must have suspected I was very suspicious of what he was doing. But then again, I was at his mercy.

He knew, apart from the damage he had caused, I was a healthy person. Crucially, in a letter he sent to Dr Duignan, my GP, dated the 3rd of July 1996 following the surgery, which I did not know about at that time, he stated that his findings were that, other than the first pneumothorax, 'she appeared to be a healthy young woman.'

There was no good, humane, valid or logical reason to put me through all those tests and, given my condition, it was cruel but there was exceptional reason to bring in a neurologist. It was not until the end of almost two weeks he finally succumbed and it all smacked of unethical power. A neurologist examined my chest wall and recommended that Dr Declan O'Keeffe, the pain management consultant at St. Vincent's hospital be brought in to my case. He administered six injections of anaesthesia on Saturday the 8th of February at different nerve points close to my thoracic spine as a temporary measure until he could perform a full thoracic nerve block.

This whole bitter experience portrayed to me the lengths Mr Lynch would go to deflect from the operative damage. After that, I refused to attend him because he was only concerned about his own position and lining his pockets. He still did not diagnose the problem with my lung and I continued to get repeated bouts of pneumonia. In my mind, he was no longer my consultant and I should have, in hindsight, written him a letter and fired him.

There was something odd that struck me about Mr Lynch and it stuck in my mind for a considerable amount of time. I received a bill from him for £929 that seemed to me to be exorbitant in 1996. He filed a claim to the VHI and on the 18th of September 1996 and he sent me a balanced bill for £501. I thought that the insurance company had paid very little for all that surgery and I rang them to find out exactly what he had filed. They told me that he had billed them for the keyhole surgery only and nothing whatsoever was mentioned about the emergency thoracotomy.

The VHI then advised me to write to Mr Lynch and ask him to refile his claim. I wrote to him on the 10th of October 1996 and asked him to do this but I never heard from him again regarding this matter. However, I do not believe he should have received any fees whatsoever for all the damage he caused. Did he not want it known that his surgery had gone so badly wrong? It was never mentioned again even though I received a bill from him for professional attendance for the period I was in St. Vincent's Private Hospital from January the 27th to the 9th of February 1997. Two years later I contacted the VHI to find out if he had ever refiled for the open surgery and I was informed he had not. Why? I have since wondered.

Once I left the hospital on the 9th of February 1997, I thought about everything I had endured from Mr Lynch and, since I was not getting better, I decided that I would contact a solicitor. I was thoroughly convinced that he was engaging in a cover-up over the surgery and his whole intimidating manner added to this belief. Nothing he ever had said made any sense to me and I was at my wit's end knowing that my career and financial security were at stake.

After I had a full thoracic nerve block performed by Dr O'Keeffe in March 1997, I returned to work. A colleague of mine recommended that I contact Mr Michael Boylan, a partner in Augustus Cullen Law in Wicklow town, who is an expert in medical negligence cases. Since I trusted my colleague's opinion and felt that 'word of mouth' was the most reliable avenue to take, I decided to go with her recommendation. Subsequently, I telephoned Michael and relayed everything that had transpired since my first pneumothorax and brought him through the whole tragic and sordid saga. However, it was very, very difficult to explain adequately Mr Lynch's temperament. I did not really have to, as Michael would soon discover his character and behaviour himself when he had to deal with him.

Thankfully, Michael agreed to look into the matter and as a first step obtained my medical records from the hospitals, but Mr Lynch refused to forward his private notes. He also advised me that I should keep a diary of my illness since the surgery, which I thought was an excellent idea. Everyone knows it takes years to bring a case to the High Court and then trying to recall the specifics becomes a very daunting prospect. On the 12th of August 1997, he sent me a letter informing me that Mr Lynch's secretary had contacted him by telephone to tell him that he was very upset when he received Michael's correspondence and I thought, *not half as upset as I am.*

Michael checked the actual operation notes and sent them to two thoracic experts in England for their professional opinions, Professor Geoffrey Smith and Mr Arthur Makey, both vastly experienced cardiothoracic surgeons.

***

I knew that to successfully win a medical negligence case the plaintiff must prove that the surgeon in question deviated from safe, standard and accepted practice and that the deviation was responsible for the injuries suffered by the patient. The notes clearly show that it was the instrumental entry through my breast that in Mr Lynch's own words caused a 'massive bleed'. He clamped the artery after I bled seven hundred millimetres, in how many seconds I do not know. Since the chest wall was already open, he excised the part of my lung that contained the blisters and stapled together the remainder. Therefore, the primary reason for this open surgery was to stop the bleeding, not to seal the lung that should have been repaired by the keyhole surgery.

The first opinion that was received from Professor Smith, dated the 16th of February 1998, absolutely floored me because he stated that, in conclusion, 'The manner in which the VATS surgery was performed conforms to accepted standards… In my opinion, the procedures followed in the surgical management of this case were those which would be undertaken by a majority of competent, experienced consultant cardiothoracic surgeons and I can detect no deviation from these norms by Mr Lynch.' He also stated that the bleed was life threatening and therefore the conversion to an emergency thoracotomy had to be performed.

However, there was one huge misinterpretation in Professor Smith's opinion and Michael, due to Mr Lynch's extremely poor handwriting, informed him that he had mistaken the word 'nipple' for 'middle'. This was quite understandable given the poor quality writing and even more so because Professor Smith could not possibly have countenanced the fact that a thoracic surgeon would deliberately make a porthole through the breast. Because of this error, the operation notes were the source of a considerably huge delay in processing the litigation.

When Michael wrote back to Professor Smith with the issues and enclosed a Polaroid photograph where the instrument had gone through my breast, he completely overturned his original opinion and stated in his letter of the 15th of June, 'I believe that the statement that the entry port was by making an incision 2.5 cm lateral to the nipple of the right breast is extremely important.'

He added, 'The whole point of VATS operations is that the small incisions for the insertions of the ports should inflict as little damage to the chest wall as possible. For that reason, the accepted area in which the incisions are placed is usually the lateral chest wall where the muscle and overlying tissues are relatively thin and where there are no important vascular, nervous or other structures. The placing of the incision would cause the port to pass through normal breast tissue and this must be regarded as a clear deviation from acceptable practice.'

What a monumental turnaround of opinion and I was so very relieved, otherwise I would not have had a case no matter how horrendously Mr Lynch had treated me both before and after that fateful day.

This revised opinion of Professor Smith's removed a heavy burden from my mind but what was even as important was that it gave me great trust in him knowing he was completely objective and I knew that if the case came to trial I would have no fear of his point of view. I then had a complete set of professional photographs taken of all my injuries and scars and Michael forwarded them to both experts.

On the 12th of January 1999, Mr Makey wrote a very detailed account of my history. He also stressed that, 'Her consent form surprisingly reads, "Operation of Laparoscopic" instead of "Thoracoscopic blebectomy". Despite the poor writing, I was able to decipher almost the entire operation note and the 10 mm port was inserted in the mid-axillary line through the seventh space, which would be usual practice. The largest port (12 mm in size) was inserted through the right breast one inch lateral to the nipple. This is not usual practice. Aberrant internal mammary vessels must be very rare and I have not seen them in an aberrant situation myself. Mr Lynch does not accurately describe their situation.'

Both experts stated they had never seen or heard of a mammary artery running more than five centimetres lateral to the sternum and that Mr

Lynch's statement to me that my artery ran down close to my side could not be true. The other main points were that if the video camera had been inserted and used properly and the chest was visualised it would have shown up any aberrancy or lesion. If clear, then the second and third instruments for grasping the lung tissue and the stapler could be placed appropriately. In my case, there was no evidence of any obstructions in my chest and the VATS should have proceeded to a successful conclusion. There was a question as to whether the instrument was placed at an oblique angle. The experts could also not understand why the third instrument was inserted at my shoulder blade when the second instrument had already severed my artery.

There was so much about this operation that was completely puzzling and, as I have already said, Mr Lynch's operation notes were very sketchy but the critical information was there. Michael advised me, after he had received Professor Smith's report, to write to Mr Lynch, which I did on the 13th of July 1998, asking him to explain to me how my artery could possibly be where he told me it was as I had been led to understand that it is located near the sternum, not out near one's side. When I did not receive an answer, I sent him a reminder on August the 18th but, not surprisingly, I never received a reply. Michael submitted both experts' reports to senior counsel, Mr Liam McKechnie for his opinion as to the likelihood that I would win a case for negligence.

It took until March of 1999 to receive all the opinions and the conclusion that I had a bona fide case. The recommendation offered was that proceedings should be issued in the high court, which had to be done before the statute of limitations of three years expired. All my contacts with Michael during this period were very professional and I was very impressed by his competence and efficiency. Consequently, I did everything to cooperate fully in forwarding any information he requested and other information I discovered myself through research.

Edward, at the time, warned me about the difficulty in winning a medical negligence action but I already was aware of that. Then one Sunday, while I was recuperating from a recent procedure performed by Dr O'Keeffe, I asked Edward that instead of attempting to dissuade me, would he go to the medical library in University College Dublin and research as much information on VATS as he could. He knew his way around the library having spent four years studying veterinary medicine. Off he went and when he returned several hours later, he was laden with copious articles illustrating diagrams of the operation from a wide range of medical journals. He also had a completely different view on things. The shift in his opinion was quite forceful as he was now convinced that Mr Lynch had, in fact, deviated from safe, standard and acceptable practice.

This surgery was not at an experimental stage, it had been established for years. All of the diagrams in the articles of how the operation should be performed were the same in that there is a 'triangle of safety' below the armpit where the three instruments should have been placed. All the research differed completely from Mr Lynch's performance of VATS. Also, when I felt a little better I went to the same library to carry out further research and in the end Edward and I had accumulated approximately fifty references that described in detail how the operation should have been performed. I read through all of them and forwarded several to Michael who found them enormously beneficial. In not even one article did I read of any other way of performing VATS and it had become standardised worldwide by 1996.

When I was making the final tough decision to take the action against Mr Lynch, it was by no means easy. I am sure that the majority of people, if they could, would avoid having to go to the courts but there was no other option for me but to go the aggressive route.

I was so ill at the time that I was prepared to risk everything as my entire future security was in total jeopardy even though I felt the enormity of what I was about to do. I also suspected that Mr Lynch would not make it easy for me, given his previous behaviour and his treatment of me as a patient. But even I could not have predicted the lengths he would go to; he was clearly out for more blood, so to speak. I did not want reprisal or revenge and certainly, the litigious route is not the way to make easy money, quite the opposite. My sole motive was to obtain some security for the future and at least I had no dependants to worry about. I am not a reckless person and much groundwork was done before Michael's recommendation and my decision to proceed with the case.

Thank goodness I was at least mentally prepared for taking this course of action even though it was an overwhelming and daunting prospect. However, throughout my career I had dealt with people from many professional disciplines, including solicitors and barristers. Also, the fact that throughout my life I had to speak in public as part of my business career and, in addition, give piano performances, helped to give me the confidence to control my nerves and anxiety. I wanted to maintain my cool when I eventually got into the witness box. My main concern was the ability to physically hold up.

The first time I actually met Michael in person was on the 21st of July 1998 after the report from Professor Smith was received. Before that, all communication was easily dealt with by telephone. We made an appointment to meet outside the law library in the Four Courts in Dublin to discuss the case. I had been there before on business when it was relatively quiet but not at the law library. I arrived at the Four Courts and walked through the ornate Round Hall and a maze of corridors that reminded me of the hospital. When I entered the anteroom of the library, it was absolutely packed. There were groups of people jostling everywhere, at tables and huddled in corners, discussing cases with their legal teams and there was a continuous flow of barristers going in and out of the library. It was a hive of activity and buzzing with energy. I found the whole experience strangely and ultimately exciting.

I had no idea what Michael looked like and finally this tall, young and confident looking man appeared and I knew it was he. He spotted me and introduced himself and we went down to the café, a den of activity as well. He had a great manner and spoke to me assuming I was an intelligent woman and I knew then that he was the best man to take on the case. I had struck lucky. I do not know what Michael expected to see but no matter how ill I felt I always swore that I would never let my external appearance decline.

At that time, to look at me, one would think there was nothing wrong; the pain lines in my face were the giveaway. If I had dressed the way I felt no doubt it would not have been a pleasant sight. Nerve pain is so intangible and invisible and the proof for all my symptoms and horrible scars were well hidden beneath my clothes. If anything, I underplayed my condition and suffered in silence although I frequently grimaced in severe pain. After meeting Michael, I have to say I knew I was in very good hands and I felt a grateful sense of relief and purpose.

***

Between the 8th of February 1997, when I had the first procedure performed by Dr O'Keeffe, I was continually fighting the enormous campaign to try to retrieve as much as I could of my pre-June 1996 condition. Dr O'Keeffe told me that he was appalled at the condition I had been left in and he performed two thoracic facet joint blocks and two rhizotomies. Over time, I also had to take a combination of medication including one drug that was originally prescribed for epilepsy and was found to help block chronic pain. In addition, I would normally go to bed with an ice pack under my thoracic area and another on top. When the nerves were 'hopping' and felt as if they were 'stretching', I found that I was constantly scratching part of my chest wall. I did not realise for a while that I had inadvertently rubbed off a large area of skin, permanently exposing a sub-layer.

Dr O'Keeffe brought up the subject many times of implanting a spinal cord stimulator along my spine that would involve placing a battery in the abdomen and feeding leads connected to the battery up along the spinal column. I have to say I was freaked at the thought of it as I was still having recurring nightmares over the previous surgery. I wanted to try to improve my condition first by exhausting my will power and every other means available to me.

What I really needed, however, was physiotherapy as the procedures and medication only gave me minimal and temporary relief and my physical structure was totally out of kilter. Dr O'Keeffe referred me to Dr Ethel Brady, a chartered manipulation and medical exercise therapist, who has her own gym and designs specific exercises for various conditions. I saw her for an assessment in January 1999, while I was off work after a rhizotomy. It was then two and a half years since the surgery. She gave me a comprehensive examination and forwarded a report to Dr O'Keeffe stating that I had 'marked thoracic joint and muscle dysfunction with evidence of spinal joint and right scapular instability.' In addition, she reported that I had neural tissue disturbance due to both the thoracotomy (open surgery) and prolonged muscle guarding and immobilisation and that my ribs were very inflamed.

Her examination showed a severe level of pain associated with thoracic movements and greatly reduced strength of stabilising muscles and noted my difficulties with my right hand. She continued in her report stating that my fitness level was approximately eighty percent below my previous active life and I was only one-quarter percent fit for work. Her opinion was that because my progress had been hampered by the chronicity of the tissue changes that she could not predict how long it would take to improve my physical structure. Therefore, I had a two-fold problem: reversing the way the structures had set and then trying to strengthen and mobilise them back into a somewhat normal position.

As a result, I began a long process of over one-hour sessions in her gym which was excruciating initially, with a programme for exercise at home as well. I was utterly determined, no matter how long it took, to improve my condition, and in 1999 alone I put in fifty-three sessions. Since I had been very active all my life, I had the capability to endure a very long-term programme but anyone who has never exercised on a regular basis would find it extremely difficult to do if they are injured and many just give up. I crossed my fingers that along with building up my strength and mobilising the structures that the pressure would be taken off the nerves and the pain would ease. Well, hope really was all I had.

On one particular visit to Dr O'Keeffe, he told me that I must have something many other people do not have because, by right, I should be flat on my back on painkillers for the rest of my life. I told him that I always had a substantial amount of will power and independence and was blessed with many people who rallied around me. Since I had not died, I was going to do everything to regain some semblance of a normal existence and quality of life. He told me, however, that I would have the nerve pain for the rest of my life and, at that time, I refused to believe him. He also warned me that I would never be the same person physically as I was before the surgery and he did his very best to try to convince me to have the spinal cord stimulator implanted. But of course, I just could not come to terms with having another major procedure at that time. People can worry about undergoing an operation and they can be apprehensive about the results but when a catastrophe does occur, it is a completely different thing; one then knows bad things, tragically, do happen.

Chapter Six

With the commencement of intensive physiotherapy and the beginning of litigation, 1999 became a precursor to a particularly onerous time in my personal life. As I lay flat on my back in bed one night, with an ice-park underneath, I tried to come up with an analogy that adequately portrayed the losses in my life that had and were continuing to occur in incremental stages.

I remember watching a splendid documentary on the rapid erosion of cliff edges along parts of the English coastline, with houses and their back gardens perched precariously on top of the cliffs. Every so often, a massive portion of the land would break away and come tumbling down into the sea, crumbling into the crashing waves that absorbed the soil and carried all the evidence down into its depths. The back gardens of those houses became distorted and ravaged.

The losses I incurred after the debilitating surgery became like those erosions. My physical structure was the first to collapse, leaving me with devastating physical pain and injuries. The next dreadful loss was my piano playing and every time I passed it by, I became terribly choked and dismayed. Then all my physical and sporting pursuits were stopped in their tracks and, alas, most of my social activities were curtailed for a protracted length of time.

As my body remained inert, my thoughts came around to a personal situation, the loss of which created a huge void in my life. That surgery had prevented any opportunity, whatsoever, of even attempting to have a child and it was even more harrowing because I always had great affinity with children. Most important to me, however, is the fact that I always loved sitting down with children of all ages and would listen to their stories and problems and have great chats in relation to their own lives. It has always amazed me how wonderfully inventive and creative children are and I have learned much from them. Even playing with them made me feel young and, like my father and grandfather before me, I was just as adept at making up gritty stories to regale them with. All those aspirations, however, were now gone forever.

It always remained in my subconscious, however, that if in the future a cure for my symptoms and intractable pain would be found, I would try to adopt a teenager. Now that that chunk of missed opportunity had crashed mightily down into the deep waters, the next harrowing and odious sadness and loss was about to crack like an earthquake on the top of that cliff.

***

When Edward and I met in May 1994, he was the man I had always hoped I would end my days with. During the two years prior to the surgery, we were constantly together when our work was finished. It was amazing we had so much in common. We were both from the country but also comfortable in the city. At the end of a week of hard labour, neither of us desired pressure in our social and personal lives. We never planned in advance but frequently, after work on a Friday, Edward would pick me up and we would travel to many parts of Ireland. I had never stayed in bed and breakfast accommodation before but even in those days, the standard was very high. We stayed in every conceivable type of place along our journeys and got to know the owners as if we were non-paying guests. Edward would always insist on doing the driving and I loved relaxing back, absorbing un-before seen landscapes in west Cork, Kerry and all up along the western seaboard. I knew the rest of the world far more extensively than Ireland. Clifden in county Galway was a place we frequently stayed in and we loved Roundstone in Connemara, a small, quaint and picturesque village with a fishing harbour.

It was always the case that we were as equally comfortable sitting together in silence reading the newspapers or while driving, as going off to some social function. If he wanted to see his friends alone as sometimes I did, it was never a problem. There was no glue between us and no hassle. Every week, if we were not scurrying off somewhere, we went to the theatre or cinema, always going to a restaurant afterwards. On Sundays, he loved watching Formula 1 or rugby, whichever was on television and I did not mind. We also took regular holidays abroad and were very contented travelling together and experienced some wonderful things. I remember on one particular trip to mainland Greece, we travelled down south to Cape Sunion where the temple of Poseidon is located. This was known to be a place to experience one of the most blazing sunsets in the world and many tourists congregated for hours so as to miss nothing.

Edward and I were sitting on rocks admiring the view and then he picked up a small, sharp stone and carved the words on a large rock, 'Edward loves Christine'. Neither he nor I were very effusive with emotional language so I decided to take a picture, but no, I did not frame it. I have it stored with myriads of photographs that were taken since I was a child. That was a special moment in a special place. True to form, when the sun did begin to set, we were totally awed by the spectacular experience. Having travelled extensively, it was the most spectacular one I had ever witnessed. Even after two years, our relationship was very intimate and we could barely contain our desire to see each other again.

It is extremely difficult to fathom just how shocked and appalled Edward felt after what happened to me in the operating theatre in 1996 as he was so used to seeing how independent and full of energy I was. To see me suffering so horrendously was something he could never have imagined but throughout the following three years, I was never demanding. However, I often woke up in the middle of the night in terror, if, indeed, I had been able to get some sleep, reliving the nightmare of coming to after the surgery and would be frozen solid in my bed. All I could do was to reach out to my telephone and ring him.

Edward gave me a great suggestion and that was to immediately switch on the radio on my bedside table. He would then talk me down, trying to ease out the fear from my mind. He was always ready to hurriedly dress and come up to me if I needed him. Most of the time, however, I calmed down by telephone and since he lived some distance away and had an extremely busy working life, I would not ask him to do so. It was enough that I had already broken his sleep during the middle of the night. He always knew I was not into drama or made undue difficulties for others so when I contacted him he knew it was urgent.

He would often, especially at weekends, bring me out to ensure I ate sufficiently and to distract me from the horrid symptoms as much as he could. He had seen me at my best and at my worst through no fault of my own. So many times I was almost passing out or did pass out and he felt grave responsibility for me. At least he knew, through his medical training, what to do and I always felt that whenever I was with him, no matter what happened he would protect and save me from dire consequences. In the five and a half years we had been together, we often sparred and had great debates but we never argued; we had nothing to argue about.

In November 1998, after Dr O'Keeffe performed the second rhizotomy on my thoracic area, I found it very severe and I was weak after it. Since it was winter, he gave me adamant advice to get to the sun to recuperate, as it was essential. He advised that I really needed to stay for two weeks to feel the benefit of it. When I rang Edward that night I told him what Dr O'Keefe advised and I was going to book a hotel right on the beach and just relax and recover. Then, if I was able to, I could take a short stroll along the beach from time to time to build up my stamina. I had intended to go on my own but Edward insisted on accompany me. It so happened a woman from my hometown was there recovering from cancer so we spent considerable time together while Edward went on very long walks. She told me she had noticed me boarding the plane and I looked dastardly pale and ill.

After Edward and I arrived back in Ireland and after Christmas, things between us deteriorated and I still had all my symptoms to cope with. Then after I began the physiotherapy, we spoke on the phone on the 28th of March and it concluded with my asking him to take time to consider our future and then to contact me one way or the other. However, I instinctively knew I was giving him a way out.

I could not blame him, as it was not his fault I was in such desperate physical condition and my symptoms were not going to just suddenly disappear. My recovery, if it ever happened was going to be long and protracted. Edward was still a relatively young man, only four years older than me and I knew he could meet someone who did not have all the physical problems I had to cope with every second of every single day. I certainly did not want him remaining with me out of sympathy and I knew it was going to be a very difficult rift. So that night, I virtually imagined the second last piece of land pulling apart from the cliff and the only remaining piece under which the houses perched related to my career.

On a few occasions, I almost picked up the phone to talk to Edward but then I would pull back thinking it probably would not be fair as it was bad enough one life having been turned on its head. At least he could get on with his life; God only knew what was going to happen to mine in the long-term. I did not know what was going on in his life and I did not keep in contact with any of his relatives because it would have been too severe a heart-breaking reminder. It was, after all, his decision to make and I had to give him space to make it.

The biggest priorities I held onto were to rehabilitate myself and continue at work and I had to ensure that everything else took second place; I was determined not to waste any opportunity to improve my condition and retrieve some normality. I was so glad that during the years

I had spent with Edward I had not neglected my friends and family, so in that respect I was not isolated and alone.

I continued to focus on building up my stamina, resetting my physical structures and kept my mind busy with work and the preparation for the trial. My determination in getting up after constant physical knock-backs did not wane and I believed one day, sometime in the far-off future perhaps, when I got up I would stay up. I also spent more time resting in my parents' home and taking long walks on the land. Fortunately, I was always an avid reader. I tried to hang on to and construct as many positive thoughts as I could feed my brain with and the hope that one day I would get a cure for the intractable pain or at least reach a level I could cope with, without assistance or intervention.

Chapter Seven

On the 14th of June 1999, after my case was lodged in the high court, an extraordinary thing occurred. Michael telephoned and asked me if I had a few moments to talk; he seemed a little hesitant which was quite incongruous with his usual self. He informed me he had just received a telephone call from Mr Lynch asserting that my symptoms were all due to a psychiatric illness. I am afraid I could not help myself and I burst out laughing which I believe took Michael by surprise. I explained this was par for the course with Mr Lynch, his intentions were so obvious and predictable and he would fight back as ruthlessly as he could. I found it highly amusing because if anyone was suffering from an illness, I thought it was Mr Lynch, given his behaviour to date. And much later on he, himself, admitted in court he had personal problems in his own home.

This was the first taste of his venom Michael had experienced first-hand. One would have to be, in my opinion, either a very irrational person or the ultimate egoist to telephone a plaintiff's solicitor to make an allegation about his client without having any basis whatsoever on which to prove it. Even if I did have a mental health problem, it would have absolutely nothing to do with what happened to me.

What Michael told me next were the most outrageous and chilling claims I had yet heard and they silenced my laughter. Mr Lynch actually told him and was adamant that he had not gone through my breast and nothing untoward had happened to me when he was performing the VATS. My breath caught because this time I was totally stunned. Michael relayed that he pre-empted Mr Lynch by quickly cautioning him and advised him that he had his operation notes in front of him.

He referred to where Mr Lynch had noted the entry made through my breast that resulted in my artery being severed. His response was that his operation notes must be wrong. Then he amazingly suggested that the scar on my breast might be the mark of a chest drain. *Was he absolutely mad I wondered, a chest drain placed in through a breast?* Then when that explanation was knocked on its head, he had the temerity to state that it must be the main open surgery scar. It was absolutely ludicrous and totally unacceptable that a consultant cardiothoracic surgeon practicing in one of Ireland's major hospitals denied his own operation notes, written and signed by his own hand, lied about his surgery.

As if the above were not enough, Mr Lynch actually admitted to Michael that he had two stacks of claims against him on his desk, some of which were genuine and others, including mine, which were malicious. Just how many claims did he have, I was afraid to ask?

Michael, of course, informed Mr Lynch that he would have to report to me what he had said since I was his client and he would not expose himself to any behaviour that could be considered unethical. Apparently, not at all happy with this, Mr Lynch became very irate and told Michael it was a 'confidential' conversation. But he had barked up the wrong tree there and he must have believed that he could have a fireside chat with Michael off the record and as a result, he would drop my case. But Michael, being his thorough self, immediately after the conversation concluded, took down a comprehensive memorandum of what had transpired and what was said.

I commented to him, 'You are a top notch solicitor and you are angered by him. Now, can you imagine what a patient, who is in a hospital bed, ill, injured and vulnerable, has to deal with?' And I believe he got the picture.

Michael added that he was impressed and glad I was taking Mr Lynch's personal remarks about me so well. I explained they were so ludicrous what other reaction could I have had when I knew the man so well and what he was capable of. In fact, that telephone call was probably the best thing that Mr Lynch could have done to jeopardise his defence. It also gave Michael a much-textured taste of how difficult it was going to be to deal with him in the future. I believed I knew the devious and malevolent mind he had and I was very much convinced, especially after denying his notes, that he was not going to be able to defend his surgery. The only other option for him was to go on the attack and try to destroy my character and credibility. Since there were many other claims against him he may have thought I was an easy target with which to clear his name or that I would wane and be frightened off and not proceed with the litigation.

But the major problem for Mr Lynch going that route was that he did not deign to get to know anything about me in the hospital or in the aftermath: not about my career, or my education, or interests and certainly nothing about my personal or social life. If he was going to try to dig for dirt he would be well disappointed. Yes, he could make up a number of unsubstantiated claims and daft allegations in court but alleging and proving are two quite different scenarios. I may have quite a few flaws but I have no sordid history and in this regard, I was not in the least bit apprehensive. Yes, I made an allegation against Mr Lynch that he was medically negligent but I would have to pursue a course to the ends of the earth and risk financial ruin to prove it.

I am always amazed by the assumptions that individuals like Mr Lynch, and I do mean individuals, may erroneously make about their patients. Do they assume we are less intelligent, when we could be more? Do they assume we are less qualified in our own disciplines, when we could be more? And do they think that we all believe ourselves to be inferior to them? If Mr Lynch assumed that I did not have the nerve or wherewithal to proceed with my case he was definitely delusional. If he thought, because he said so, that everyone else would believe his opinion over mine, he was equally delusional. As he tried in January 1997, in my opinion, to pin my symptoms on another part of my anatomy, he was now trying and would keep attempting to try to slander my character. I knew he was going to feverishly fire up a dirty campaign.

When our conversation concluded I began to question that if many of Mr Lynch's patients were suing him, how many were out there who had not had the wherewithal to take an action against him if they thought they had meritorious cases? I am certain the lucky ones will swear by him but what percentages of injuries and deaths were there compared to international statistics? It became a real worry in my mind that if this man could lie so easily to me, my family, my partner and to my own solicitor, denying his own operation notes, he had lied to other patients and their families.

I was not prepared for yet another astounding revelation so soon after my telephone conversation with Michael. The seed was planted when I signed a consent form authorising Dr Duignan, my GP, to release copies of my medical records to date. By this time, I had informed Drs Duignan, O'Keeffe and Brady that I was taking an action for medical negligence against Mr Lynch. I informed them they could expect requests from Michael asking for reports on my treatment, current condition and future prognosis.

Then, in August 1999, when Michael received my medical records from Dr Duignan, we discovered another major untruth. Unbeknownst to me, Mr Lynch had written him a letter on the 3rd of July 1996 reporting on my surgery. It had been summarised on Dr Duignan's computerised records. Mr Lynch told him a shocking lie: that he had performed keyhole surgery on the 5th of June 1996 and, '*That night* she developed a massive bleed as she had an aberrant internal mammary artery in her right chest wall. I therefore had to convert to a right open thoracotomy.'

My gosh, I dreaded to think, even three years before he made the claim to Michael that no complication had occurred during his VATS procedure, he also told my general practitioner that the 'massive' bleed occurred copious hours later as post-operative haemorrhage. I really did believe I had been sufficiently shocked by Mr Lynch's behaviour and lies before this but obviously I was wrong. No wonder he had not released his own records.

One way or another Michael was going to get a copy of the original of that letter. So here was another piece of vital evidence we would have for the trial. Michael also noted a second letter Mr Lynch had written to Dr Duignan after my two-week stint in the hospital in January and February 1997, so we awaited the complete text of this as well.

***

As Christmas Eve approached that year, 1999, my thoughts were constantly interrupted by what could have happened to Edward. I had received no contact from him and we had spent every holiday season together, breaking only on Christmas morning to go to our respective parents. I thought after all we had been through, I could not let it pass by without wishing him a happy Christmas. I rang his home number on Christmas Eve reaching his voice-mail. I left a brief message extending good wishes. I was not to know until much later that that telephone message unintentionally set the cat among the pigeons.

The year 2000 arrived and, unexpectedly, a partner of one of Edward's friends telephoned me with shocking news. He had become engaged at Christmas and the wedding was planned for Easter. My immediate instinct was that this was not in keeping with Edward's normal behaviour. I knew he might go along with it for a little while but would then kick to touch. I remember thinking of that song, 'I know him so well', and I instinctively believed I knew Edward thoroughly.

Then a short time later, one of his cousins telephoned me with the same news. She was appalled at the situation but felt she had to tell me. She told me that Edward's family could not understand what he saw in his fiancé and they were all praying he would come to his senses before the wedding. However, beauty is always in the eyes of the beholder and Edward obviously saw something in her he liked, at least for a brief while. I believed it was a classic case of a rebound situation.

As I predicted, it did actually transpire that only three weeks before the wedding, Edward bowed out. Everyone was so relieved, apart from me. That surgery and its consequences did not only affect me; it impacted on all those around and close to me.

***

By April of 2000, we had yet to receive a response from either Mr Lynch or his insurance company, the Medical Defence Union (MDU). As he had failed to report my claim against him or indeed his other claims, Michael issued a Motion for Judgement in Default of Appearance. On the 10th of April, Mr Lynch turned up in court to defend himself. Mr Justice Declan Budd who, according to Michael, is an incredibly patient man, lost such patience with Mr Lynch that he told him in no uncertain terms to take legal advice. In any event, he granted him eight weeks within which to deliver an appearance.

The junior counsel for my case, Ms Karen O'Driscoll had appeared in court that day on Michael's behalf. In a letter to him she reported, referring to Mr Lynch, 'He reiterated this point which he has previously made to us that he had a confidential communication with your good-self and that you repeated the remarks in a letter back to him. I confirm that the judge took absolutely no notice of this claim and proceeded to point out to the defendant that he was talking to the plaintiff's solicitor and the unspoken words were that there should be no expectation on the defendant's behalf in this regard.'

Karen went on to say that, 'The defendant indicated to the court that the plaintiff's only complaint was that she had a sore chest and he made no reference whatsoever to the allegation made against him that he had actually severed the plaintiff's mammary artery. He again made the statement that he had a number of such claims on his desk and some were genuine and he indicated that this claim was not.'

After receiving Karen's letter, Michael wrote to the MDU in London and enclosed a copy of the plenary summons that had been issued and served upon Mr Lynch. He asked the MDU to confirm that they would be insuring him in respect of this matter. Upon receipt of their confirmation, he would forward them all the relevant details relating to the claim.

Almost a year had already been wasted because of Mr Lynch's attitude and behaviour and it did not bode well for the trial to proceed anytime soon. The wheels were grinding and turning very slowly but at least now there was some movement and Michael was very proactive.

Then, on the 4th of May, he advised me that the MDU had made contact with him. A representative would be travelling over to see Mr Lynch in Dublin within the following week to discuss a number of cases, including my own. Michael felt that this was indeed good news that they would become formally involved and the matter would proceed in proper order.

However, an extraordinary mix-up occurred when the MDU representative contacted Michael and he began to discuss a different patient, a woman who had tragically suffered locked-in syndrome. This is a condition where the patient is alert but paralysed. Michael advised him immediately of his error and when I was informed of this, my mind immediately switched back to when I was in hospital after the surgery and the young woman opposite me who could only blink 'yes' or 'no'. Was this the same patient's case the representative had begun to discuss? I desperately feared it was no coincidence.

Following that conversation, the MDU appointed Arthur Cox & Co., Solicitors, in Dublin, to represent Mr Lynch. Michael wrote immediately to them requesting that they enter an Appearance in the matter as per the Order of Mr Justice Budd that they proceeded to do on the 19th of May. Up to that point, I had already sent Michael the originals of my entire out-of-pocket medical and physiotherapy bills, prescription receipts and other expenses, a huge sum by this stage.

Since Mr Lynch had still not furnished copies of his records, including the two letters to Dr Duignan we knew to exist by the end of January 2001, Michael informed me that an Order for Discovery was made against him on the 1st of February. He was allowed a period of eight weeks, again, in which to make Discovery of all of his records which he held relating to his treatment of me. If he did not comply with the Order then a Motion for contempt of court would be brought against him. Michael informed Arthur Cox & Co. of this and said that he regretted having to make a threat of bringing a Motion for committal if Mr Lynch did not comply. He stated that they should appreciate that there had been wholly unnecessary and avoidable delays of at least eighteen months in prosecuting the proceedings due to the attitude which had been adopted by Mr Lynch to date.

By the 29th of March, Arthur Cox & Co. believed they had received all of Mr Lynch's records and they forwarded copies of them to Michael along with a copy of the Affidavit of Discovery Mr Lynch signed on the 28th of March 2001. He swore he had provided every document he had in his possession relating to my treatment. It turned out to be another blatant and fateful lie and the gravity and seriousness of swearing a false oath did not elude me.

I could imagine their reaction, or thought I could, when Michael replied to Arthur Cox & Co. and advised them of the non-disclosure of Mr Lynch's two letters to Dr Duignan. He requested that they proceed to obtain copies, which they did and forwarded on the 4th of April. I wondered and waited to discover what they were going to do about the fact that their client swore a false affidavit and I believed there would be repercussions. Surely, I thought, there was going to be a reprisal for Mr Lynch because he compromised their defence of him. I worried about what such reprisal would mean for my case. I was now beginning to believe Mr Lynch was not only a chronic liar but also a notorious one.

The complete letter that was sent to Dr Duignan by Mr Lynch on the 3rd of July following the surgery stated, 'This lady was admitted to St. Vincent's Hospital under my care on the 30th May 1996. She was found to have a right pneumothorax. Going into her past history, she also had an earlier pneumothorax in April of 1996 in this lung.' *There was no mention of any other previous medical history, an issue that would eventually become very contentious in court.* 'Otherwise she appeared to be a healthy young lady.' *Of course the statement that I had 'a massive bleed that night' was there, recorded succinctly in black and white. One other note made in his letter was,* 'Post-operatively she made a satisfactory and uneventful recovery' *when in fact, instead of leaving the hospital in two to three days with just a little soreness, I left physically destitute, raw, debilitated and traumatised after two weeks. Where will his lies end, I wondered.*

In June of 2001, everything came to a head and another extraordinary situation developed that would cause major repercussions for my case. Michael first informed me that my case had been fixed for hearing in the high court for the 6th of November 2001. Finally, I thought, what long-awaited relief. But then the bombshell. He had been advised by Arthur

Cox & Co that the MDU had withdrawn instructions from them on the basis that Mr Lynch had not co-operated fully with the investigation of the claim and had prejudiced the preparation of a proper defence. An application was made to the court by Arthur Cox & Co. to come off record for Mr Lynch, which was fixed for the 23rd of July, as they could no longer represent him. On the day, Mr Justice Kearns granted the Order that now meant Mr Lynch had no insurance cover.

Michael told me that Mr Lynch showed up in person and was quite aggressive towards the judge, arguing that he had fully complied with his solicitors. Then he repeatedly made strange and outlandish statements saying this time that the cause of my pain after his surgery was not his negligence. It was caused by injections I had been given in hospital the first time my lung collapsed. I wondered, not for the first time, if there was anything this man would not make up. First a psychiatric illness and now injections I had been given in the hospital and this when I was under Dr John Hegarty's care. My goodness, I wondered, what else was there to come?

Michael also related that of course he knew this was absolute nonsense and Mr Lynch appeared to be quite irrational about the whole matter. His behaviour apparently was so grave and out of control that Justice Kearns eventually had to have him removed from the court by the Gardaí. I remember thinking that if his behaviour in front of two judges of the high court and now his tussle with the Gardaí did not convince my legal team of my ordeal as a patient at his hands, when I described the appalling lambasting, bullying and harassment he subjected me to in hospital, then nothing would.

Now I was in a real dilemma and in hindsight who could have predicted such a startling outcome? The whole case was going off the rails and taking on a life of its own that none of us would have wished for. I wondered how my legal team was going to handle this situation. Would Mr Lynch try to stall the trial? Since he now had no insurance cover, if I won the case and was awarded damages and costs, then he would have to personally pay both. That meant we could have a real battle on our hands securing funds from him and I could imagine him doing everything in his power to avoid paying at any cost. If he had not made it easy for his own solicitors and had not cooperated with them, then I was certain he would stop at nothing to drag me through hot coals. Obviously, he must have been hugely wealthy to take the risk of losing and often money and power go hand in hand.

Looking back, the enormity of the whole situation struck me forcefully. Instead of worrying about the 'what ifs' and trying to predict outcomes, I found the only way I could mentally cope with this horrible situation was to deal with it one step at a time. I focused only on each stage as it developed. In the business world, I was used to forward strategic planning but I had to quickly understand that the territory I was now in was, for me, completely unchartered. I had no option but to adjust to it.

All we could do now was to ensure that we had everything prepared for the upcoming trial and Michael would fight any move for a postponement. Any chance I thought that this entire matter would be settled out of court was now blown asunder.

***

While all the litigious proceedings were going on between March 1999 and November 2001, I was battling away trying to improve my physical condition. It was like trying to climb a mountain, slipping back a little and then having to surge forward again. In the physiotherapy gym, I had put in approximately fifty-three one, to one and a half-hour sessions in 1999, twenty-six in 2000 and twenty-seven in 2001. I also transferred the exercises Dr Brady had taught me to the local gym I had attended prior to the surgery.

When I first began the physiotherapy exercises, I do not know if I could have handled them without the rhizotomy that Dr O'Keeffe performed on me in December 1998. Trying to change one's physiology when it had set in the wrong position was extremely difficult and I was forced to rely on sheer will power if I was going to make any headway. While medication helped with the muscle, rib and breast pain, it could not control the pain from the damaged nerves. I did believe at the time, however, that when I rebuilt my structure the pressure would ease off the nerves. That was the goal I set myself and I remained the ultimate optimist. If one does not have hope, it is very difficult to survive and I kept reminding myself of that.

By the time the year 2000 came around I was getting a little stronger, although after a long day's work I would continue to collapse on the couch as soon as I arrived home. I still could not sit for any continuous length of time nor play my precious piano. Because, however, I had to gain the maximum benefit out of the exercises, I often felt very drained and exhausted.

As the physiotherapy exercises became more and more demanding, I found that I had to increase the amount and number of times I used ice but I soldiered on. I also began to learn deep breathing exercises that I found useful in easing out my chest wall. I had tried everything available to date but absolutely nothing helped ease the nerve pain. I knew, even though my right side would always remain weak and sore, that I would improve a little every year that passed. But nerve pain is a totally different type of pain and still there is much to learn about how to curb or cure it.

By March 2001, having been in hospital on a number of occasions for treatment and at various times collapsing at my work place, I inevitably missed intermittent periods of time from my duties trying to recover. I was barely able to keep going and my physiotherapy regime was being hampered.

My body took control out of my hands when one morning, in agony and distress, I attended Dr Duignan who rightly gave me no choice and pulled me from work. I went to see Dr O'Keeffe immediately and he wrote a letter to my employers advising them and insisting that it was essential I take an unbroken year from work to concentrate solely on my rehabilitation as I was in no fit state to carry on at the time. Obviously, it was quite a sum of money I had to forfeit in salary, being in senior management, but my health was far more important.

And so I began a new phase in my life because I was not worried about having to cope with work, when I would get a massive flare-up. I was able to push myself harder and harder at the physio and local gyms because I could rest whenever I needed to. In addition to the loss of salary, I still had my mortgage and other household bills to pay, people to hire to clean my home, taxis to rent and pay for groceries to be delivered because I could not lift, the costs had mounted substantially. I was very worried, however, that I would not have enough funds to cover all future medical bills and keep a roof over my head. It can be difficult to earn money but so easy to lose it.

Chapter Eight

I was now in the wilderness not knowing what course of action Mr Lynch was going to take in relation to defending himself. All my legal team could do was to finalise matters on our side and Michael succeeded in ensuring that the trial date was not deferred. He also informed me that there were rumblings that the powers that be were trying to bring the MDU back into the case to insure and defend Mr Lynch. I did not realistically believe that would happen given the fact that he obstructed their work. What was to occur next, however, was the most outlandish tactic Mr Lynch would yet perpetrate, and in my opinion demonstrated nothing short of what I believe was unlawful.

On the day when I had my appointment with Dr O'Keeffe to conduct an up-to-date assessment for his final report, I arrived and sat in the waiting room in St. Vincent's private consultants' clinic, not in the least expecting what I was going to walk blindly into. When Dr O'Keeffe came out and called me in to his rooms, I noticed he was quite agitated, certainly not his normal temperament. Before we had even seated ourselves he told me, in a clearly rattled voice, that Mr Lynch had unexpectedly stormed into his office that morning and threatened to destroy his practice if he appeared as a witness for me. Dr O'Keeffe had to demand that Mr Lynch leave his office. He also advised me that, in addition, Mr Lynch launched into a tirade of very slanderous statements about me. By now I had sat down, startled and mortified and leaned back in my chair in silent astonishment.

The first thing I wondered was how Mr Lynch could perpetrate and succeed in this threat. Secondly, just how many times had Dr O'Keeffe picked up the pieces of Mr Lynch's grandiose and inflated sense of competence, if my case was anything to go by? Surely, I thought, tampering with a witness by threatening him if he appeared as a witness had crossed the threshold into a completely unconventional and illegal realm. I really began to feel fear. What if he tried to intimidate me somehow before the trial commenced? After all, he had done it before in the hospital.

At the time, I could have felt extremely worried that Dr O'Keeffe might rethink his position of appearing for me but I knew he had more courage and integrity than that. However, clearly he was very unsettled. I think we were both equally shocked at this outrageous behaviour and I wondered just how far Mr Lynch would go to try and scare my witnesses off. In addition, it transpired, and what we were unaware of at the time, that he had also brazenly trampled into the rooms of another of my medical witnesses. It was another shocking incident that would come out in evidence much later on. This I felt was the stuff of the underworld, not the real lives of ordinary people.

As the trial date loomed we still had no idea as to how Mr Lynch was going to deal with his embattled situation. There was absolutely no movement on the part of the MDU to restore his privileges. I heard from Michael that he thought he was going to defend himself in the high court. Now, I respect everyone's right to represent themselves but I thought surely not and then I hesitated; well, we are talking about Mr Lynch. Perhaps, I sardonically wondered, since he had such grandiose opinions of himself and his abilities as a thoracic surgeon, he may have thought he had the makings of a genius barrister in addition.

When one had insurance and legal representation to start with who would choose to go down this route unless one had an almighty ego and powerful wealth and had to maintain the pretence of his lies? It was an extremely difficult prospect that my legal team now had to face. I could only imagine, going on the previous experience two other judges had with him, that it would become an extremely difficult proposition for any trial judge to either instruct, advise and keep order if Mr Lynch continued to behave in the same notorious fashion. This man was not going to be cogent in his defence; I was certain he would continue his misplaced sense of omnipotence.

It was now very clear to me that I would have to go through a difficult, unpredictable and protracted trial. I was in the appalling situation of being cross-examined by the very man responsible for destroying my life as it was, in his practised stride, without one ounce of empathy for me but bucket-loads for himself. How very ironic it was that I thought, after Dr O'Keeffe assumed my care, I would never have to deal with this man again. Now I would have to come directly face-to-face with him as he cross-examined me. The thought of it almost made me retch but somehow I would have to stomach it. At least this time, I would not be in a hospital bed and he would have no control or power over me. I would develop a strategy to block and stop him in his tracks and take back control. I was determined he was not going to faze me.

***

The experts, Professor Geoffrey Smith and Mr Arthur Makey, arrived in Dublin on Monday the 5th of November and Michael arranged a meeting late that afternoon to include the experts, Senior Counsel Mr Denis McCullough and myself. We discussed the case in detail and I found both experts to be real gentlemen and, in my humble opinion, very experienced thoracic surgeons. It was the first time I met Denis, my senior counsel, and I was exceptionally impressed by his easy manner, his quiet confidence and the way he took my own comments on board. All of those present respected my opinions and I hoped and trusted I had made a good impression on them. This was very important because every legal team wants a good witness in the box who can handle the situation confidently.

At the end of the meeting Michael told me that the way things stood, I should be prepared to be called to give evidence the following day. No one ever advised me how to answer questions or ever suggested what I should say. What I had to do was relate the whole sorry saga as clearly and logically as I could. All I had to do really was to simply tell the truth.

When I arrived home at around eight, I trawled through all my records. Even though the evidence was cast in stone in my head, I decided it would be prudent to memorise dates so that in the witness box I could make the evidence flow and not waste the court's time or frustrate the judge. Since I was not allowed to bring a prepared script of any kind into the witness box, I spent approximately three hours memorising as much as I could as if I was cramming for an examination.

As I was about to retire for the night I tried to appeal to a higher power to help me get through the opening of the trial the following day but I found it of no benefit. I needed to tap into inspiration from someone more concrete. I thought of many people who were deceased and who had loved me and vice versa including my paternal grandfather and my godmother. Even after he died, he never left my mind and when he was alive, we were particularly close. As a child, I could not wait for Saturday mornings to come around and I would run into his bedroom and lay my head in the crook of his arm while he told me story after story, most likely conjured up by him. I was always riveted and fascinated by the way he described his tales and sometimes I would laugh in stitches and at other times he would leave me woeful having put the fear of God in me.

When I lay down with an object and photograph, I tried to connect in my mind with both of them and others. It transpired that it was my grandfather I instantly felt was close by. This might seem strange and I had never really had an opinion of what happens to us after we die since I was always comfortable with not knowing. I never searched for the 'meaning of life' as I was always far too busy living it, but that night I thought it was a very comforting feeling. I required no ice and fell asleep from exhaustion knowing what I had to do the next day. I relinquished my anxiety to my grandfather who, I believed, would watch over and guide me.

***

I arose very early and had a leisurely and substantial breakfast to boost my stamina for the foreboding day ahead. Having dressed smartly as though I was going to work, in an about-turn I paused in front of the tall mirror in my bedroom and thought that to casually observe me no one would think there was anything physically wrong. For a moment I wondered if it was a mistake to look externally better than I felt but I quickly discounted the notion. No matter how ill I had been since that surgery I had never let my outward appearance decline and I knew I would never go down that road. In front of the presiding judge, I wanted to look and sound credible.

Unless people actually saw the scars and state of the right side of my body, no one would understand but my legal team had the photographs. After all, I would have my doctors and physiotherapist to testify about the agony I had gone through and was continuing to go through. However, even at that time I was still in far too optimistic a view of my future and that the offending nerves would eventually burn themselves out. Because I'd had to achieve so much exercise since January of 1999, I actually appeared trim and fit.

I took a taxi in plenty of time to the Four Courts and as I entered through the front doors into the Round Hall it was so crammed it was difficult to spot any specific individual. There were barristers, solicitors and clients everywhere, seated on benches, huddled against walls, groups in the middle; there was very little standing room unoccupied. After peering around, eventually I saw and joined the medical experts and then Michael came over to us. On the directory in the Round Hall were listed the cases to be heard that day and the courtrooms they were assigned to. I also met for the first time my junior counsel, Ms Karen O'Driscoll, who had a great personality, an exceptional wit and she was extremely intelligent. I was immediately impressed by her and she was to become a great, constant and reliable support to me during the entire trial.

It was noted that my case would be heard in Court Number 2, one of the original courtrooms circling the Round Hall. I watched out for Mr Lynch for ages, suddenly spotting him, a lone figure seated on a bench with what appeared to be a holdall with him. I thought it was very odd because surely, if he had documents he would be carrying them in either a briefcase or a folder. I was very intrigued and it was not until well into the trial that I was to discover its mysterious contents.

Michael went into Court Number 2 to check when the Judge would be sitting and when he came out again Mr Lynch had already gone in. He told me that Mr Lynch did not want a record of the trial taken because if he lost he would appeal the decision. I, therefore, had to pay the entire costs of the stenographer. So already we knew, even before the trial commenced, that if I won I would be facing the supreme court. Since he had now retired, I presumed that Mr Lynch had all the time in the world to play barrister. If he lost the case he would just appeal it and if he won, I could imagine how exceedingly gloating he would be, especially because he had represented himself. But before we got to an appeal, we would first have to win the trial and that would be our only immediate focus. It was certainly going to be an arduous and torturous journey to its final conclusion.

When I entered the courtroom with Michael, I thought I was walking into the Old Bailey with its wooden benches, wall panels and the judge's bench and witness box next to it looking down onto the pews. The ceiling was very high and ornate and the room had an airy feeling with a great sense of space. I think I had watched too many English courtroom dramas because I felt very comfortable in the surroundings.

Michael directed me to sit on a side bench next to the medical experts and I thought my case was going to commence immediately. However, the courtroom filled up with other barristers. The scene became decidedly hectic and I was rather perplexed not knowing what was happening. Then, as the judge appeared, he turned out to be none other than the President of the High Court, Mr Justice Richard Johnson.

We all stood up and after being seated again, each of the other barristers started directing questions to him in relation to their cases, asking him for approval for certain decisions, actions or to confirm a variety of matters. It seemed so overwhelming I was absolutely amazed how the judge could keep abreast of everything. I thought for a second I was watching a scene from the floor of the stock exchange and this was normal practice on a Tuesday morning. One of the medical experts said later that the whole thing was totally chaotic, yet it seemed to work.

After all the extraneous decisions were made the courtroom cleared, except for people in the public gallery. I began to take long deep breaths to try and prevent my chest wall from tensing up and to appear relaxed and confident. Then, at long last, the proceedings that were going to affect the remainder of my life commenced and one man was going to decide my fate.

Opening the case, Denis informed Judge Johnson that the lawsuit was for medical negligence and went on to give him an account of my life up to the time of the surgery. I had given him my curriculum vitae to refer to when questioning me in relation to my career to date. Immediately Mr Lynch butted in and the judge informed him that Denis was opening the proceedings and then presenting witnesses and, at that time, Mr Lynch would be at liberty to cross-examine those witnesses if he chose to. Then, of course, Mr Lynch wanted to correct some minor point and the judge told him, 'That is a matter for cross-examination, Mr Lynch.'

Denis continued on to describe the nightmare I endured when I came round post-surgery and he also informed the judge how Mr Lynch conducted the operation and the way he should have performed it. He actually described in great detail how VATS is conducted in accordance with safe, standard and accepted practice.

Then, as it approached lunchtime, Judge Johnson directed a question at Mr Lynch, 'By the way, there is something I think I should say, Mr Lynch, am I not correct in thinking you were in court yesterday?'

'That is correct.'

'You said you had an application to make of some kind, a preliminary issue; is that correct?'

'No, I'm sorry.'

Denis interjected, 'We had a preliminary application, my Lord. It was just in relation to the rules of disclosure, my Lord. What we understand is that Mr Lynch in fact has no expert reports.'

Fantastic, I thought. I did not know whether it was the case that he could not secure the services of a thoracic expert to support the way he performed the surgery or he just assumed he would be vindicated because of who he was. The trial then adjourned until 2 p.m.

To clear my mind I decided to go out and get a sandwich and take a stroll in preparation for the testimony I was about to give. As I opened the double fronted doors of the Four Courts and began to tentatively walk down the granite steps, I thought I saw a few flash bulbs going off but I dismissed the notion because reporters would not be interested in me; I was no VIP. When I returned to the Round Hall, I informed Michael about the camera flashes and he also thought that my case would not attract much attention. I would have to wait until the following day to find out. I still had some doubts.

When the trial resumed Denis continued with his evidence and he informed Judge Johnson, 'I think your Lordship will be satisfied that she has suffered genuine pain, which is now intractable pain. The doctors, my Lord, will say that it is not likely to clear up now, and that is what she faces, my Lord, into the future with a constant effect on her life and on her working life and her career, my Lord. You will be satisfied on the evidence, my Lord, that Mr Lynch was unfortunately negligent, my Lord, and that the plaintiff in consequence has suffered devastating pain and injuries, which have seriously affected her life.'

During the course of Denis's evidence, he got around to the letter that Mr Lynch sent to Dr Duignan following the surgery. 'My Lord, there is a clear reference there, my Lord, to the plaintiff developing a massive bleed *that night*. My Lord that simply is inaccurate, my Lord. That is not in fact what happened, my Lord, as is clear indeed from Mr Lynch's operative notes made at the time that the bleed occurred early on in the procedure. It occurred, according to his notes, my Lord, where he had made or had inserted the second port. Indeed, the plaintiff's evidence will be that Mr Lynch told her subsequently that as soon as he went into the right breast he realised that he had damaged the artery.'

He continued, 'Notwithstanding that, my Lord, Mr Lynch apparently made or inserted the third port for some reason, even though there was a bleed. But the fact is, my Lord, that that bleed occurred in the course of the operation and did not occur that night. As I say, that letter and the reason for it being written, my Lord is a mystery at the moment.'

As I sat listening to Denis I thought, well it is no mystery to me. I felt that anything Mr Lynch ever said or did was to detract attention from how he carried out the operation. Why would a surgeon tell a blatant lie to a patient's general practitioner and her solicitor, contradicting his own operative notes, unless a cover-up was not his motive? I certainly cannot think of any other reason and no one I know can think of any other explanation.

When Denis had concluded his lengthy and comprehensive opening statement, he advised that I was ready to give my evidence and Judge Johnson asked, 'Now, Mr Lynch, are you familiar with court practice?'

'I've been to court frequently but I am not familiar with the court practice.'

Judge Johnson informed him, 'Well, no, the situation is the plaintiff will now give direct evidence. When she is finished, you will be at liberty to cross-examine her then each of the witnesses being called by the plaintiff, you will be at liberty to cross-examine them when they have given their evidence. Then you can address the court subsequently or give evidence yourself, as you wish.'

'Thank you, my Lord.'

'With regard to the cross-examination, I recognise that you will be required to live within the limits of the rulings which I make regarding as to what is relevant. Therefore, questions which may be relevant to be asked of some of the medical experts would not be relevant to the plaintiff, if you follow me, regarding the intricacies of the various operations.'

It appeared to me, and quite rightly, that Judge Johnson was going to assist Mr Lynch conduct his own defence to the best of his abilities. However, I also hoped that Mr Lynch did not expect, or receive preferential treatment because he chose to defend the case himself.

***

When I was summoned to the witness box, I tried to suspend my emotions so that my evidence would be clear, factual and flowing. I was almost certain I had memorised the trauma of the previous five years sufficiently and could give my evidence without indulging in emotional hiccups. Therefore, I walked slowly up to the witness box, was sworn in and promptly took my seat. I peered down and saw Mr Lynch's eyes focused menacingly on me.

It appeared to me that he had thought all along I would not go through with the litigation and that I would just 'go away'. Because I had never been impolite or 'lost my head', I believe he mistook manners for stupidity. This was the time now to draw upon the experiences I gained in the world of business and the confidence I developed giving piano performances. I wanted to show that I would not be fazed when Mr Lynch eventually cross-examined me. I also had media training during my business career when I learned how to field questions by interviewers and not be tricked. I was not nervous as I looked out at the sea of faces and I purposely decided not to look in Mr Lynch's direction until such time as I had to. I focused on Denis and Judge Johnson and blocked out everyone else.

Denis addressed me by asking me direct questions about my background to date including my upbringing, education, my social and personal lives and business career. After answering his questions in a concise and I felt coherent manner he then went on to ask me to describe the circumstances which led me to go to the accident and emergency department in St. Vincent's Hospital the first time my lung collapsed and the subsequent trauma I suffered at the hands of Mr Lynch over the following five years. I described in detail and chronologically the state I found myself in and the copious treatments I had received over the years.

The time and effort I put in the previous night seemingly assisted my case. Without embellishment, I tried to relate to Judge Johnson the horrific and never-ending ordeal I had found myself in. Apart from one time when I became a little choked remembering the horror of it all, I took a sip of water to pull myself together. Presenting my evidence in a mostly detached emotional manner was credible but not difficult.

Judge Johnson interjected a number of times and asked me a myriad of questions about my current position in senior management in relation to my responsibilities and demands. I gave him an overview of my position with its inherent pressures and that I had no time to be ill. I described the consequences of the surgery, noting all the physical and social activities I had previously enjoyed and had to relinquish, and the huge losses in my personal life. I also related how the problem with my hand affected my piano playing which had been very precious to me and was my greatest passion.

Denis asked me, 'You were quite a keen pianist?' I replied that I had played the piano from a very young age and that I now played badly.

Then, suddenly, Judge Johnson interjected and asked me if I had been 'any good at it' and for a split second, I was caught off guard. I knew instinctively this question would test my credibility and was of vital importance for the remainder of the trial. I wondered how on earth I was to answer that question; it was so subjective. I still remember the capacity of the brain to process information in what seemed ages but actually only took a few seconds. I racked my brain to produce an answer that would satisfy him and would portray the modest raw talent I had in my genes.

I wondered if I should tell him that I had achieved first class honours in all the Royal Irish Academy of Music examinations and in my Leaving Certificate, I had obtained very high marks in honours' music. Also, I considered if it would be prudent to tell him that while growing up I was the pianist for the Musical Society and frequently had to sight-read scores of music in rehearsals and perform solidly for two-hour shows. Since then, I had continued to give amateur performances in the US and played with fervour until June 1996. No, I decided, those qualifications and experiences were not unusual and certainly at the low end of performance experience.

I looked at Denis and I could almost feel him willing me, intently, to give the judge a good response. And then it suddenly came to me, like a thunderbolt out of the blue. Of course, an example, that was it. Throughout my career, I had interviewed hundreds of prospective employees and regardless of the position I would always ask them to provide an example of a particularly difficult situation they had been in and how they had managed it and another hypothetical situation to see how they would apply their skills.

Then I heard the words come from my mouth because one always remembers one's first love, and I remembered my first performance, 'Well, when I was only thirteen I played a version of Tchaikovsky's Concerto No. 1 in B flat minor,' the first time I had performed formally on stage. As I looked at Judge Johnson, I knew I had struck a chord and established my credibility. I was succinctly put on the spot and what a relief I had successfully thought on my feet, so to speak. I could observe Denis's reaction and his relief was palpable. I believe it satisfied Judge Johnson since he nodded his head knowingly; I believe he knew his classical music. I felt such relief that whatever evidence I proffered from then on would be credible.

Afterwards, Denis told me that he was standing there, waiting and willing me on to come out with a good reply and he said, 'You came out with an absolute gem.' All those years of interviewing had finally paid off and for a change I had been at the other side of the interview table.

By 4 p.m. Denis wrapped up my testimony by discussing my prognosis for the future, including the probability that I would need a spinal cord stimulator which would be inserted by Dr O'Keeffe. Then Judge Johnson advised Mr Lynch that he would be able to cross-examine me first thing the next morning.

The judge retired to a meeting and I left the witness box feeling satisfied as it had been the most important performance of my life and I had only one shot at it. I never once looked at Mr Lynch, which certainly helped, but I am sure his eyes had been boring into me probably hoping I would collapse under the pressure. At least day one was over with and now I had to try to cope with Mr Lynch the following morning. In discussion with my legal team, Michael informed me that other barristers who had come into the courtroom to hear my testimony, although I had not noticed them, thought I made a very good witness so that gave me great confidence for the following morning. I could tell Michael was relieved and because the members of my legal team and counsel had put so much time and energy into my case, I certainly did not want to let them down. I did the best I could for all our sakes. Their credibility was on the line and so I went home contented even though the ordeal had left me in physical agony.

After friends called in to see me that night and having answered numerous telephone calls I went to bed to rest even though I knew I would not get much sleep. I pondered what sort of questions Mr Lynch would ask but, again, all I had to do was answer them truthfully. What I was afraid of were his behaviour and the lies I was certain he would trump up and throw at me. I just had to be confident of both Denis and Judge Johnson and I left it, finally, in the lap of the gods and my grandfather during the black hours of the night.

Chapter Nine

I awoke at dawn, after a short, fitful sleep, two ice packs under my thoracic area having completely thawed and I wondered what was in store for me that day, Wednesday, November the 7th. I decided to arise immediately and perform some stretching and flexibility exercises on my chest wall in preparation for the anticipated onerous morning. I had to get to the Four Courts by nine to meet my father who was coming to Dublin to stay with me for the duration of the trial. Something was nagging at me about those camera flashes the previous day and my gut instinct kept prompting me to think my case had hit the media.

I sauntered across the road to my local newsagent and purchased *The Irish Times*, sat down and spread the paper across my coffee table, slowly and tentatively turning the pages. And there, on page four, was a large picture of me on the steps of the Four Courts with the caption, 'Retired Dublin surgeon is sued over alleged negligence.' So, it had not been my imagination. The article briefly relayed what had happened to me during the surgery but more importantly, it contained the information about Mr Lynch representing himself in the high court because he had not cooperated with his indemnifiers. It also mentioned that his solicitors, Arthur Cox & Co. had taken him to court to come off record. I was very glad I had dressed well the previous day and applied a little of my usual make-up; a bit of vanity certainly gets one through a difficult time.

As I approached the Four Courts in a taxi that morning I saw Mr Lynch, still a lone figure, walking sprightly down the quay carrying the same holdall and my curiosity was even more piqued. My father arrived and I told him I was still a little apprehensive about the media coverage. However, when I enquired of one of the medical experts if he had seen the photo and article, he laughed and said in jest, 'Well, when you are good looking, you are good looking.' I, in turn, saw the humorous side and began thinking about it in a completely different and amusing context, wondering what I had been concerned about. I had overcome another obstacle along the precarious route I had taken. Media attention was just something I was going to have to contend with on a daily basis.

At approximately 10 a.m., we all filed again into Court Number 2 and Judge Johnson opened the proceedings for the day. I took a few deep breaths and walked slowly but stoically up into the witness box again, to be cross-examined by Mr Lynch. The irony of it did not elude me. I was not nervous, however, and felt that he was not as intelligent as he probably thought he was. I believed he just used intimidation and lies to get his way.

As soon as I took my seat he immediately jumped to his feet and addressed Judge Johnson in relation to the letter he had sent to Dr Duignan after the surgery, 'My Lord, before I ask Ms Carroll a few questions, I would just like to refer to one item yesterday, a letter that was presented by the senior counsel here, Mr McCullough, to you. The letter is totally out of context. You probably remember the claim is that there was a bleed at night, whereas we know the bleed was during the operation.'

Ah, backtracking are we Mr Lynch, knowing you were caught out in your lie? You told the same untruth to my solicitor. Now that he was going down this line, I realised that there was going to be no stopping or controlling the man and that there was absolutely no telling what he would come out with over the coming days. But even I could not have imagined the allegations he was going to proffer the court without any substance. The best, or worst, was yet to come. It was going to pan out as more of a thriller than an actual civil court case. Only for the fact that I was a participant in this surreal drama, I would not have believed it. It was as if I was looking through a glass mirror at myself.

Judge Johnson responded, 'When evidence has been taken, you can address me on that. There is no difficulty. You will have all the opportunity in the world to address me on that, but at the present time, at this stage in the case, your opportunity is now to cross-examine the witness on any evidence to which she may be able to assist you.'

Finally, Mr Lynch commenced his cross-examination but I was eager and determined not to allow him to intimidate me so I assumed a steely expression. I felt I was strong enough to answer his questions in a cool manner as I had really had enough of him. So I provokingly thought, *'Now, Mr Lynch, do your worst in court as well as you did in hospital.'*

He started off with, 'Ms Carroll, I am sorry we are meeting in such circumstances. Basically, you came under my care on the 5th of June 1996, when you were transferred from the unit of Professor Keogh, his theatre; is that correct?' *Pardon? Had he forgotten I was his private patient? Had he forgotten he wrote to Dr Duignan,* 'This lady was admitted to St. Vincent's Hospital under my care on the 30.5.96?' *At this stage, I was confused as I did not know the reason behind his denial of this but there had to be a sinister motive.*

'I don't know, I just know that you were called in as my consultant.'

'Yes, but basically…'

'I don't know Professor Keogh.'

'Basically, you were on the medical unit on that day, you then went to theatre and then you went back to the surgical unit, St. Agnes' Ward; is that correct?'

'I have no idea.'

'All right. Now, I attempted to carry out a video-assisted thoracic surgery on you and I ran into a bleed and I had to convert that to an open thoracotomy. I did the open thoracotomy and I did a blebectomy. Now, the primary objective of the surgery was to prevent you having further collapses of your lung.'

Gosh, Mr Lynch, you are very adept at making it seem so minor. Why don't you state the complete facts, that I had a 'massive' bleed because you severed my artery? And the primary purpose of that surgery was to remove those blisters in the most untraumatic, safe, acceptable and standard practice there is. You were not capable of carrying out what you promised and lauded yourself for.

He continued, 'I saw you on approximately five occasions at my outpatients in the Blackrock Clinic. On the first occasion I saw you, you were complaining of a stinging pain along the wound. Would that be correct?'

'Yes.'

'It was also noted on that occasion that the right breast showed that it was minimally enlarged compared to the left breast?'

Wrong, wrong, wrong Mr Lynch and you know it.

'No, it was not minimally, it was very enlarged.'

'That is what I have written in my notes on that occasion.'

You are a blatant liar, Mr Lynch, and I have read your notes. Then, my absolutely brilliant senior counsel immediately interjected, apologised for interrupting Mr Lynch and informed Judge Johnson that his notes read, 'right breast much larger than left.' So, as well as having contradicted his own operative notes, he was now lying about his private notes. Incredible,

I thought.

I was extremely pleased that so early in the trial Mr Lynch showed his propensity for telling untruths that could so easily be disproven. I imagined that since Judge Johnson had put me on the spot the previous day, this must have indicated to him who was espousing the truth and who was not. Immediately into the trial, Mr Lynch began to show his true character. It could not have been more propitious.

He blundered on, 'The reason I have had an interest in that was in 1978 I published a paper where I had two young ladies who started lactating from the breast. It is a rare…' To which Judge Johnson interjected, 'Sorry, Mr Lynch, that is a matter, really, for your own evidence. Of the questions which you have asked her, she has disagreed with you on the question as to whether her right breast was minimally enlarged or not.'

I began to feel I was sitting there pointlessly as Mr Lynch was making more statements than grilling me on the evidence I had given. And if he had only thought about what he was saying he would have realised that he had just backed up evidence I had given the previous day in relation to my breast and the phantom pregnancy. He would not have made a very good barrister if he could walk himself into trouble so easily and I excitedly thought, the more he talks the more he trips himself up and I just had to let him 'dig his own grave' because Judge Johnson had all the documents referred to in his possession.

Since Mr Lynch's so-called 'cross-examination' had not proved fruitful for him he then went down a different track. 'On the first occasion that I saw you I ordered you therapy, I ordered you DF118?' *I looked at him wondering what relevance that had to the horrid surgery.*

I replied, 'Yes.'

'That is an opiate drug; is that correct?'

'Pardon?'

'I ordered that drug for you; is that correct?

'Yes, you prescribed DF118.' *What was he up to now?*

He went on, 'I then saw you again on the 29th of July and on this occasion you were complaining of pain beneath the right shoulder blade. You said that you were very sore in the right anterior chest and you also said you were numb low in the right chest; is that correct?'

'On both occasions I complained about the very bad pain I had in my back along with the stinging pain and the enlargement and the soreness of my breast and the pain in my ribs.'

'The other thing that you complained to me on that date was that you could not write properly with your right hand?'

'That is correct.'

'I next saw you on 28th of August and you were complaining of soreness in the right chest along the line of the wound and you also complained of pain in your anterior chest, and you also complained on this occasion of pain between the shoulder blades. In addition, you also complained that you still could not write properly with your right hand. Are those statements of fact?'

'In relation to the pain between the shoulder blades, it was around the shoulder blade area on the right side, but all the other facts are correct, yes.' *Had he not remembered he had pushed a third port under my shoulder blade? I sighed with exasperation.*

By this time, I was getting more and more confused wondering where he was going as he was all over the place. He was actually, again, backing up my testimony and serving it up to Judge Johnson on a platter.

'I then saw you on 10th of September and on this occasion you said that you just had a little pain in the back, no pain in the chest, but that your main problem was that your energy was terrible. Would that be correct?' *I stared at him dumbfounded. I thought, are you mad? Are you saying I somehow had a miracle cure in only two weeks? An amazing recovery, I do not think.*

'No, I had exactly the same complaints I had from the first time I saw you, they never decreased; the pain increased.' *He was not going to get the better of me in the witness box. I was literally fed up of his nonsense at this stage.*

Since this pack of lies had not worked for him, he then changed tactics again and became really abhorrent and malicious in an attempt to attack my character. He thought he could just spout out anything he liked and everyone was going to believe and bow to him.

'I did not see you until 27th January 1997. During that six-month period after the operation, were you getting pain relating drugs?'

'I was taking the medication from you and I also went to my GP in between.'

'What did your GP order for you?'

'You gave me enough in the end of September to last me…' *And immediately he jumped in, blatantly preventing me from completing my answer.*

'I have no record. I have only a record of ever giving you DF118 after your first visit. There is no record of my giving you any other analgesic therapy.'

Now, Mr Lynch, after denying your own operation and private notes, do you seriously think anyone is going to give credence to anything you are maliciously suggesting?

'My GP may have renewed the DF118 prescription. I cannot remember, but that is what I was taking.'

'You know a DF118 prescription; they will not renew it because it is a Schedule 4 drug.' *What is a schedule 4 drug, I wondered? And what are you talking about? Of course one has to get a prescription to renew medication and I had never even heard of DF118 until you prescribed it to me. You are being silly and malevolent.*

'That is all I was taking.'

'You presume, am I correct, that it was ordered by your GP…'

'No, I just remember you had prescribed DF118 for me.'

'On 27th of January you came to me and you were complaining of pain in your right upper back.' *Yes, in a wheelchair after collapsing in my office.*

You said that you were extremely tired. You complained that the pain was sharp and knife like, and that it radiated from the back through to the front of the chest, from the back straight through to the front of the chest; is that correct?'

'My whole chest wall was very inflamed and I was in very severe pain.'

At this stage, Mr Lynch had me really perplexed because all he succeeded in doing was corroborating the evidence I had sworn.

'I went over with you in great detail on that occasion and I was going into your past history of endometriosis, because I thought I was running into a rare syndrome called catamenia pneumothorax?'

'No, never.'

You are like an addicted gambler, Mr Lynch, with no limit to the amount you will bet. It was I, in fact, who gave this in my medical history on admission and when I asked you on January 27th 1997 if you ever discovered what caused the blisters it was only then you asked me if I had any other pre-existing conditions. You dismissed the endometriosis as irrelevant and it had been cured in the early eighties. I know what deviousness is going through your mind. Obviously for the trial, you have trawled through all my records and spotted this in my admission's record. Little did I know in 1997, however, that you would use this information in a malicious way because you are going to grasp at anything you think you might use to your advantage.

'When I saw you I thought that you looked pale and distressed and I found that you were tender between the shoulder blades. So, I brought you into hospital and I had you seen by a number of other consultants. I had you very extensively investigated. You were seen by Dr Walter McNicholas, a respiratory physician, I had you seen by Dr Moore who is a cardiologist, I had you seen by Dr Michael Hutchinson who is a neurologist, and I had an extensive range of investigations of your cervical/thoracic spine, your chest and your abdomen; is that correct? In fact, I even had an MRI of your spine done?'

'Yes, that is correct.'

But what good reason had you for checking out my heart when I never had a problem with it? What good reason had you for checking out my abdomen when I never had a problem with it? What good reason was there for any of it when all the pain I was experiencing was in my right chest wall from your surgery? You should have had the neurologist see me immediately and I would have avoided two weeks again in hospital on morphine that only you prescribed. So obviously, you knew I needed it. And now you are trying to persuade Judge Johnson that you had been very thorough and had put me through all those tests for my own good rather than having an ulterior motive for doing so.

'All these tests were reported as normal?'

'The neurologist did not say it was normal.'

'Basically, what I am asking you is why are we here in court, why do you bring me to court?'

'I have been in extreme pain since the operation.'

'Are you sure that all this was caused by the operation?'

'One hundred per cent.'

'One hundred per cent?'

'Yes.'

'That extreme pain, you are not really able to tell me who was supplying you the analgesics, who was writing the prescriptions?' *But you have just said, 'I ordered you DF118' and I did tell you if you had just listened to me. Oh Mr Lynch, the gloves are off and by God you are fighting dirty, right into the gutter.*

'You did.'

'I wrote one prescription?'

'No, every time I went to see you, you wrote me a prescription for DF118.'

'No, I have no record of that.'

'That is it.' I finished.

Judge Johnson then had to intervene and call Mr Lynch's bluff as he had to put an end to this charade and he asked me which chemist I used and after I gave him the details he responded, 'Very good'.

What was incredible was the fact that I had given my solicitor the original prescription receipts for any medication I had purchased and which were in the book of evidence, for all parties to see and shame on Mr Lynch for the absolutely scurrilous accusations he was trying to get Judge Johnson to believe. But he proceeded, 'Basically, you are complaining of terrible pain since your operation; is that correct?'

'Yes.'

'This is affecting your life severely?'

'Yes.'

'My Lord, everything in Ms Carroll's case…'

'You are addressing me now, I want you to ask questions.'

'Ms Carroll, is it correct that you were admitted to St. Vincent's Hospital on 19th of April 1996, through Casualty, to the care of Dr John Hegarty?'

'I was admitted, yes, that is correct, yes.'

'Is it correct that you had local anaesthetic put into your chest, that you were given a dose of 75 mg of Pethidine intramuscularly, and Stemetil 12 mg intramuscularly, at 19:40 hours that day?'

Judge Johnson intervened, 'Ms Carroll, unless you know precisely the answers to that question…'

'The only thing I can say is that I was given a local injection in the side so they could put in a chest drain. I have no idea what I was given by the doctors.'

'Do you not remember getting those other two injections at the same time?'

I thought, for God's sake, I was lying on my side getting a drain shoved up into my lung. I could not even see what the doctor was doing; never mind what he was giving me.

'No, I don't remember what medication was given to me.'

'Well, they are documented. Later that evening, at 23:00 hours, you were given Voltarol 75 mg intramuscularly. The drain that was initially put in was a size 32 drain and the next morning that was found not to be functioning satisfactorily, so that was taken out and changed to a tiny size 20 drain.'

Judge Johnson, tiredly it seemed, from hearing all these statements, interjected, 'Mr Lynch, it is the problem of the cross-fertilisation of cultures. The vast majority of people when they go to hospital know as little about what is happening as the vast majority who come into court. Now, this witness, I doubt very much if she knew what were the exact drugs that were being given to her. You can give evidence yourself, you can call witnesses to give the evidence, but there is no point in asking this witness to know precisely what drugs she was given in hospital unless she was in a position to know.'

'My Lord, this lady worked in a hospital.'

I did not, Mr Lynch. You are so busy trying to throw out ridiculous assertions that you never listen, but make no mistake about it, Judge Johnson does.

'She worked in administration. Does every patient ask precisely what drugs they get when they are getting an injection or the volume?'

'Well, now, I will keep it very simple, my Lord.'

'Just ask the questions.'

Then showing complete contempt for and ignoring Judge Johnson, and in a blatantly arrogant voice he continued, 'On 20th of April, according to your hospital notes, you were given six injections of 75 mg of Pethidine, two injections of 50 mg of Voltarol and three injections of Stemetil that day. In other words, you had eleven injections that day for pain; is that correct?'

'I have no idea. I had a chest drain in, my lung was still collapsed, I was still in pain. I do not know what I was given.'

You will not succeed in riling me, Mr Lynch. But I was, however, aghast and dumbfounded by this information. I knew it could not be true but I did not have the records in front of me to check and see what I had actually been given but certainly it was not even close to what Mr Lynch was stating. Otherwise I would have been dead, I was so unused to any kind of drugs, especially six injections of Pethidine.' He was just tossing out all these names and volumes, trying to impress and I had not a clue what he was going on about. But I did check out later what Stemetil is and it is not even a painkiller, it is administered for nausea. I wondered what Dr Hegarty would think about Mr Lynch's assertions since it was his care I was under and I had absolutely no complaints.

Judge Johnson had already warned Mr Lynch not to ask me questions I could not possibly answer but he flouted his authority. He was obviously trying to deflect attention from his surgery and turn it on its head, dropping Dr Hegarty into it. *Who is free from your venom, Mr Lynch?* However, he would not be controlled and blundered on and on and I silently wished Judge Johnson would demand he stop.

'I have no idea as to the accuracy. All I know is I had a collapsed lung, I was in a lot of pain, I had a chest drain in through my side, it was all very distressing and I know the doctors gave me pain medication while I was going through this process. I do not know any other details.'

'I agree with you,' interjected Mr Lynch. 'I have been a chest surgeon for almost forty years and when a person comes in with a pneumothorax, at one end of the spectrum they feel nothing and at the other end of the spectrum they feel horrible pain. You were obviously one of these people that when you got your pneumothorax you got horrible pain?'

'I had almost a totally collapsed lung flapping against the spine I was told.'

'The other problem that you had was you had to get this chest drain put in, and getting a chest drain put in is generally very painful. Would you agree with that?'

'It wasn't that bad.'

'Well, generally, it is very painful.'

'Well, I didn't experience that.'

'My experience of dealing with hundreds and hundreds of people like you is that when a person gets a pneumothorax and has severe pain you give them one shot of an opiate drug and, generally speaking, that takes care of the situation.' *People like me? How could it take care of the situation when my lung was still collapsed the following morning, Mr Lynch?*

Judge Johnson had finally had enough, 'Mr Lynch, once again you are making speeches or else you are giving evidence, but you are meant to be cross-examining and cross-examination is a question of putting your case to them or else asking them questions which they may be capable of answering.'

'All right, my Lord. My Lord, could I take Ms Carroll on to the 30th of May 1996?'

'Of course.'

Then he went on to cover the period of time when I was admitted to hospital the second time. He argued that he never used the word 'cinch'. But he did use it and I swore it under oath. He was acting, in my opinion, just like a terrier with a rag and all he did was to replay the same obsolete record, questioning me over and over again about the medication I had been given. One would think I was responsible for selecting and administering my own medication in hospital for a pain in my toe, not because of a collapsed lung, or that I had not been brutalised by Mr Lynch. It was crazy because whatever drugs I was given, I was under his care.

What continued to puzzle me, however, was that he kept repeatedly disputing that he had immediately taken over my care. It is true that when you are admitted to the public hospital you are assigned to a consultant physician automatically and on April the 19th 1996, it was Dr Hegarty.

I noted from the hospital records later that Professor Keogh's name was written down automatically but that was just standard procedure. But Mr Lynch became my private consultant immediately and planned to perform the surgery on May the 31st, so I was really confused as to why he was bringing this up in the trial and disputing the fact that Professor Keogh was not my doctor. I was to discover, however, the following week, what his motive was in insisting that I was under Professor Keogh's care and he was, true to form, intentionally implicating others in his conspiracy.

Because I could not remember Professor Keogh, I looked up my hospital records that evening and his name was typed in but there was only one entry made by him, 'recurrent pneumothorax – would Mr Lynch kindly review?' Professor Keogh was obviously not up to scratch with what decisions had been made by Mr Lynch while I was in A&E. It seemed to me that the level of communication was not very impressive. There was no other entry by Professor Keogh and no matter how much I tried I could not recall having met him. I also checked the insurance claims for the time I was in hospital and it is a telling fact that there were no fees claimed by Professor Keogh. Dr Hegarty had, indeed, claimed his fees for the previous April.

He hurried on, 'This therapy was continued each day on that unit until you were transferred to my care.'

'I was transferred to your care the day after I was admitted to St. Vincent's Hospital.'

'No, you were not. You were transferred to my care the day after you left theatre.' *Haven't you forgotten you also told Dr Duignan in your letter of the 3rd of July 1996 that 'this lady came under my care on the 30th of May?' Are we all taking this 'out of context' as well?*

'I saw you on the Friday.'

So on and on it went but I knew he was 'up the creek without a paddle'. He had to have a motive for this but I was not going to let him get away with it. I was far beyond being harassed by him at this stage and Judge Johnson had to intervene again and say, 'That is a dispute.'

'Now, Judge, I am finished, I have just one more…'

'No, no, just that that is a clear dispute.'

But he still droned on and on about the medication he was responsible for even when I was under his care, until we were all 'blue in the face'. He even asked me to confirm what I had been given immediately after waking up screaming from the surgery. This line of questioning was really becoming obscene and I felt he was trying to push me to react angrily but I just sat there looking at him in a surreally calm fashion. It again did not make any sense because he was the surgeon; he knew what he had given me during and after the surgery while I was writhing in vast agony. But he continued to blatantly ignore Judge Johnson's instructions.

And then the shocking motive. 'That suggests to me that you have developed a tremendous tolerance for morphine.'

Ah, so I was right, and it just reinforced my opinion that, indeed, he was being vile. *In your thrust to blemish my character, Mr Lynch, you have forgotten one major point. Why did you administer two weeks of morphine in January 1997 if there had been any question about previous medication? Forgotten that, haven't you? You and you alone were responsible for admitting me to hospital. You cannot accuse anyone else can you? Not Dr Hegarty or Professor Keogh?*

And then Judge Johnson addressed me, 'It is being put to you that you had a big tolerance for morphine.'

'I had never taken any opiate drugs in my life before I had a pneumothorax.'

Then Mr Lynch went on about the morphine pump that had been inserted in my hand after the surgery, at his request, when it was written down in the notes that the pump had not worked and I did not want it replaced.

But Judge Johnson intervened again for the umpteenth time. This was going absolutely around in circles and if Mr Lynch thought that the Judge was a fool, he had calculated wrongly. But why again lie about everything that could be shown to be untrue by looking at the notes? I could only think that he thought Judge Johnson would automatically be biased against me because he was a surgeon. But the proof was all against him.

'I keep on pointing out to you, Mr Lynch, you are not here to make statements at this time, you are here to ask the witness questions. What is your point? Are you suggesting she was a morphine addict?' *Of course he is. Judge Johnson understood his motive very lucidly and I thought to myself, you have failed yet again, Mr Lynch; now you are being put on the spot.'*

'I am not suggesting anything…'

But still he whined on and Judge Johnson turned to me and asked, 'Ms Carroll, did you ask for specific drugs when you went into hospital?'

'No.'

'Did you accept what was given to you by the doctors?'

'Yes.'

'Did you ever ask them for specific drugs at that time?'

'Never.'

'Now, that is it.'

And thus it was over. Judge Johnson had finally put an end to it. There I was, having to go to bed at night with two ice packs for company and there he was, not only being incapable of defending his surgery but suggesting that I had somehow got to the top of my career and achieved all my academic qualifications by having a psychiatric illness and being a morphine addict. But of course, I believe 'the dogs on the street' knew what he was up to. But would he stop? I very much doubted it. I knew he would continue on his rampage for the remainder of the trial.

Then Denis, apparently having put up with enough himself, asked me several questions that reinforced the nonsense and put paid to it. I could sense that Mr Lynch was not too happy with Denis's competence and retaliation but he still wanted to 'flog a dead horse'.

'My Lord, may I reply to that?'

'No, no, you may ask another question if it arises out of that.'

But of course, all he wanted to do was to make statements and make himself heard. He knew there was nothing he could ask me which could not be refuted and he was well on the way to having dug a hole that he could not climb out of. He knew exactly what he was trying to achieve. As he testified himself, he had been to court 'many times' and only someone with arrogant confidence would even attempt to try and pull the wool over the eyes of the President of the High Court. Judge Johnson gave him every assistance and opportunity but he abused it.

That was it; good for you Denis, I thought. As I left the witness box I had the feeling that Mr Lynch was seething but I did not look at him because I did not want daggers coming at me; I was ready to duck just in case. I realised by then that he could not possibly defend his surgery and his only method of attack would be to continue to make defiantly ugly, various and slanderous allegations against me for the remainder of the trial. But was I worried? No, but I can honestly say I was going to be frustrated with boredom on several occasions.

Chapter Ten

To win a case of medical negligence I knew that the most important witnesses would be the expert consultant thoracic surgeons since it hinged on proving that Mr Lynch had deviated from safe, standard and accepted practice. It had to be also proved that it was, in fact, the alleged negligence that caused the severe personal injuries I sustained. It appeared a totally black and white case to me but who knew the complexities that could arise? I had begun to postulate that anything was possible and highly probable.

After I vacated the witness box, Denis called Professor Geoffrey Smith to give evidence and began by questioning him in relation to his experience as a consultant cardiothoracic surgeon. After listening to his extensive list of district, regional and international appointments and publications, I felt unequivocally that he was eminently qualified.

The evidence Professor Smith gave would bring the proceedings up to lunchtime and necessarily was very technical. However, the salient points against Mr Lynch's method of performing VATS were probed by Denis.

'Do you consider yourself, Professor, to be an experienced cardiothoracic surgeon?'

'I have a lot of experience, but I am still learning.'

'What is your knowledge, Professor, in general terms, initially, of what I described to his Lordship as video-assisted thoracic surgery, known as VATS, I think? What is your knowledge about the development of that, how recent a development has this been?'

'VATS began to be introduced in a formal way in modern electronic imaging in the mid-80s. At that time, I was a Senior Officer for the Society of Cardiothoracic Surgeons of Great Britain and Ireland, and we anticipated that this sub-specialty would grow. I was involved nationally in setting up standards by which this could be organised. Locally, we decided that we would embark on a programme in my unit on this and we discussed protocols and the instrumentation necessary, including the approach into the chest.'

Denis continued, 'I described to his Lordship in opening the case, Professor, that my understanding of the techniques involved were that a number, perhaps three openings or ports are made in the lateral chest wall. In other words, the area underneath the armpit; is that correct?'

'That is correct, it is called the triangle of safety.'

'If you would just describe it, where is the triangle of safety?'

'It lies in the lateral side of the chest, above the level of the 6th interspace, between the 6th and 7th ribs, and it lies behind or at the back of the big pectoralis major muscle, which is a very vascular structure. At this triangle of safety there are obviously some structures in the chest, but at this point there are relatively few, the chances of causing extensive tissue damage at these points is low.'

Judge Johnson wanted clarification, 'If I may, broadly speaking, in layman's terms, is the area you are speaking of, the triangle of safety, generally speaking, is the area of the axilla of the armpit, underneath the armpit?'

'Yes, generally speaking.'

'It is on that side of the body as opposed to the front of the body?'

'Oh, indeed.'

'What you have been involved in Professor, as I understand it, and what you have an expertise in, is in the siting of the ports or the access points to get into the area of the chest?'

'Indeed. May I say this is not peculiar to that surgery. Any chest drain put in, any diagnostic procedure which involves penetrating the chest wall carries dangers and this is the area which carries the least danger.'

'Leaving the video-assisted technique aside, if a thoracic surgeon wants to make an entry into the chest for the purpose of inserting a drain or some other instrument, which is not video assisted at all, is this the point from which he would enter?'

'Indeed.'

'That is because, as you have said, there are less structures to be damaged if you approach it in this way?'

'Precisely.'

'In 1996, in general terms Professor, what was the quality of the equipment that was available for carrying out video-assisted thoracic surgery?'

'The major advance had been in the visualisation – there were major advances; one in the visualisation of what you were actually doing, which was electronically enhanced and in beautiful colour with great precision and accuracy; the second one was the development of specific instruments and techniques which were not among the usual surgical skills to be expected of a cardiothoracic surgeon.'

'You were asked by Ms Carroll's solicitors to look at the available relevant documentation relating to Ms Carroll's case and the treatment which she received from Mr Lynch and to express an opinion in relation to the treatment or the quality of the treatment she received, is that correct?'

'Yes, sir.'

'I think you had for that purpose all of the relevant records from St. Vincent's Hospital dealing with Ms Carroll's two admissions, is that correct?'

'Yes.'

'Both pneumothoraces. You also had, I think, the records that were obtained from Mr Lynch himself.'

'Eventually, they did not come with the original documents, there was some difficulty obtaining those.'

'Had you originally met Ms Carroll when you furnished your first report?'

'Not at all.'

'I just want to bring you through that report. You knew the history, that Ms Carroll, on the 19th April had her first pneumothorax, which was treated and the lung reinflated and she was discharged from hospital; is that correct?'

'Yes.'

'She then was readmitted to St. Vincent's Hospital on 30th May 1996, and she told us in evidence that she complained of increasing right-sided chest pain and shortness of breath.'

'Yes.'

'This, I think it was accepted, was because she had another right-sided pneumothorax. What, in fact, is a pneumothorax, Professor?'

'Pneumothorax is air occupying the space, which is very small, between the lung and the chest wall.'

'Where that space becomes occupied with air, what is the source of that air, generally speaking?'

'It depends on the age and type of patient. Sometimes it can be a knife wound, for instance, introducing air from the outside. It may be a leak from an air containing structure within the chest, the oesophagus, the gullet, or more commonly than that, the lung. In younger people the source of the air is often a defect in the structure of the lung at its apex towards the top of the chest. I am not sure that anybody understands why that lesion happens, but it happens in young people, particularly the long, thin young person who is very fit.'

'This would be at the uppermost portion of the lung; is that right?'

'Yes.'

'Ms Carroll has told us in evidence that on both occasions when she had the pneumothorax it was painful, she was in pain. Does that seem to you to be reasonable or unreasonable.'

'I think it is entirely reasonable.'

'We are primarily concerned, I suppose, with the second admission on 30th May and we know – and I do not think is disputed by Mr Lynch – that Mr Lynch saw Ms Carroll on 1st June and surgery was arranged for 5th June. Ms Carroll has told us that she was in pain throughout that intervening period and she was treated with analgesia. Again, is that reasonable, that she should be in pain during that period of time given that condition?'

'Yes.'

'Is it reasonable that she should be treated with analgesia?'

'Oh, yes.'

'If a patient complains of pain, is it reasonable for the medical staff to prescribe analgesia to deal with that?'

'Not only reasonable but mandatory.'

'In what position would a patient in Ms Carroll's situation be placed to have this operation performed? How would she be laying, in what way?'

Professor Smith went on to describe the entries that Mr Lynch made and explained that a trocar is usually made of some high-grade stainless steel and is extremely sharp and I shuddered knowing that one of these went through my breast. It had been difficult to decipher at the beginning Mr Lynch's handwriting and he interjected, 'My Lord, can I help Mr McCullough with my horrible writing?'

'Certainly, Mr Lynch.'

'The first line is 10 mm port, 7th intercostal space, mid-axillary line, MAL. The second line is 12 mm port, 2.5 cm lateral to the nipple line, and it is also in the 7th intercostal space.'

That is wrong, Mr Lynch, actually you did not say nipple 'line', you said 'nipple'. Why now the addition of 'line'? Trying to detract from your operation notes again, are you?

'The third port is 5 mm and it is six finger breadths above the posterior axillary line.' Mr Lynch then felt he had to give a lecture on chest surgery but Judge Johnson intervened. He had tried to make so many statements that would only be appropriate when he took the stand as a witness. And, yet again, Judge Johnson had to instruct him, 'Mr Lynch, you can do all this…' To which Denis quickly interrupted, 'I am grateful to Mr Lynch for translating, my Lord, but I think I had better proceed.'

Judge Johnson then very politely addressed Mr Lynch, 'We will do all this now, Mr Lynch, in due course, but thank you for assisting us with the translation.'

How the Judge still remained perfectly reasonable with Mr Lynch really showed his objectivity even though his instructions were continuously and blatantly ignored. Could Mr Lynch, by now, not grasp the most basic procedures in a court action? I believe of course he could, he just refused to do so and I was astounded by his constant audacity to ignore Judge Johnson's instructions and I had the feeling that he was trying to rankle him.

Denis asked Professor Smith to clarify certain information in the operation notes and he replied, 'This port hit the internal mam. vessels, by which I mean internal mammary vessels, and the next words are I think are "which were aberrant in position".'

'That legend appears to relate to the 12 mm port?'

'Yes, the second port.'

'Firstly, what are the internal mammary vessels?'

'Internal mammary vessels are an artery and a vein which originate in the neck. The artery is the important one because it originates from the major artery supplying the arm.'

'Are these vessels on either side of the sternum, one on the right and one on the left?'

'They are, yes.'

'There is an indication then, I think, that there is a 400 ml blood loss as a result of that?'

I always wondered about this because in the notes there was a distinct disparity between Mr Lynch's estimation of blood loss and the anaesthetist's estimate of 700 ml. It was an important point because the fact is that, if the bleeding from my artery had not been stopped, I would have died.

'Yes.'

'I should ask you, you can tell us yourself, what do you understand the rest of the operative notes to mean then?'

Professor Smith went on to describe the rest of the operation notes that were very technical. Judge Johnson then adjourned the case for lunch until two o'clock.

After breaking, Michael and his assistant informed me that they discovered Mr Lynch had put his home up for sale with Sherry Fitzgerald. Because he had lied to his insurers, I was very worried that he may transfer his assets to someone else but Michael informed me that the courts have the authority to track such a move and take a dim view of such transactions. However, since I knew that unless one is completely paralysed or babies are born with profound mental and physical disabilities through negligence, the award would not be high even if I did win. I was certain Mr Lynch was wealthy enough to pay but I instinctively felt that he would be hell bent on stalling it.

When I looked up 'MyHome.ie' on the internet this enormous mansion was advertised for nearly four and a half million euro called 'Carrickmoleen, Killiney Hill Road', in South East Dublin. I heard some days later that Mr Lynch had changed his mind and decided to hold onto the mansion. I could only surmise that this was some sort of financial tactic on his part for reasons I can only guess.

The advertisement stated that the mansion was, 'A magnificent Victorian family residence and coach house of instant aesthetic appeal set amid exceptionally secluded grounds of in excess of two acres approximately in this highly convenient and sought-after location.' I took a virtual tour of the house and I felt genuine disgust and contempt. There was I, having been butchered by this man and he had not shown me one ounce of compassion afterwards, fighting for my life and now needing security. And there he was, with a seemingly vast amount of wealth in his possession. It did not settle very well with me.

I seriously questioned whether I would get any justice but surely, in the end, I would get some measure of security even though I would have to live with a life sentence caused by unnatural means. It was really devastatingly and mightily difficult to stomach.

Mr Lynch, in my estimation, probably thought he would just come into court, give it a lash and lie his way through it. If he lost, he would just appeal the judgement. Obviously, I do not know for certain what his motives were, but that was my opinion. As I have said before, I did and still do believe that he had every right to defend himself in court but not by constantly contradicting his own operative and private notes, telling copious lies, not to mention his constant attempts to smear my character. Surely, he must have known he would be found out very easily, but was it the case that he was so arrogant he thought everyone would bow to his word and that Judge Johnson would never decide a case against a surgeon? Since he had no expert thoracic witnesses, I did not think he could ever defend his surgery and so I believed he was going to try every other course of action and he was just making a complete farce of the court.

Chapter Eleven

The afternoon of Wednesday November the 7th was to produce such drama it could never have been predicted. If I had thought that Mr Lynch's behaviour was bizarre up until then, what was about to transpire really unnerved me. The case was becoming more inconceivable by the hour.

Denis, ready and eager, recalled Professor Smith to the stand to continue his direct examination. 'Just to go back to the position of the internal mammary vessels, you told us where they are normally, on either side of the sternum, running down to a point at the diaphragm where they divide. Have you, yourself, in your practice as a cardiothoracic surgeon, have you had much experience of dealing with these vessels?'

'I started to dissect out the full length of the internal mammary artery in the early 1980s, I think it was 1982, as a routine procedure in coronary artery bypass grafting, to use that vessel as a conduit during the operation, and I guess since that time I must have dissected out – I said 2,000 originally, but thinking about it, it may well be more than that – mainly on the left side, but at least five hundred on the right. During the length of that experience I have never encountered a deviation from the expected anatomical course of more than a couple of centimetres. In addition, if I might say, I have also been a thoracic surgeon opening the chest and I have never seen the internal mammary artery under the lateral chest wall in the way in which this operative note describes it.'

This is great, I thought, because it totally undermines Mr Lynch's assertion that the 'massive bleed' was due to my artery being out towards my side and even if it was he should have picked it up with the video camera. Regardless, there was no reason to enter my chest through my breast.

Then Denis, referring to the operative note that read, '2.5 centimetres lateral to the nipple' asked, 'Is that something which should or should not be done in the course of this procedure?'

'It is standard teaching in thoracic surgery that any incision, no matter how small, on the chest for the purposes of chest surgery should avoid the breast, for both aesthetic and surgical reasons.'

'You explained to us this morning, Professor, you described the triangle of safety and you indicated where that was, and you said in your evidence that thoracic surgeons, when entering the chest, would do so in that area because, I think you said, that is where the least damage can be caused to other structures. How does an entry in that area compare with an entry through the breast?'

'The breast in a woman of this age is a vascular structure with active glandular tissue in it. Once you start entering the tissue of the breast you are in danger of causing fatty necrosis, infection, and there is a danger of haemorrhage before one actually meets the tissues of the chest wall itself.'

Denis continued asking, 'If one were to insert the instrument through the breast, as in this case, how would that affect the angle of entry or would it affect the angle of entry?'

'It should not, but I have difficulty interpreting the reason why the incision was put in the breast itself. I cannot make any inferences from that, I am afraid, as to the angle of the insertion of the cannula.'

'In your view Professor, based on your experience and your skill and expertise in this area, is it good practice to place a port in the breast?'

'Never.'

'Of the three ports that are made, and are made I suppose routinely in this sort of video-assisted thoracic surgery, through which of the ports does one normally insert the visualisation equipment, the video, the camera?'

'The first port.'

'Why is that or is there a reason for that?'

'In order to see what the problem is in the chest, but also to enable one to insert the subsequent cannula in an area which appears to be free of any hazards. You can judge this from the inside of the chest by pressing with the finger externally and you can show an indentation of the soft tissues where the cannula will go.'

'Just to be clear on that, having put the camera inside, as it were, does the surgeon then press with the finger on the place where the next port he believes should be placed?'

'Yes.'

'Can you see the effect of that pressing on the camera from inside?'

'Yes.'

'You see the indentation?'

'Yes.'

'Are you able to judge then whether there is anything in the way or whether anything is going to be affected?'

'You can make a reasonable guess, you cannot be absolutely certain, but at least as far as you can see, there are no hazards inserting the port at that point…'

'In your opinion, should a careful surgeon make the next port without testing in this way to see whether it is safe or not?'

'No.'

'It appears, Professor, subject to what Mr Lynch might say, but it appears that it was on the insertion of the second port, the 12 mm port 2.5 cm lateral to Ms Carroll's nipple, it was on the insertion of that port that the damage to the mammary vessels occurred. Is that your understanding of what…?'

'I have difficulty believing the internal mammary artery was there.'

'Why is that?'

'Because, as I say, my experience has shown that the internal mammary artery does not vary, and I have done a literature search electronically and found there to be no evidence of significant variation to that point of the chest.'

'That would mean that it would be coming down at a point, it would be 2.5 cm lateral to the nipple.'

'That would be an astonishing deviation.'

Suddenly Judge Johnson interjected, 'Professor, can I ask you the following? Having regard to the position of the first port, if the camera had been put in – I just want to get this right – and this device was used for the purpose of ensuring the safe placing of the second port, (a) it would have revealed where the safe place to put the second port was; and would it (b) have revealed the positioning of the mammary gland if it was in this unique position?'

'The mammary gland, my Lord?'

'No, the mammary vessel, if it had been in this unique position. If it was, as stated, in this unique position, would the camera have revealed it prior to the insertion of the second port?'

'I believe so.'

Then Denis continued, 'If the camera had revealed it, as you believe it would have done, what then should Mr Lynch have done or not done in those circumstances?'

'Avoided that area.'

And Judge Johnson followed up, 'If that is so then, once you see where you are going, this should not happen?'

'You reduce the chances of getting a bleed enormously.'

'Yes, but this particular vessel ought to have been visible. If it was looked at and examined, then it ought to have been avoided.'

'Yes.'

Resuming, Denis questioned, 'Taking the area of the breast, Professor Smith, are there more vessels in the breast than there would be in the triangle of safety that you described earlier?'

'Many more, especially in a young, sexually active woman.'

'As between the chances, such as they may be, of striking a vessel if one goes in through the triangle of safety and the chances of doing so if one goes in through the breast, how do the chances compare?'

'I think, obviously, the tissue trauma is going to be greater by going through the breast, you are going through vascular tissue, and therefore, your chance of getting a significant bleed are greatly increased.'

'Again, it would appear from Mr Lynch's note that having placed what seems to be the second port, the 12 mm port, which caused the bleed, he then placed the third one. Assuming that the bleed became apparent as soon as he placed the port, does the placing of the third port make any sense in that context to you?'

'Not to me.'

Judge Johnson interjected, 'Sorry, why does it not make sense to you?'

'If there were a bleed of the dimensions described in the operative notes, the next step would have been to proceed to open the chest to control the bleeding.'

'And not insert the third port?'

'That is right.'

Denis continued, 'You could not safely proceed with the video-assisted thoracic surgery in the presence of such a bleed?'

'No.'

'Therefore, no point in making the third port, because you were not going to go on in that way?

'400 ml of blood in quite a short time is a significant bleed.' *I envisaged that if it were seven hundred and not four hundred, as the anaesthetist had estimated, then it would have been even more dangerous.*

'What are the benefits, Professor, in your view, of this video-assisted thoracic surgery over a thoracotomy or ordinary, if I may say, thoracic surgery?'

'The amount of surgical damage inflicted on the chest wall in dealing with the problem is much less. This gives rise to three benefits, one of which is a series of wounds that heal much more quickly and are more immediately controlled by analgesics. The second one is the metabolic effect of an operation. The effect on the general body system of having a big muscle-slicing operation is profound, you lose nitrogen, you lose body weight. The third is that many patients – and it depends on the literature you read – somewhere between ten and thirty per cent of patients having a lateral thoracotomy end up with persistent pain.' *And how much worse, I wondered, because it was an emergency thoracotomy.*

'Are you more likely or not to have serious continuing pain if you have a thoracotomy than if you have the video-assisted thoracic surgery?'

'Oh, very much more so.'

'Is that a major reason for choosing one over the other?'

'Yes.

Denis went on then to ask Professor Smith to describe the operation and came to the incision. 'Having made the incision, what then does a surgeon have to do to gain access?'

'He has to go through the skin, the subcutaneous fat, some fibres of serratus anterior, which is a muscle just above the ribs, and then the ribs and the muscles between them become apparent. It is usual then to divide the muscle between the ribs on the top of a rib, rather than below the rib.'

'Is that because the nerves tend to be below the rib?'

'Yes, when that happens, you are left with a long, rather narrow slit in the chest wall between the ribs.' Professor Smith continued, 'I do not want to be facetious, my Lord, then you have to take a car jack sort of thing and get the whole thing open in order to get your hand in, and this means spreading the ribs, sometimes straining them, occasionally breaking them.'

Denis then asked, 'Is it possible to gain access without doing that?'

'No, because you have to get your hand in.'

'In layman's terms, is that a severe procedure? Is it a fairly forceful, invasive procedure?'

'In layman's terms, it does not look particularly pleasant.'

'There was a blood loss of 700 ml. Is that average or above average, or how does that…?'

'It is above average…'

'Just to go back then, Professor, to the first procedure, the procedure that it was intended to complete. How should that have been performed, in your view?'

'I think the port should have been inserted through the triangle of safety. I can see no reason why the second port should have been inserted through the breast tissue in the way it was described and in the way I have subsequently seen photographs of the scar. I can see no justification for that at all, I am afraid.'

'If it had been performed in that way, Professor, in your view, as a matter of probability, would it have gone to completion?'

'Yes.'

Justice Johnson interjected again, 'It just occurs to me this is a very serious matter. The Professor has been operating on photographs. Is there any reason why there should not be an examination?'

Denis quickly responded, 'I was going to put it in two ways, my Lord. We do have some photographs, not at the moment a full set, which do in fact demonstrate the point, but it may well be necessary to have an examination as well.'

'These are very serious matters and I think it is proper there should be a physical examination. In my view, it should be conducted sooner rather than later, and certainly before cross-examination.'

Little did Judge Johnson know when he gave this instruction that it was to set in motion a dreadful ordeal for me and at the same time completely blow apart Mr Lynch's credibility or what was left of it.

'Indeed, my Lord. Your Lordship is suggesting that the doctors and Mr Lynch…?'

'Mr Lynch has seen it already. This is the witness who is criticising the situation.'

'Your Lordship is quite correct and maybe if your Lordship rose it could be done now.'

'I will certainly rise now. I think the sooner it is done, the better, because this is a matter which is of great seriousness and I think all medical witnesses should have physical evidence. I will rise, you can let me know if and when you are ready.'

I thought this a good strategy because Judge Johnson was being extremely thorough and, in the end, if things went my way then he could not be accused of not covering all angles. Mr Lynch's assertion that he would appeal the judgement was constantly preying on my mind.

'May it please your Lordship.'

During the short adjournment Denis, Michael and Karen discussed Judge Johnson's request and told me that a room would be organised for the two medical expert witnesses to examine my scars, especially the culpable one on my breast. But then they approached and informed me that Mr Lynch wanted to be present. I immediately felt sick and I asked, 'Why does he want to see it again; he put it there?' I had this very creepy feeling and I did not wish to undress in front of him. These were not his rooms in the Blackrock Clinic and he was not playing a medical role in this. *Now what am I going to do?* Even Judge Johnson saw no reason for Mr Lynch to be present. The thought of him looking at me naked in this context made me feel queasy and very anxious.

While I was pondering the most advisable means of handling this, I was suddenly struck by a brainwave and I did not know then that it was to become one of the most important decisions I made during the trial. Then the words came out, 'Well, I will allow Mr Lynch to attend as long as Judge Johnson is present also.' My biggest fear was that Mr Lynch would say or do something outlandish that the judge would not hear or see. He had become such a chronic liar that I did not trust him in any capacity and

I also wished to be shielded from his oppressive behaviour.

Judge Johnson duly returned and Denis asked, 'My Lord, a matter has arisen and I just want to ask your Lordship if your Lordship would consider dealing with it in a certain way, my Lord. Mr Lynch takes the view, and he has expressed the view, my Lord, that as an Irish citizen he is entitled to be present when Ms Carroll is being examined.'

Now the veracity of that I doubt. What difference does being an Irish citizen make? But Denis indulged Mr Lynch nevertheless and he went on, 'That does not cause a difficulty… I would prefer if an examination in those circumstances could be carried out in your Lordship's chambers, in your Lordship's presence, with Ms Carroll and with Mrs O'Driscoll on our side and with the doctors. There is going to be an issue about this, I think, as an objective fact and I think that your Lordship as trial Judge should see what there is there to be seen. Ms Carroll has no objection to that, my Lord, and would welcome that, but she would prefer if it were done in your Lordship's presence. I think, my Lord, in the interest of the trial, that should be done, if your Lordship agrees, because I think there may be a dispute about this and it is of some significance to our case.'

Judge Johnson replied, 'I want you to consider this now, because there is a problem with this. Does not this make me a witness? It is not like the valuation of a scar, Mr McCullough.'

'The fact which I think your Lordship will have to determine in the case is whether or not there was in fact – depending on which Mr Lynch may say in his defence, your Lordship has to determine as a fact whether or not there was an entry made in Ms Carroll's breast. The evidence of that, my Lord, there is some photographic evidence taken two years ago, but it is what is to be seen on her breast now, and it seems to me that it is a matter which your Lordship, as Judge, can judge.'

'What does Mr Lynch say to this?'

Mr Lynch replied, 'My Lord, I am delighted that you made the suggestion…' *Why is he so elated, I wondered?*

'I am sorry, do not mind the suggestion, do you have any objection to me being present when…?'

'Absolutely none.'

'Very good. Well, then, we will set up the room and we will do it straight away.'

Denis responded, 'I am obliged to your Lordship.' *This was perfect because now Judge Johnson would also see the scars for himself and Mr Lynch's approval of Judge Johnson's presence would be on record.*

Thank goodness for Karen though. Just to have a female present and be by my side would make it easier to undress. I would have to say that throughout the entire trial, she was of fantastic support to me and I was constantly amazed by her intellect, stamina for work and her great sense of humour. She lightened many a strained hour for me and little did I know the next was going to be one of them.

We proceeded down one of the many corridors to Judge Johnson's chambers. He positioned himself with his back to the sole window in the room. To my left was Karen and in front of me stood Professor Smith and Mr Makey. Remaining at the door was Mr Lynch. He was only supposed to be an onlooker and I wanted to keep my distance from him as much as possible. I took a few inhalations and avoided looking in his direction. I abhorred his presence but I had little choice. Then, in front of staring eyes, I peeled off my clothes in a hurried fashion. Judge Johnson asked me to point out all my scars to the medical experts. When it came to my breast through which the offending instrument was pushed, the scar was not immediately visible as my skin was very white and I was not turned towards the dim light coming through the window.

Then the most incredulous thing happened and we all looked, startled, in Mr Lynch's direction. He obviously thought, because the scar could not be seen in the gloom, that there was no mark of an incision. Suddenly and frighteningly, he started prancing around with absolute glee saying repeatedly, 'I told you there is no scar there. I told you there is no scar there.' He was like a child skipping around in joy. I completely froze at his behaviour and I stared at him aghast, rooted rigidly to the floor and, luckily, that meant I did not react immediately, thus allowing him to make a complete fool of himself and repeat his lie in the process.

Even in the presence of Judge Johnson, when he knew he had operated through my breast, he could not contain himself. If a surgeon can lie and behave so ridiculously in the presence of the President of the High Court, one can just imagine how he could treat a patient scared and alone in a hospital bed. I can and unfortunately, I do.

It took me a little while to recover from the startling shock of his unhinged display but when I lifted my right arm up and turned my breast towards the light from the window there, completely visible, was the evidence of Mr Lynch's scar and all of a sudden, evidently prepared, Professor Smith stepped forward with a measuring tape noting its size without actually touching it. It was exactly as stated in Mr Lynch's operating notes. Judge Johnson had absorbed it all and I could only imagine what was going through his mind. Mr Lynch's lies had finally caught up with him.

Then we turned our attention to Mr Lynch again. It was now his turn to be shocked, so much so that his whole face contorted and slumped in disbelief. Then, without warning, he sprang forth and lunged at me with a clawed hand out to grab my breast. With the luck of God I was very alert and I only had a split second to react before he succeeded in assaulting me. I slapped down with my hand preventing him from mauling me and jumped backwards. It was awful. I always had my suspicions that he was truly unhinged but I was in doubt no longer.

This, in my opinion, was attempted assault on an intimate part of my person and it terrified me. The only privilege Mr Lynch was granted was to be present. He was not given permission to approach or touch me. The man, in my opinion, was totally beyond redemption at this point. I was not in his clinic in the role of patient and I felt that this attempted assault was an unlawful act on top of the threats he made to Dr O'Keeffe as my witness. To this day, I have that horrible image in my mind and I still cannot believe that he was so arrogant to act out all of this drama in front of Judge Johnson. I felt of the strong opinion and I still believe that he should have been arrested there and then for attempted assault.

As I quickly dressed in a shaken manner, I was still distressed, and as we were leaving Judge Johnson's chambers, he apologised to me. I know this was a horrendous thing to happen but I can only say that I was very thankful for that brainwave I had, asking for Judge Johnson to be present. I know that everyone seemed stunned leaving his chambers. Mr Lynch's bizarre behaviour was so well ingrained in my psyche I had predicted something dreadful would happen. At least this allowed Judge Johnson to both see and hear Mr Lynch, in his own words, denying again his operation notes. I actually felt queasy and fearful from the experience and from then on I was physically afraid of what he could do to me and I stayed glued to my father for protection.

When we returned to the courtroom after that insane incident, I was deflated. Without any assistance, Mr Lynch had by now, dug his own grave deeper through his notorious behaviour and deceit but I knew that would not stop him from attempting more. As I sat down beside my father and tried to expunge the entire episode from my mind, Professor Smith returned to the witness stand to conclude his testimony. Judge Johnson resumed the case and gave a synopsis of what had occurred in his chambers, although leaving out Mr Lynch's attempted assault on my person and I wondered why.

Denis began, 'Professor, I think I had asked you whether, if the procedure had been done by Mr Lynch as you say it ought to be done – in other words the placing of the ports where you say they should have been placed – whether, in your view, as a matter of probability, the video-assisted thoracic surgery would have gone to completion?'

'It was highly probable it would have been successful.'

'Just to be clear on this point, what do you say about the actual placing of the ports as happened, in fact?'

'My Lord, may I mention the facts that I have just seen?' and Judge Johnson acceded.

'Thank you. I detected a 4 cm mature scar about 2.5 cm lateral to the right nipple on the substance of the right breast.'

Denis continued, 'Was what you saw, Professor, consistent or otherwise with the entry on Mr Lynch's operative note as to where the 12 mm port was sited?'

'Yes.'

'Just to be clear, what do you say about siting that port where you believe you saw it had been sited?'

'That is an unacceptable port of entry.'

Then Denis brilliantly employed a pre-emptive move, knowing full well that Mr Lynch would continue to try and assassinate my character, he asked Professor Smith, 'Just to conclude, Professor, two things. I am not going to bring you through the hospital notes. I think you were in court when Mr Lynch was suggesting this morning to Ms Carroll, as I understood it, that she had an excessive amount of analgesia, in particular an excessive amount of opiate-based analgesia, and there was something strange about that. Have you had an opportunity to look at the hospital notes and records as to the analgesia which Ms Carroll received?'

'I have.'

'What do you say about it?'

'I think the amount of analgesia and the frequency of dosage given in that period lies within the normal expectations of a patient after surgery.'

'You were in court, I think, Professor, for the evidence given by Ms Carroll as to her condition since the operation and I think you heard what she said about pain and disability and all of that. Having heard that evidence, Professor, do you have a view as to whether or not her complaints are consistent with what she went through?'

'Yes.'

After some further questions were posed, Denis concluded, 'Thank you.' *That signalled the end of Professor Smith's evidence. Great work, Denis, I felt appreciatively.*

What an afternoon it was. I was still reeling from the episode in Judge Johnson's chambers and thought this was more the stuff of a John Grisham novel rather than reality in an Irish courtroom. But what was to occur next, when I thought things could not get any worse, was to eventually have major repercussions for me. No one would have predicted the fallout and we proceeded, blindly unaware that the remainder of the trial, with all its twists and turns and proving more and more unfathomable, was in the end to become totally and utterly irrelevant in the wisdom of certain powers that be.

Chapter Twelve

It was now Mr Lynch's opportunity to cross-examine Professor Smith and, as I gazed at him in baffled regard, I wondered how he was going to handle Mr Lynch's questions after what he witnessed in Judge Johnson's chambers.

Mr Lynch stood up and faced his critic, 'Mr Smith, it is nice to meet you and I think that we are playing with words here. When you see in my operation notes, I say a "queried" aberrant internal mammary artery. There is a question mark in front of that. From the position that you see those scars and those ports going in at right angles to the skin, do you, who has a lot of knowledge about internal mammary arteries, see that hitting the internal mammary artery if it is in a normal position?' *What was he attempting to do now? There was no such query in his operation notes.*

'No.'

'Would you state emphatically…'

Then Denis, completely alert, immediately arose and interjected, 'My Lord, I do not want to interrupt, but I would like Mr Lynch to point out, if he would, where the question mark appears in his operative notes.'

Judge Johnson, frowning, replied, 'Yes, I cannot see the question mark. I do not see a question mark and I do not think the Professor saw one when he was reporting.'

Mr Lynch then pointed to something and said adamantly, 'There is the query there.'

I was still actually capable of being stunned. This was a clear and emphatic statement and I could only think that the reason he was introducing this was to change the meaning of his operation notes. Because he was so insistent, the only conclusion I drew from it was that he had either lied about my artery being aberrant or was trying to suggest that he had not, in fact, severed my artery at all but some other, more minor, blood vessel. I was becoming absolutely fuddled with the man's different spins.

'Can you say which page?' asked Denis. 'I have to say, my Lord, and I am careful about saying this, my Lord, Mr Lynch is pointing to something which does not appear on the copy that I have.'

'It is certainly on that copy,' angrily retorted Mr Lynch.

'Perhaps it could be handed in to his Lordship.'

'Can I just have a look at that?' asked Judge Johnson.

And then Mr Lynch interrupted, 'Quite honestly, my Lord, I do not think this is significant.'

'Mr Lynch, I want to see it,' demanded Judge Johnson.

Denis added, 'Mr Lynch pointed out to me, as I understand it, a small black squiggle which is just to the left of the word we believe to be "which", and it certainly, my Lord, is not in the copy that I have. Perhaps I should hand it in to your Lordship…'

Judge Johnson responded contemplatively, 'This is most interesting. Number one, what has been handed to me here is a Photostat. That which was in this book is also a Photostat.'

'That is so, my Lord,' confirmed Denis.

'There are a number of additions to this that has been handed to me by Mr Lynch, a number of things down the left-hand side, which, on examination under a light, it is quite clear they were added by a real pen and penetrated the paper. The same applies to that matter which is now stated to be a question mark. It is quite clear looking at the back of the paper it is there.'

Responding, Denis said, 'Thank you, my Lord.'

To which Mr Lynch could not resist interjecting, 'I cannot see that.'

Judge Johnson replied, 'If you look under a close light you will see it, Mr Lynch. It is a photostat and that penetrates the paper. Mr McCullough, if that is what Mr Lynch is relying on, I think it should be examined by professionals. I am merely passing an opinion.'

Denis requested, 'Could I ask Mr Lynch to produce that, my Lord, when he has finished his cross-examination, because…' To which Judge Johnson acceded, 'It has been produced in court, it is now a document for the court to examine.'

'I wonder would your Lordship retain that document…'

'Mr Lynch, I will require that document to have it examined.'

'Yes, you may have it.'

Judge Johnson informed him, 'You may use it for the time being, give him the photostat, but I want that kept by the court.'

Oh Mr Lynch, what have you tried to do? Change my operation notes? You have not only added a question mark to the record in evidence but you also stated in your own words, 'When you see in my operation notes I say a "queried" aberrant internal mammary artery. There is a question mark in front of that.' *You have both written it and spoken it.*

Mr Lynch continued with his cross-examination of Professor Smith or statements I should say, 'Professor Smith, it is a trying day for us all.'

Then he continued, again and again, ignoring all of Judge Johnson's instructions, making statement after statement. During this tirade he said some very strange things. One was that he had performed VATS 'about one hundred and fifty times' when he had told me before the surgery two hundred times and that it was a 'cinch'. Then he added, 'I started doing it in 1990 and I was the first person in the country to bring in this particular equipment.' *Well, this surgery, according to all the literature I have read, has been performed since the 1980s.*

He then went on to say something that really showed his arrogance and ego, which were mighty. When he spoke about the 4 cm scar on the main substance of my breast he actually said, 'It is a tiny scar, it is darned difficult to pick up, it is so good. Would you agree with that?' *This was obscene and I shuddered. Now this man was applauding himself for putting a lovely scar on my breast. If you were a woman Mr Lynch, you would know how sensitive a breast is, never mind that you shoved an instrument right through it into my chest.*

'No, I do not agree with that, Mr Lynch. It is four centimetres long, it is within the substance and it is overlying the lower lateral quadrant of the breast.'

'Yes, but surely to goodness that is a mini-thoracotomy…?'

'No, no, I am talking about the 4 cm incision lying on the breast tissue immediately lateral to the nipple, which I have seen both clinically…'

'Four centimetres?'

'Yes, you saw me measure it.'

And then another lie, 'I did not see you measure it, but that surprises me.'

Did I hear correctly? You put the scar there and now you are saying you are surprised? What kind of surgeon are you, Mr Lynch, being surprised by your own surgery? Are you deviously pretending to mix up the main thoracotomy scar around my side with the scar on my breast as you had done with Michael?

Then he started going on about the ports and where you place them, still making more statements. I was surprised at this stage that Judge Johnson did not interrupt and remind him again to ask questions but perhaps he concluded that no amount of telling Mr Lynch how to conduct a cross-examination would work.

He continued, 'Surgery is not perfect, surgery is an art, it takes years and years to learn this art and no matter how you do your cases, they will not be perfect.' *Oh no? I had 'perfect' keyhole surgery performed in the US as far back as the early eighties but then, that surgeon was competent. If surgery is an art, as you say, well then would you not take all the precautions you can? Why did you not adhere to the 'triangle of safety' as other thoracic surgeons have done? That seems to me to be extraordinarily contradictory.*

On top of this, he made another strange statement, 'Now, Professor Smith, you have done a lot of coronary artery surgery. This lady is complaining of pain in her chest following a blebectomy.' *No, Mr Lynch, that statement says nothing. I am complaining of terribly severe pain in my chest wall after both the aborted VATS and the emergency open chest surgery.*

'Now, if a patient after coronary artery surgery in Dublin was brought to court with a stroke, no one in their wildest dreams would say to him, "Ah, look, you are responsible for that stroke and you have just got to pay up".' *Well, Mr Lynch, it depends on whether the surgeon was negligent or not. A surgeon does not perform operations out of charity. You are paid handsomely for it and a patient then expects you to be competent and if you are not you should not be performing surgery. If you make yourself out to be an expert then a patient has expectations the least of which is to have an operation performed in a way that provides the highest level of safety possible.*

Then Professor Smith said, 'I am not quite sure how to answer your question.'

'It is not a question,' interjected the judge.

To which Mr Lynch replied, 'It is a statement.' *This was turning out to be a joke and I was becoming very exasperated.*

'No, you are meant to ask him questions; the time for statements comes later.'

Then Mr Lynch continued to dig the crater more deeply, 'Have you any views on that?'

To which Professor Smith asked, 'Do I have any views on complications arising from surgery?'

'Yes.'

'I think any surgery, particularly of a major sort, and that includes nearly all cardiothoracic surgical operations, carries complications, some of which are unavoidable, some of which are avoidable, and it is necessary, as part of the surgical craft, to organise your operation and organise the care in such a way that the avoidable hazards are detected and the situation dealt with. I believe that bleeding will follow some insertions of a cannula through the chest wall no matter how careful you are but I do believe that putting a cannula in through the breast is going to increase your chances of having a complication which must be regarded as avoidable by many factors.'

'If that bleeding did occur from the breast, where would it occur from? Would it occur from the chest wall beneath the breast or from the actual breast itself?'

'It would occur through the holes you made, Mr Lynch, whether they be internal or external.' *I laughed silently at that even though I am sure Professor Smith did not intend it as a joke.*

'But what would the source be? Would it be the muscular wall of the chest or would it be the breast tissue?'

'It can be anywhere.'

'I agree.'

But then Professor Smith, I thought brilliantly, replied, 'But, you said in your operative notes the "int. mam. vessels". That is not just any old mammary vessel. I accept there are mammary vessels coming off the intercostals and supplying the breast, they are without specific names, but the internal mammary vessel which I take it that refers to…'

'Unfortunately, you are correct and that is the way the court is going to look at this.'

But Professor Smith was going to finish his point, '…is a special vessel. We are not playing with words here, we are being precise with words.'

'Do you feel that that particular port had a significant effect on this lady's subsequent health?'

'I do, because it led to an avoidable bleed, the bleed led to you opening the chest in order to control that bleed and she is now suffering with the consequence of a thoracotomy.' *Performed in a brutal emergency situation, I added silently.*

'Have you any idea of what percentage of video-assisted thoracoscopic procedures end up being converted?'

'It is around two per cent.'

'In my hands it is fifteen per cent.' Then, 'In that year, 1996, I presented a paper in Heidelberg at the European Society on this,' and then he had the gall to say, 'I think we are going around in circles.' *Have you not realised what you have just admitted to, Mr Lynch? You have a thirteen per cent higher rate of conversion than the international average which is certainly not something to be proud of. If this is your conversion rate for a straightforward VATS, what is your rating for more serious operations like cancer? I dread to think.*

'With respect, Mr Lynch, I do not think we are going around in circles, because I am stating that there is a port that was inserted through breast tissue in the wrong place which caused the bleed which led to a thoracotomy. I do not believe that is going around in circles, I believe that is a straightforward statement.'

'Was that bleed dealt with properly or not?'

'Yes, it was, but my point is that the bleed was avoidable. On the balance of probability, that bleed was avoidable.'

'Is that not a holier than thou approach?'

'No. Every thoracic surgeon that I know would avoid breast tissue.'

Judge Johnson interjected, 'Sorry, before you start on that, where is the original of this particular piece of paper?'

To which Denis immediately asked, 'The operative note, my Lord?'

'Yes, where is the original, the actual original? I am issuing an order for it now.'

Then Mr Lynch proffered, 'The point that I am trying to make, Mr Smith, is that the breast in a young lady who has never had children is actually much larger than is apparent.' *What an absurd assumption to make. As it turned out I did not have children but he never knew that. I never gave out personal information about my life or family and no one ever asked me.*

'The breast tissue, no matter how big or small the breast, if you are 2.5 cm lateral to it…' [meaning the nipple], '…you are going to go in through breast tissue.'

Mr Lynch continued then with an extremely long barrage commencing with, 'I think there is an element of truth in that and I have to concede that point, your Honour. But I do not see the mere fact that a port had been put in there led to this lady's ongoing problem.' *The 'mere' fact? Pushing an instrument through a breast to get into a chest is a mere fact?*

Then he continued, 'The point that I was trying to put across to this court this morning was that this lady, during her two admissions to St. Vincent's Hospital, during the pre-operative phase, had huge doses of narcotic analgesics.'

Ah, here we go again, back to his old tricks. His malice is now really showing through and he is slipping further into the gutter. *But yes, Mr Lynch, I certainly did have frequent doses; right after your brilliant work which left me screaming.*

'Now, you can get me on some little point about an internal mammary artery or you can get me on some little point about the particular site of a port or something like that, but that is completely different. She is complaining about three things, (I) the pain in her chest; (ii) the problem in her arm and (iii) for a period of time after the operation she was complaining of swelling of that breast.'

You mean rupturing a main artery is a 'little' point? The siting of a surgical instrument is a 'little' point? Are you demented? Then he whined, 'Now, I am caught with the horrible dilemma that I am being held responsible not only by this court, but by this whole country of inflicting on this lady chronic pain, and I know deep in my heart that she had that pain seven weeks before I operated on her.'

That's choice, Mr Lynch, because I am left with the 'horrible dilemma' of a lifelong disability and having to have further surgeries as technology develops, not to mention personal and financial devastation. And you have not been held responsible by the court, not yet anyway; are you not jumping the gun a little? The trial is not over by a long shot so are you saying this because you know you were negligent and your lies are coming home to roost?

Judge Johnson interjected again and by this time I had completely lost count of just how many times he had to tell him, 'Mr Lynch, when you have taken the oath and wish to give evidence, if you want to, or indeed when the evidence is finished and you wish to address me, I would ask that you address me and there is no jury over there and no jury up there, so address me, but in the meantime could we get on with the cross-examination of this witness?'

'I think that Professor Smith is honest and many of the points that he makes are accurate but what I want to ask you again, Professor Smith, is there any relationship to where that port went in and this lady's subsequent pain?'

'There is an indirect relationship.'

'What does that mean?'

'Because the port, in my opinion, went in through the wrong place, a bleed was caused which I believe was potentially avoidable, which led to a thoracotomy which led to this lady's chronic problem. That is my opinion.'

Judge Johnson asked Professor Smith, 'Can I ask you a question? Is it your evidence that if there had not been a thoracotomy, on the balance of probabilities, she would not be in her present situation?'

'Yes, my Lord.'

Then Mr Lynch asked, 'Mr Smith, is video-assisted thoracic surgery not a form of thoracotomy?'

'Yes, but it involves less tissue trauma. That is the whole point of doing it. It is not to be clever with electronic instruments.'

'Instead of making one incision we make three incisions?'

'But you do not spread the ribs.'

'Well, is that important?'

'Yes.'

'Well, that is your view.'

And very quickly Judge Johnson had got the point, 'Mr Lynch, I have got the question, but when you give evidence you may well be asked the question: If it makes no difference, then why did you introduce it into the country in the first place? Do not answer it now, think about it. That is the kind of question you may be asked. I am not saying you will be but I think it is a possibility.'

So, Judge Johnson indulged Mr Lynch again, purposely assisting him in a way to prevent him from incriminating himself. He then concluded his so-called cross-examination.

Judge Johnson then asked Professor Smith, 'Will you be here tomorrow by any chance?'

'If you wish it to be so.'

'Lest there be any further matters arising, Professor, I think it might be as well.'

'Thank you, my Lord, I will then.'

'There may be certain matters that need to be cleared up.'

'Yes, my Lord.'

Judge Johnson was being very thorough indeed and was leaving it open for Mr Lynch to cross-examine Professor Smith again if he so wished. But I remember wondering how many hours he would be up during the night trumping up more malicious plots before the next morning's deliberations.

I felt so relieved that Professor Smith's evidence definitively supported all the literature I had researched and read to date. The way the keyhole surgery should have been conducted and the trauma to my body because of the emergency chest surgery were all topics I had digested repeatedly. Now it was time for the second expert, Mr Arthur Makey to give his evidence and if he presented it at the high standard of Professor Smith's then I would go home a contented woman.

Chapter Thirteen

With no time to waste, Denis called Mr Makey to the witness box and commenced his examination by taking him through his professional experience. Like Professor Smith, he was also vastly qualified as a thoracic surgeon. The substance of his testimony matched Professor Smith's and he gave the same conclusion in relation to the triangle of safety.

During the giving of his evidence, Denis asked him what advantages keyhole surgery had over open surgery and he responded, 'I agree with the remarks that Professor Smith made. The disadvantage of a thoracotomy is that it is a painful operation. You can open up somebody's abdomen, that is painful, but it usually passes off fairly quickly, but opening a chest does cause more problems, chiefly related, I think, as Professor Smith intimated, to the fact that you cannot just make your incision and open through into the pleural cavity, you actually have to distract the two sides of the wound to give you enough space in which to operate.'

'Does distraction mean the pulling apart or the holding open of either side of the wound, or what does it mean, in fact?'

'It means, yes, the moving apart, shall we say. The more gently you can do that, obviously, the less likely you are to cause trauma.'

After considerable time, Denis asked a very pointed question, 'Again, Mr Makey, from your point of view as a thoracic surgeon, should a thoracic surgeon, in seeking to make an entry for whatever purpose into the chest cavity, make that entry through a woman's breast?'

'No, I would not go through a woman's breast, no.'

'Why not?'

'It is a very vascular structure, to start with. I do not think if you asked if you would be allowed to do it they would agree, and I would not want to do it, there is no need to do it.'

'Having done that, it seems then that Mr Lynch became aware of there being a bleed, which he certainly indicated in his notes was the internal mammary vessels. The notes that we have been working on up 'til now says "which were aberrant in position", although Mr Lynch, I think, was inclined to contend that there was a query in front of that, but what is your experience as to the aberrancy, or otherwise, of the internal mammary vessels?'

'I must have opened several thousand chests at least and I cannot ever recollect seeing an internal mammary artery in a markedly aberrant site.'

'For it to be where it would have to have been for that particular port to have damaged it, how aberrant would its position have to be, in your view?'

'Grossly aberrant.'

'You have heard Ms Carroll's evidence, Mr Makey, as to what happened to her after the surgery and how she felt and how she has been since and she has made complaints of very serious and continuing pain. Do you have an opinion as to what is the cause of that pain?'

'I think the answer is that, that when you make an incision through, say, the abdomen, you are not going through, apart from the skin perhaps, you are not going through most of the tissue that has got a markedly sensitive sensory nerve supply. So, it fairly quickly can be ignored, the body will ignore it. When you are going into the chest you are opening between the ribs and you are bound – there is no way that you cannot have an interference on at least the nerves in the intercostal space you open.

'You put your retractor in and you are putting pressure on it, and if the operation took an hour or two hours, that is pressure for two hours. Also, there is a certain amount of traction sometimes at the proximal end, which is stretching the nerve. But that is not all I think if your chest wall is retracted fairly open, you are probably having some effect on the bundles above and below as well.'

'In your view, Mr Makey, as a matter of probability, what has been the cause of Ms Carroll's pain?'

'I think one has got to say it is related to this thoracotomy, yes… because the retraction, especially if it is being done in a hurry because you want to get in through that space in a hurry, you are going to be likely to retract it a little more forcefully and more rapidly than you would do in the ordinary course of events.'

'Would you be in a hurry if you thought you were getting in there to deal with a bleeding mammary vessel?'

'If you saw a vessel bleed, you would want to get in and stop it, wouldn't you, because until you really saw it well you would not be certain of the size of the injury to the vessel and the amount of blood coming out of it.'

'You are familiar with the case, I think, and you have heard Ms Carroll's evidence given yesterday. Given that the pain of which the complaint has gone on for this long, do you have a view as to what is likely to happen in the future?'

'It is a very difficult one to answer. My feeling usually – I have seen this more in males than females, and my feeling has been that if they have had this sort of pain for three years or longer, that the chances are they will continue to have it…'

'You were present for the examination which took place in his Lordship's chambers. Did you see a scar on Ms Carroll's right breast?'

'Yes.'

'Where was that scar in relation to the nipple, so far as you could tell?'

'Roughly 2.5 cm from the nipple and it was quite a good-sized scar. It appeared to be 4 cm.'

'In your view, is the presence of that scar there consistent with the entry in the operation notes, about the 12 mm port being sited 2.5 cm lateral to the nipple?'

'I cannot think of any other reason for it to be there.'

'Thank you,' Denis concluded.

***

What is in store for us now, I wondered, after the drama surrounding the change to the evidential copy of the operation notes made by Mr Lynch? As soon as he stood up to cross-examine Mr Makey he was true to form, but again I was perplexed at his oft-times support of my witnesses' answers.

'Mr Makey, I read your report, it is a very fair report. I think it seems to be accurate that that port did go through the breast tissue. I had a bleed and I had to deal with it.'

Judge Johnson interjected, 'Sorry, was that a statement? Did you say the port beside the breast did go through breast tissue?'

'Yes.' *Gosh, I just cannot keep up with this man. One minute he did not, the next he did; he even seemed to have Judge Johnson perplexed and that was no mean feat.*

'You agree with that?'

'Yes, I did think that, yes. Yes, I think so; I was not sure when I saw it today.' *I was beginning to think I was a participant in a crazed and surreal movie.*

It had taken so long to get him to admit to his operation notes and, of course, since everyone in the Judge's chambers had actually seen the scar on my breast, it was rather difficult for him to continue to lie about it. And then when he could not succeed in persuading Mr Makey to agree with him in relation to his VATS procedure, he reverted to his continual attempts to smear my character. He pursued a barrage of the same old medication and volumes I had been administered in hospital. It was all 'old hat' and since he realised that between Professor Smith and Mr Makey he could not gain any ground in his defence he was back to his old fixation. He had tried to make his allegations sensational and by now it was just boring hogwash. I totally switched off and gave no credence to what he was spouting out.

***

The afternoon drew to a close and Judge Johnson announced, 'It is now 4:00, Mr Lynch. We are going to stop shortly, but I understood the whole point of this operation was to get rid of the pain.'

'The whole point of the operation was to fix the lung so that it would not collapse again, and that is what I did.' *What, by Tudor standards? The end justifies the means and it is of no relevance how you actually achieve it?*

But Judge Johnson repeated, 'Was to get rid of the pain. Very good we will adjourn until 11:00 tomorrow morning' Then Denis informed him, 'I understand, my Lord, that the documents that we seek will be brought to court tomorrow at 11:00.'

'Can I merely point out as another matter, I just think having regard to what took place today I do feel that what I suggested yesterday for today, in particular, might be appropriate, a transcript.'

'May it please your Lordship.'

'This day, in particular, would be of some use.'

Thank goodness this harrowing day had reached closure. I was very weak and in pain sitting most of the day on a wooden bench. All I wanted to do was to get home, put ice packs under and over my chest wall to ease it out and numb the area, perform some exercises and finally rest. I had a brief discussion with my legal team before I left and it appeared we were all a little stunned and wondering how the following day would pan out.

What I had not thought of were the consequences of the newspapers having printed my full address and my telephone number was not ex-directory. My father and I had barely stepped foot into my apartment when I heard the telephone ringing and I answered what was to be the first of many calls from injured and helpless patients who were anonymous to me. I did not know what I should say because I had no precedent in life for this situation. I just listened to their stories and my heart went out to them because the majority I suspected did not have the wherewithal to do anything about their situation. I would never influence anyone to take, or not, litigious action.

It is difficult enough taking a case when one is in perfect health but quite another story when suffering from severe physical injuries. What I could do for them, however, was to listen to their stories and hopefully they got some satisfaction from talking to a person who could understand their pain, fear, helplessness and vulnerability.

I was never a proponent of litigation but in this instance, since the tragedy had completely destroyed my life at its peak, I had no choice. I would think that unless one is very seriously injured, only a minority of people would choose to go through this adversarial process. I was only two days into the trial and knew that anything could happen along the way so if one has to risk everything and has a family to support, losing can result in lifelong debt.

Even if a patient believes there was negligence involved then there is the matter of finding an expert solicitor, who unfortunately has to go outside Ireland to obtain experts' opinions, even if the case is seemingly black and white. Before a final decision is made to proceed with a case, the process can have considerable financial outlays.

It is extremely unfortunate and wholly unacceptable that there is no other avenue available to people who are injured through either a medical mistake or negligence. Because of that, I would imagine the majority of people are left to suffer for the rest of their lives, without the ability to earn an income and who can lose much more in addition. And if a case is settled without liability then a rogue surgeon in the system can go right back and continue to practice incompetently and unabated. If I had done anything seriously wrong at work, and especially in the position I held where mistakes could have a detrimental effect on peoples' lives, I know what would have happened to me.

But what occurs when a surgeon continues to repeat mistake after mistake and is incompetent? How does the system trigger a review of his or her cases? It still appears that very little is done unless a patient or member of staff has the nerve and capability to try to get to the truth. Whistle-blowers take enormous risks. So what confidence can a patient have going into any hospital in this country especially through A&E? In many cases, it can be a roll of the dice.

Unfortunately, it is not until many tragedies happen that result in serious injuries or death that laws and regulations are put in place. So many things in this country are reactionary rather than planned and prevented. God only knows the damage Mr Lynch has caused to peoples' lives throughout his career if what happened to me and the other patients who sued him are anything to go by. As he admitted himself, he had piles of claims against him. What were his overall statistics of morbidity and mortality compared to the international average? I dread to think if for a routine operation like mine, 'in his hands', it resulted in a failed rate of thirteen per cent higher than the international average.

Eventually, I had no option but to silence my telephone because I was so exhausted and needed to try to get some rest to face the day ahead. I reckoned that even if I took a limited number of calls every night at least that would be of some help to other injured patients. So, like my father who was also in need of restoration, I retired to bed and the last thing I did was set the alarm clock for 7 a.m., even though I knew I probably would not need it. I would be lucky if I got a snooze after hearing those heart-wrenching stories. After I wished my father good night, I asked my grandfather to maintain his constant vigil over me.

Chapter Fourteen

As dawn segued into daylight I was already up performing non-vigorous flexibility exercises to ease out my chest wall and distract my attention from the ordeal ahead. It was now day three of the trial and it already seemed like three weeks. The quality of my future life was quite literally in the hands of Michael, Denis and Karen and ultimately Judge Johnson and rather than being apprehensive I became more contemplative. I had a role to perform to the best of my abilities, even if only to present myself in court. If events transpired as they did the previous day, I was in for further startling revelations.

Before the morning began in earnest, however, I had to take care of the most important priority of the day after breakfast. I brought my father to the West Coast Coffee Company, situated on the quays within the vicinity of the Four Courts, for his first taste of freshly brewed coffee and a read of the newspaper. It became his favourite haunt; he was particular about his coffee.

It was always rather difficult persuading my father to come to Dublin at the best of times and we established a pattern every morning of sitting back and relaxing with plenty of time to spare, scarce moments I really enjoyed. The gods still shone down on us with the weather and after a leisurely stroll in the crisp, bright November air to the Four Courts, we were prepared as well as could be expected. And, for both of us, the whole process of the trial with its drama, twists and turns was a real learning experience and eye opener.

It might seem a strange thing but I always looked forward to seeing my legal team in the mornings and I became very comfortable in the surroundings. It was like having an extended family. Just as well because at that stage I could not have predicted just how long I would be ensnared in a litigious route that would eventually assume a life of its own. The only consistently annoying and increasingly frustrating situation I did not get used to and could not endure with any grace whatsoever, was the same surly photographer chasing after me and snapping at my heels at every opportunity. I felt he went grossly beyond the boundary of decency.

Of all the photographers and, indeed, reporters, he was the sole one I have to say who subjected me to such complete invasion of personal space. At least within the solid walls of the Four Courts, I was protected from and spared the ordeal.

As usual, that Thursday, I noticed Mr Lynch carrying the same holdall and wondered what he had up his sleeve for the day. I did not imagine how he could possibly surpass his extraordinary performance in Judge Johnson's chambers. Then again he still had not reached the limit of his consistently, I believe, narcissistic behaviour. I purposely stayed well away from him and avoided glancing in his direction as much as possible. After my usual pre-trial chat with Michael, the proceedings commenced.

Mr Makey, still under Oath, was prepared and patiently waiting for Mr Lynch to continue his cross-examination. However, the person who had been charged with the task of bringing my original records from St. Vincent's Hospital had also arrived in court and, standing up, Denis announced, 'My Lord, I think Mr Makey is still in the witness box. I do not know whether your Lordship wishes me to hand in to your Lordship now the original operation notes.'

'I want that proved, I think it should be proved. You can hand it in to me, but I will need it proved eventually.'

'I can prove it, my Lord, in the sense that the person who brought it down from the hospital is here and it is Mr Lynch's own note.'

'Yes, it is from the hospital records.'

Denis called the administrator from St. Vincent's Hospital and after confirming she had my original hospital records, asked her, 'Are the records open at an operation note or a note of an operation which was performed on the 5th of June 1996?'

'Yes, that is right.'

'What is the surgeon's name on that note?'

'Mr Lynch.'

'If you would just hand it to his Lordship, please.'

'Then Judge Johnson asked, 'Mr Lynch, have you seen this?'

'I just caught a glance of it. I see the various…'

'You'd better examine them, Mr Lynch, I do not think you should say anything, because I am going to give you advice now. Is that the original of the note which you made on the day of the operation?'

'That is correct.'

'Very good. Well, now, Mr Lynch, before you say anything else I think I am going to give you advice, not about this case, but I think you should take legal advice from a solicitor or from someone else regarding this document which you produced yesterday.'

'Thank you, my Lord.'

'Because I am now forced to take certain steps which I will have to take later in the case.'

The seriousness of Mr Lynch's, in my opinion, calculated change to his evidential copy of the operation notes and supported adamantly by his own words, was evident to everyone on my team. And as he was to testify, he had spent copious hours trawling through my records so this alteration I concluded was premeditated and not something scribbled in a hurry five minutes before the trial.

Mr Lynch then posed a request to Judge Johnson, 'My Lord, would it be possible for me to ask questions of the two expert witnesses that we had yesterday?'

'Mr Makey is still in the witness box, and if you wish to recall…'

'Could I, just to get into proper chronological order, I wonder could I call back Professor Smith to the witness box?'

'Professor Smith, would you come back to the witness box, please.' And then to Denis, 'Can I now have that original record myself, please?'

'It is there, my Lord.'

'Very good.'

When Professor Smith re-entered the witness box for a repeat cross-examination, Mr Lynch began by asking a strange question, 'What does the word "surgeon" mean?' *In an about-turn, I wondered if the courtroom had been transformed into an examination hall.*

He then proceeded to match up to his previous dirty tricks campaign by trying to force the Professor to agree with him about his old friend 'medication' and when the Professor kept repeating, 'No,' Mr Lynch replied, 'I am afraid you attempted to evade the answer.'

Judge Johnson had to intervene, 'That was the answer he gave in evidence, he did not evade it under any circumstances, it is the same answer.' *Mr Lynch must have been up all night concocting more nonsense, I thought.*

Then he insisted on rehashing the previous day's evidence subjecting us all again to rhetoric on his way of performing VATS as if he was lecturing to an audience of doctors in training instead of cross-examining Professor Smith. As usual, after the very few questions he did ask instead of making points and speeches, with Professor Smith constantly disagreeing with him, I just sat there painfully stiff and mentally bored, already wishing the morning was over. Judge Johnson absolutely failed to succeed in getting Mr Lynch to adhere to the most basic of court procedures and I certainly appreciated the difficult task he had.

'Mr Lynch, ask the questions, you can give evidence of what you did yourself subsequently, Mr Lynch.'

He then went on to describe the anatomy of the breast.

Judge Johnson interjected, 'Mr Lynch, the only allegation made against you is that you put an insertion through the breast.'

'Correct. That is the point I am trying to make.' *Pardon? Now I was completely baffled.*

Judge Johnson repeated, again, 'You may put anything you want to the witness…'

Denis, I believe, was also confused because he also interrupted, 'I should say, my Lord, I do not know where Mr Lynch is going with this, but Mr Lynch yesterday, in the course I think of his cross-examination, conceded that he accepted that he had, in fact, placed the port in Ms Carroll's breast, a matter which he only realised yesterday.' *I thought Denis was being very sensitive and reasonable saying 'realised' rather than 'admitted to'.*

'Yes, that is exactly the words he used.'

And Mr Lynch astonishingly added, 'That is perfectly true.'

But he was on the warpath, relentlessly pushing Professor Smith to agree with him and when the Professor again said, 'No,' he could not resist making another statement, 'The point that I am trying to make…' *Then the whole purpose of his 'point' hit me.*

'What I am saying loudly clearly is that when a surgeon puts three ports into the chest of a female, doing a VATS procedure, more than likely one of those ports will generally go through breast tissue.'

But this time Professor Smith did not let it go and asked Judge Johnson, 'May I answer that?' to which he agreed.

'Thank you. Surgeons do not operate on Gray's Anatomy, they operate on individual patients and the structure is variable and the limits of that structure are determined by palpation under clinical examination or under anaesthesia. It is perfectly obvious to an operative surgeon where the breast is. There may be microscopic breast tissue outside, but we are not talking about an incident here, we are talking about a cannula that was pushed through the major substance of the breast.'

When Mr Lynch still had no success in goading Professor Smith to agree with him about another technical point and to which the Professor refutably answered, 'No,' Judge Johnson announced, 'Very good, that is your answer.'

But would Mr Lynch cease his antics? 'That is that point but what I am saying is accurate, it is true.'

Judge Johnson had to put a stop to it, 'You have asked the question, he disagrees with you.' *At this stage, I was pulling my hair out. I will not need another trim for a while, I mused.*

When Mr Lynch went on then to ask Professor Smith under what conditions a surgeon would convert from keyhole surgery to open chest surgery my ears pricked to attention.

'What may I find when I go in with my camera that tells me, look, it is not wise to proceed with this method of surgery, I should go back to the older, excellent, conventional way?' *But it was perfectly wise Mr Lynch if you had competently performed the VATS. You did not 'choose' to perform the open surgery; you had no option. The fact is you did proceed with the VATS after you inserted the camera. You became 'unwise' when you shoved one of the ports through my breast into my chest and severed my artery.*

I know what deviousness you are up to. You are now trying to set the scene that it would have been better to have performed the thoracotomy in the first place rather than the VATS. So why did you choose the VATS procedure in the first instance? Not once in the hospital did you mention open surgery and I had never beforehand heard the word 'thoracotomy'. I really think whatever story you come up with now, because you have told so many, that your credibility is shot.

It is astonishing that Judge Johnson had warned you the previous day that you might be asked to explain why you brought VATS into the country if you believed planned, open surgery was the 'older, excellent' way but you did not take his tip-off. He did not have to warn you about the possibility of being asked this question but he was trying to assist you as much as possible to conduct your own defence and not land yourself in deep waters. Now I have begun to realise you have been given far too many advantages.

When Professor Smith gave his convincing and experienced reply, Mr Lynch began to question his authority to speak about VATS. But the Professor adeptly retorted, 'I was asked to comment about the method by which the ports had been inserted. That evidence is available to me. I based my evidence on personal experience and the general principles of thoracic surgery, which is that you do not knowingly injure the breast.'

Judge Johnson repeated, 'You do not knowingly injure the breast,' and asked Professor Smith, 'in this particular case, was it possible to avoid knowing the cannula was going through the breast?'

'It was possible to avoid injuring the breast, sir, yes.'

Of course Mr Lynch had to interrupt, 'My Lord, the point that I am making, and in making this point with great authority…'

'Sorry, ask questions.'

'Yes, sorry my Lord,' *as if he was going to take any heed.*

Judge Johnson had a dreadful situation on his hands. The problem was, however, that by ensuring that Mr Lynch, because he was representing himself, had every opportunity to present his defence and that his constitutional rights were protected, but Mr Lynch refused to follow instructions, I began to seriously and anxiously think that it was my constitutional right to a trial being fair to both parties that was being jeopardised, not his. I had to be confident that Judge Johnson wanted to ensure that absolutely nothing could be criticised in his treatment of Mr Lynch in such an important and obviously unusual trial.

He was not to blame for Mr Lynch's propensity for lying or his appalling behaviour and he must have experienced just about everything and anything during his long career. I only hoped that what I had experienced at the hands of Mr Lynch would not get totally lost in all the lies, surrealism and drama.

Finally Judge Johnson had enough and rightly so. 'You are meant to be cross-examining. I have not done an operation, but you have come into this bailiwick to conduct your own case and you must conduct it in accordance with the rules.'

But I could not help but think that Mr Lynch was antagonistically confident that he could make his own rules in the high court as he did in

St. Vincent's Hospital. No one and nothing, I believed, could control him.

Judge Johnson interjected, 'He has already stated he is not familiar. If you wish to take it up, swear it and produce the books, that of course is a completely different thing. That means taking the oath and producing the books.' *Which, of course, he failed to do. Then after a lead-up he introduced a totally new scenario and I asked silently, are there no bounds to the lengths you will go to cover-up what you have done?*

He started to set the plot, 'I was talking about VATS conversion rate and the reasons for conversion. Sometimes we run into a bleed, sometimes we run into adhesions and in a pneumothorax there are varieties of emphysema such as…' And he subjected us all to a list of anatomical diseases and finished by saying, 'So, that will determine your policy. Would you agree with that?'

But, as Professor Smith had previously stated, and which I knew anyway, I had no obstructions or disease in my chest to prevent the VATS successfully going to completion. He responded, 'I believe that the surgeon should enter a chest always with a firm diagnosis having been made and a clear idea of what procedure is to be undertaken. That applies to any sort of surgery, whether it is VATS surgery or open surgery.'

After a few more exchanges Mr Lynch finally let the bomb drop, 'There was one unusual feature about this lady and that was that she was known to have had endometriosis. When you look in there, Professor, with your scope, what two particular things would you be looking for?'

I knew it and so did my legal team. *How do you live with yourself Mr Lynch? How do you sleep at night with your lack of conscience, knowing you are balancing on a cliff edge?* He was going to use the condition I had, and was cured from, back in the early nineteen eighties in a malicious way. I just imagined him sprawled over my records and in minute detail picking out any word or phrase he could scrounge up and latch on to, to proffer different scenarios to the court.

In the myriad of pages of my hospital records the word 'endometriosis' was mentioned once, by me and only by me. I had in hindsight handed Mr Lynch ammunition on a platter. Even the letter to Dr Duignan in the immediate aftermath of his horrendous surgery confirms that the only medical condition he mentioned in my history was the first pneumothorax.

I only wished that Judge Johnson would see it for what it was and I anxiously awaited Professor Smith's reply, but I need not have worried.

'I would be looking for a hole in the lung somewhere in this particular patient. The aim of this operation was to seal a lung leak.'

'You would be looking for two particular things…' lectured Mr Lynch, proceeding to provide a long-winded account of the first and then the second. 'Now, to come back to my question, this patient is known to have endometriosis.' *So now it is 'have' not 'had' I noticed.* 'I agree that you have got to see when you are doing that surgery, you have got to see the whole of the intrathoracic cavity.' Then, continuing to weave the web, 'Now, to come back to my question, this patient is known to have endometriosis. Would you worry about any particular features in her chest?' *Seriously, this was getting out of hand because the endometriosis had been cured by laser treatment more than thirty years ago.*

So Professor Smith answered blindly, 'I would say that the ports had to be placed in such a manner that the whole of the chest could be visualised in order to determine what the problems were, and the best way to get a view of the whole of the chest is to put three ports through the triangle of safety.' *Oh excellent, Professor Smith.*

'Where would you look for the problems with endometriosis?'

'Our policy in Sheffield was to look at all parts of the chest that were visible and to put the ports so that we could see all parts of the chest.'

'Would there be any problem with the diaphragm in these patients?'

The diaphragm? What had my diaphragm to do with the issues?

'We would always inspect the diaphragm.'

'That is frequently present in catamenia pneumothorax. The second thing that we generally find in these patients is that there is evidence of endometrial tissue on the surface of the lung, and that could be detected by the presence of a blood stain in that part of the lung. That is something I had to pay particular attention to in this case.'

Absolute news to me Mr Lynch and God forgive me but I thought, 'Oh, you horrible liar.' Indeed, when I did contract endometriosis it was confined to my lower abdomen. It had not travelled to my diaphragm or lungs; the surgeon who cured it was thoroughly competent. Even if I did have any other problems, a surgeon would never go through a breast to determine the problem.

Judge Johnson interjected, 'Is this what was there, Mr Lynch, or not?

Are you putting that to this witness?'

'I am putting it to this witness that things are just not as simple as he is making out.'

But mine was very simple, the only problem I had were some blisters on the top of my lung and that you do know. You are backtracking and obfuscating because you did state you paid 'particular' attention to it.

'We want to know what precisely you are saying,' Judge Johnson emphasised. 'The case against you is perfectly straight forward and simple, that you put the port in the wrong place, through her breast, thereby making it necessary for you to do open thoracic surgery.'

'That is the point that I am making, my Lord.'

'Are you saying you put the cannula in the correct place, through the breast?'

Judge Johnson asked the Professor, 'Now, Professor Smith, what do you say to that?'

'I do not believe that what you say is true. I believe it is possible to push three ports into the chest in order to get good visualisation of the intrathoracic cavity without going through not just the anatomical limits of the breast, but also what the lay public would call the breast. This port went through 2.5 cm lateral to the nipple, that is through the substance of the breast, which is not an anatomical definition in the textbooks, it is available to every *Sun* reader.'

I laughed at that, silently of course; a little humour in the midst of a nightmare but I do not believe Professor Smith intended it to be funny.

'A triangle has three reference points.'

'You are going on a lot about this triangle. I do not hold with this, but what I am trying to say to you we use four vertical lines of reference and I will tell you what they are…'

Judge Johnson interrupted, trying to obtain precise clarification, 'You are rejecting the concept of the triangle of safety?'

'I am not rejecting the concept of the triangle of safety…'

'You cross-examined two witnesses yesterday without ever mentioning that the triangle, the three ports were wrong.'

'This is something in surgery. There is no such…'

'That is a surgeon,' Judge Johnson interjected, referring to the Professor. 'He gave evidence there was a triangle of safety, you are now introducing a fourth port.'

Professor Smith continued, 'The definition of the triangle of safety is the sixth or seventh intercostal space, the anterior axillary line and the mid-axillary line. Those are three sides of the triangle of safety. If you adhere to those, you do not go through breast tissue, you do not damage the diaphragm, you do not damage any important structures within the chest wall, and you do not go through muscles which are highly vascular or any structures which are highly vascular.'

But Mr Lynch continued making other points and after the last question at this stage, Professor Smith answered, 'I agree you have got to have room to work, but I reiterate that the correct way of entering the chest is not to damage important structures to which damage can be avoided.'

'Everybody agrees with that.' *Well you didn't.* 'Now, Professor, describe your method of putting in your first port.'

Judge Johnson reminded him, 'You went through all of this yesterday in your cross-examination yesterday, as well, Mr Lynch, but carry on Professor.'

Professor Smith confidently reiterated his technical procedures again which I think antagonised Mr Lynch because, since I had already switched off, my attention was swiftly brought back when I heard Mr Lynch cutting him off and in an angry tone lectured him again, 'Professor, I do not want to be contentious but doing that, you have done significant damage to your patient's lung. The first thing you must do, Professor, is…'

'Mr Lynch, not if I have had an immediate pre-operative chest x-ray and I know that the lung is away from the chest wall, as should have happened in this case.'

'Professor, there are two methods of dealing with that problem and the first method is…' This was too technical for me to pick up. 'Would you agree with that?'

'If the lung were abutting against the chest wall, that is something I would do, but this lung was not abutting against the chest wall.'

'The second thing that you must do…' Again, too technical for me and he went on to stress, 'Professor Smith, I do not like doing this, but I want to defend myself and people are listening to you as a person who is speaking with great authority in this particular operation…' And he went on to criticise him in a vitriolic temper.

Judge Johnson had to interject again, 'Mr Lynch, you can criticise the witness in many ways, but do so by way of cross-examination. You may comment to me at the end of the case. I have said this to you repeatedly.'

'I am sorry, sir.' *Another empty 'sorry'?*

'Will you ask questions and stop making speeches. Now, I am not going to talk to you again, because you are quite incapable of taking any form of direction. So, ask questions.'

Mr Lynch's flaunting of court procedures had by now become so extremely farcical I believed he was deliberately trying to rile Judge Johnson so that he would have ammunition for his appeal.

Then he continued, 'I would just like to ask one question, Professor. Do you feel that on reflection that the statement that you made yesterday was correct?'

'I think you will have to tell me which statement you are talking about.'

'The statement about the ill effects of inserting a cannula that went through the breast, a port?'

'Yes, I stand by the statement I made yesterday, which was a surgeon should not insert a cannula knowingly through the substance of the breast.'

'We all agree totally on that but the point that I am trying to make clearly and the point that I would love to get you to accept and to express in a sincere and genuine way, the point is that the breast is a much larger structure than we surgeons realise and that these ports are frequently going through the breast tissue.'

'No, I will not accept that.'

And then bringing up Dr John Hegarty's treatment again during my first pneumothorax and knowing it was false said, 'Well, I think we will have to differ on that. In closing, I am just going to ask you a question – and, maybe, my Lord, this is the wrong thing to do – a patient getting twelve doses of narcotic drugs…'

But Judge Johnson, with his remarkable memory, interrupted immediately, 'You have asked that question four times already. How many times have you asked the question, Mr Lynch?'

'At least four times.'

'We have got the answer, Mr Lynch. We try and make things not too repetitive here. I got the answer first time.' And suddenly it was over; Mr Lynch had run out of steam and contradictions.

Everyone on my legal team knew by that point, if they believed as I did, that Mr Lynch could not possibly defend his surgery. He was trying everything he could to pin my condition on anything he felt would take the limelight off his incompetence. There seemed to be nothing he would not say or do to get away with what he did to me.

It was becoming extremely difficult sitting there listening to the various lies and venom he was spouting out. I had a life sentence to endure after his butchery and he was now retired on probably a fat pension with all the time in the world to manipulate and introduce completely false information to the court. I hoped that at the end of the trial a travesty of justice would not prevail and it would all come back to haunt him.

And while I knew Mr Lynch had introduced the issue of endometriosis for a malicious motive I was yet to know the beforehand unheard of reason for introducing my diaphragm into the case. What farcical explanation would he come up with next?

Chapter Fifteen

As Professor Smith left the witness box, I surmised what thoughts were going through his mind after what I can only describe as an onslaught but, naturally, whatever I suspected was only conjecture. Now, as Mr Makey replaced him and faced Mr Lynch again, I pondered ruminatively if he would deal with his 'points' as effectively as Professor Smith had done. However, I have to admit, I felt far more optimistic than apprehensive.

Mr Lynch kicked off by making a bold and surprising statement, 'I have nothing contentious to ask you…' and yet what he went on to ask Mr Makey was extremely so. He launched into a tirade of criticisms of both experts in their experience of VATS, so much so that Denis stood up and intervened.

'With respect, my Lord, I am not certain that that is a fair way of putting the question. Professor Smith has inserted the ports, which is what this case is about.'

'Precisely,' confirmed Judge Johnson. 'I have quite clearly got the point from everybody. I know exactly what the case is about.'

Not at all happy, Mr Lynch continued, 'You were listening to the discussion between myself and Professor Smith…'

'Yes, it was a discussion, not a cross-examination. Now, can we have a cross-examination this time, please, Mr Lynch? I do not use your instruments you carry there in your bag.'

Oh dear God no, I thought alarmingly. Did I hear correctly; not his surgical instruments? I was dumbfounded. So, that was what Mr Lynch had in his holdall. What was he going to do with them? I detected something creepy and foreboding around the corner and a frisson of terror coursed through my veins.

Then, after attempting to dominate Mr Makey again with another tedious and rambling oration he asked, 'Mr Makey, you have done thoracotomies?'

'I have done thoracotomies.'

'Have you often noticed that there is some breast tissue in the wound?'

'No, I would not have thought that, unless I happened to be operating very high in the chest wall and I would normally be operating from the back and, therefore, I would be restricting my forward extension.'

After rendering answers to further technical questions, Mr Makey earnestly affirmed, 'I do not think I can say honestly that I have ever seen anything looking like breast tissue as I have gone through those incisions.'

'It is very difficult, of course, to tell as breast fat looks much the same as ordinary body fat.'

'Fat maybe, but not actual breast tissue.'

Attempting then to re-assert his domineering position, Mr Lynch, in a very curt statement admonished Mr Makey, 'But, this means that frequently we surgeons must be going through breast tissue.'

'I would be very surprised if I had been going through breast tissue in the numerous operations I have done.'

We continued to be further subjected to a catalogue of diseases of the lung and the placement of the ports and after some length Judge Johnson inquired of Mr Makey, 'Tell me something, Mr Makey. I understood that the purpose of putting in the cannula, the port and the scope was for the operating surgeon to see where the various condition was.'

'Exactly, yes.'

'That was the whole purpose, you put it in, in order to ascertain what you had to do.'

'May I just elaborate slightly?'

'Yes.'

'You would have some information from the x-ray, but probably not very much, as has already been agreed. In some you might, because you might see quite big air spaces. It has always been agreed that even if you did a CAT scan or otherwise you might not get much help unless the spaces were quite large, but after that you are then dependent on the first inspecting telescope to give you what is there in the chest.'

'The first inspecting telescope tells you where next to go?'

'Yes. Then you choose yourself if it is at the apex or in the front or the back and you could vary where you put your other scopes, yes.'

Mr Lynch could not fail to resist interrupting and lauding himself, 'Mr Makey, I have had a considerable interest in this operation and have presented papers at international meetings.'

'That is a statement Mr Lynch,' repeated Judge Johnson. 'Please ask the questions.'

'Yes, but I am leading into something.'

'Yes, but you can lead into a question by asking the question as opposed to making a speech.' Mr Lynch did not appear at all chastened.

'Do you feel that this port that there is a lot of discussion about, would you agree with your colleague's comments about that or would you agree with the comment that I made, that suggests that, look, the breast is far larger than we all realise?'

And as competently as Professor Smith, Mr Makey replied, 'I cannot agree. I will accept what your statements are, that Gray's Anatomy may have given the extent of the breast as larger than it appears visually and perhaps to palpation with your hand, but I think that does not excuse the fact that you put the cannula through what must have been a major part of the breast. That, I think, would be an error that I would consider that was made.'

'Do you think this lady is suffering any problems due to that?'

'I think it is difficult to know exactly what damage that did. If we accept that the bleeding came from the internal mammary artery, then there may have been extra bleeding coming from the breast tissue into the chest through the track. There would also be the fact that putting it through a fairly sizeable part of the breast there must have been considerable contusion and bleeding into that breast substance. Therefore, there would be post-operative swelling, pain and a need for some period of time for this to settle back to normal.'

'The other point that I would like to get across to you is that when I am referring to the internal mammary artery, I may not be thinking of the same internal artery…'

Ah, so there we have it. You have just succeeded in supporting the assertion you made yesterday when you added the change to my operation notes. You have repeated it and I do not believe there is now any ambiguity in your motive for doing so. How can you explain yourself when you know you sutured off this artery and having again tried to deflect from it? You are slipping down a treacherous slope to your own demise.

Judge Johnson, seemingly, knew exactly what Mr Lynch was up to and if I figured it out he certainly was able to. 'Internal mammary vessels is what you talk of.'

'Same thing.'

'You wrote down "internal mammary vessels." You cross-examine him on "internal mammary arteries." Let's at least stick to the same terminology.'

'Mr Makey, would you also agree that there are a number of internal mammary arteries going to the breast?'

'There are lots of tiny little vessels coming off the intercostal vessels,'

'Coming off the internal thoracic artery and also coming off the axillary artery. Would you agree with that?' *No, Mr Lynch, it is not going to work. You lacerated my mammary artery; it is sutured off. You will not succeed in attempting to suggest you hit some other blood vessel.*

'Not really the axillary, no.'

'Is it possible that one or two of these vessels may be larger than usual?'

'I have not seen that, but I am not in the habit of dissecting that area myself, so I do not know, but I would not have thought, from the information in the anatomical books, there were normally sizeable vessels coming from those arteries.'

'Do you feel this patient was managed properly?'

But Judge Johnson wanted clarification, 'Pardon? What was that question?'

'My Lord, I asked Mr Makey does he feel that this lady was managed properly.' *What a totally absurd question and I felt disgusted.*

Mr Makey agreed by saying that his decision to perform the VATS operation, was 'perfectly reasonable and correct,' because my lung had collapsed twice. But then he proceeded to stress succinctly, without embellishment, 'The only point that I disagree with is that I would not have put my second port through what to me is a fair-sized portion of the breast.'

Pursuing a different tack then and with further debate, Mr Lynch stated, 'So, frequently, you would agree, the surgeon has to determine the site of his ports with the site of the pathology.'

'I agree with that, but you had done that with your first port, so you knew exactly where it was. On your evidence, the lesions were confined to the apex, because all you did was to remove the apex of the upper lobe.'

'Would you like to make any other comments about how…'

Judge Johnson had to interject again, 'Mr Lynch, just ask the questions. This is a cross-examination, ask the questions. He gave his direct evidence, gave all his comments yesterday.'

'This lady is now six years after her surgery. She has had no further collapse of the lung. Do you feel that her surgery was done well?'

Mr Makey, after stating that in the sense my lung had not collapsed again, although there is no guarantee that it will not, went on to what seemed supernumerary criticism, 'If her lung apex is well stuck to the chest wall and she has not got disease elsewhere, then she is not likely to get a recurrence. You, at the time, did not particularly undertake any other procedures that can be undertaken to try and make sure there is good adherence of the apex, you removed the disease, and I think the only procedure you used to help produce pleuracentesis was installation of antibiotic, which one knows is an irritant and does so. Some surgeons, and I must say I would have been tempted, I think, to have stripped the apical pleura as well, because that leaves a raw area that bleeds and is therefore more likely to become adherent. But that is a matter of opinion.'

And in a menacingly curt statement, Mr Lynch informed Mr Makey, 'I achieve my thoracotomy by putting in a chemical.' *I shuddered.*

As he approached the end of his purported cross-examination, Mr Lynch asked a completely irrelevant question, 'Mr Makey, do you think that it is fair to bring a surgeon to court for a patient who has persistent pain in her chest following an operation?'

'That is a legal question to my mind.'

Judge Johnson interjected to clarify a matter with Mr Makey, 'The pain in the chest before the operation is caused by what?'

'…it was probably coming from the pneumothorax.'

'Yes. Her pain now is not from the pneumothorax?'

'Her pain now is in the chest wall, I am sure, yes.'

Judge Johnson addressed, Mr Lynch, 'The question as to whether it is fair or not is a matter for me.'

But Mr Lynch was going to try and squeeze blood out of a stone by asking Mr Makey, 'Going back to what you gleaned about this case, do you think that there were any pre-existing complaints prior to surgery that may have caused her present pain?'

'Not as far as I was aware. Reading through her previous history, I have no reason to think that, no.'

Then, in a vehement outburst, he could not desist from his deceitful and sinister stratagem, referring again to medication. *Oh give it up Mr Lynch, I frustratingly thought. You never learn and you are somebody who lectured medical students. Are you not an astute man to be able to ask questions when they are malicious and pretend you cannot understand the rules the rest of the time?* Now I was finally pushed to anger.

But Mr Makey was competently insistent, 'I have no idea, because I was not aware, I did not see it happen, I do not know what things were like, but reading the notes, when I read them I did not get any impression that she had excessive medication following the first pneumothorax.'

But Mr Lynch did not take too kindly to that reply and proceeded to almost coerce Mr Makey to agree with him with the result that Judge Johnson had to emphatically interject, 'He did not consider it was excessive medication.'

Then Mr Lynch made the most appalling comment, 'Judge, Mr Makey is giving an *impression* he is a very fair and honest person and I am worried about…' *How ironic I thought, the dishonest talking of 'honesty'?*

But Judge Johnson got it in one, 'Mr Lynch, if she got all these drugs, it was under the supervision of a doctor; is that not correct?'

'That is correct.'

'Well, then, we may very well have to get the doctor who actually gave it to her or prescribed it for her. But, if she did not need it, are you criticising the doctor who gave it to her?'

Fantastic. Again Judge Johnson, you have called his bluff. It was really preposterous, however, because all the originals of the prescription receipts were there in court and Mr Lynch could have gone through them but no, he just wanted to slander me as much as he could. However, he would get nowhere with that strategy.

You are so ruthless Mr Lynch and your callousness so palpable you do not have one ounce of compassion in you for what I endured at your hands in that hospital and afterwards when you failed to refer me for rehabilitation. I have never met a more insensate person as you. Now I am beginning to become angry at your abuse and cruelty. And brutality it was. But you have wrecked your own credibility right from the beginning of this trial. All you have succeeded in doing so far is to make yourself sound and look utterly ridiculous and ultimately a chronic liar.

He did not relinquish his venomous verbal attack, however, and Mr Makey, of necessity, had to repeat himself and drive his point home, 'There was no evidence to suggest, that, whatever those doses are that you are quoting, that she was over sedated clinically. There was no evidence to suggest, I do not think, that she was knocked out by these drugs. Otherwise, she would have probably been lying there pretty stuporous and not responsive.' *But no, Mr Lynch refused to accept Mr Makey's response and move on, and in the end Judge Johnson had to pull the plug,* 'All right. Now, any further questions of this witness, Mr Lynch?'

'I am nearly finished. She came in a second time, Mr Makey, and on the second occasion she came in with a small pneumothorax on 30th May, and again she was under the care of a physician. On this occasion she had no chest drain and again she was constantly complaining of terrible severe pain.' *I was under your care, Mr Lynch. And yes, I was in pain because my lung was collapsed and I never used the word 'terrible', I said 'severe'. Terrible I ascribe to your dastardly surgery. Still flogging a dead horse?*

He continued, 'She is complaining of the pain and she is getting a narcotic drug. Would you agree with me that prior to her operation that this lady had severe pain in her chest?'

'One can only surmise that from the notes and the fact that in response she was given appropriate narcotics.'

However, Judge Johnson was quick, 'Mr Lynch, if you remember, the plaintiff herself said she was in severe pain at that time, in the witness box.'

Then Mr Lynch said, 'Before the surgery…'

'Before the surgery she said she was in pain.'

'Thank you, my Lord. That is the point that I want to get across.'

'She said it herself, if you had listened to her, Mr Lynch.'

And, finally, it was over. By the end of his cross-examination Mr Lynch was 'up a creek without a paddle', all of his own making. His stories and lies had crept up on him and there was no turning back. He would never stop digging and the more he went on the more he fuddled himself.

As Mr Makey left the stand I wondered what he thought of Mr Lynch's statement that he was trying to give the 'impression' that he was being 'fair and honest'. Was no one beyond his vitriol, arrogance and ego?

The worst was over, or so I thought. After cross-examining the two thoracic surgeons twice, Mr Lynch had got nowhere. With all his statements, discussion and points I knew exactly what he was going to say when he himself got into the witness box and I felt an unequivocal sensation at that moment that he had absolutely no valid defence for his actions. I just wished he would continue to lie and conjure up even more ridiculous stories and this time, under oath and with any luck, he would perjure himself. In addition, while I was sitting on the bench a strange, eerie feeling came over me and I knew that Mr Lynch could surpass his out-of-control conduct in Judge Johnson's chambers.

But before that happened, even more intimidating behaviour and ubiquitous untruths would be revealed over the next two days and I did not cease to be gob-smacked. Mr Lynch did not wane in startling us in his forthcoming testimony.

Chapter Sixteen

The testimonies given by both experts, Professor Smith and Mr Makey, had been crucial to prove the case of negligence against Mr Lynch. They established that it was indeed this negligence that caused my severe and debilitating injuries. Now we had reached the stage when we had to validate the trauma and the long, frustrating, arduous and expensive journey to try and recover some semblance of my pre-existing strength and fitness. It was going to take insurmountable and mammoth attempts to reduce the level of chronic pain I had been left with.

The first witness Denis called was Dr Ethel Brady, the physio and medical exercise therapist I had attended for a number of years. However, although I had continuously gained incremental improvements in my physical structure, nothing to date reduced the nerve pain. It was like, not only one toothache, but all my teeth on fire concurrently. However, unlike being able to cure the pain by filling or extracting teeth, the damaged and stretched nerves in my chest would not respond to treatment. So in that respect I was living in a state of constant misery, endlessly seeking a lighthouse to guide me through the dark turbulent waves towards a method that would provide some relief.

Denis asked Dr Brady how I had come under her care and she replied, 'She was referred by Dr Declan O'Keeffe who was seeing her with regards to pain management.'

'When you saw her in January 1999, what complaints did she make to you?'

'She had extensive pain in the region of the right thoracic spine, running from the cervical spine right down to the lower limit of the thoracic spine.' And after further explanation she concluded, 'She also had a very persistent, troublesome, aching and sharpness of pain in the ribs anteriorly on the right side, around the level of ribs 4, 5, and 7.

'Were there certain things and activities which she indicated to you she could not do?'

'I found her to be very debilitated in comparison to her reported previous level of activities. Firstly, she was not able to work. She was not able to sit for longer than about forty minutes to an hour without her pain increasing. She was not able to tolerate driving long distance. After an hour, she would be very much aggravated in her pain. She found her right hand was weak; her writing had deteriorated. She would not be able to lift shopping, for example, or do household chores in the normal way. They would be very aggravating activities for her. Her overall tolerance for exercise and activities was very much less. She had previously been active in using a gym and doing exercise of various sorts, and at the time I met her she was unable to do any of those things.'

'Did you examine Ms Carroll when she came to you first?'

'In fact, I examined Ms Carroll every time I saw her. My initial examination showed that her range of movement of the thoracic spine was about fifty per cent below normal due to pain.'

'Was there pain in any particular areas that you can recall, on examination?'

'The worst pain she felt was in the right side of the thoracic spine. Movement aggravated pain anteriorly in the chest wall, that was the worst pain, but also posteriorly close to the spine on the right paraspinal region.'

Denis continued by asking her about the therapy she had given me and she provided a very lucid account of her manipulation treatments and the exercises she taught me in her physio gym. 'Since she came to you first in January 1999, with what regularity has she been attending?'

'If it is all right, I have here just a summary of her attendance and in that year, 1999, Ms Carroll attended fifty-three times. When planning a treatment for someone like Ms Carroll, whose injuries and her presentation is chronic, and whose initial presentation and my understanding will indicate that her treatment is going to be on a long-term basis, I am trying to look for a treatment frequency that will be enough to ensure recovery without being too intense to actually be counter productive.

'These treatment sessions are quite painful and difficult for the patient. If we do too many per week, it is going to aggravate her pain more than help settle it down. Attending fifty-three times in one year is spectacular regularity. It is not something that is achieved by a person who has got a minimal presentation.'

'Is there hard work involved in this from the patient's point of view?'

'I think sometimes for patients even to turn up at the clinic is hard work. They have to battle through traffic and whatever inertia they have, and pain, to actually get there, and then they know the treatment may be painful. Even if the treatment itself is not painful, they may suffer pain afterwards for quite a few days before they visit the following week.'

'How long does a typical session last?'

'An hour. It would involve a series of manipulations which are quite painful and exercises which are demanding and strenuous, because I am trying to – I am focusing all the treatment on the tissues that are weakest and most affected by her presentation.'

'In the following year, the year 2000, how frequently did she attend?'

'I have marked here a total of twenty-four visits.' *And I recalled, twenty-seven times in 2001 to date.* 'However, in a couple of those months she was in hospital for treatment. In the year 2000 it was reduced because she had successfully managed to rehabilitate independently for a few weeks at a time in her own gym.'

Denis then reached the stage where he focused on my future abilities. 'Looking into the future now, as far as you are concerned, do you envisage continuing to treat Ms Carroll and if so, with what regularity and in what way?'

'In fact a person needs to be about eighty per cent fit to successfully complete a job and living requirements and a reasonable quality of life; in other words, about a level three to four. However, in the case of a person like Ms Carroll who has had chronically reduced spinal function for a couple of years, they have to aim for a higher level of fitness than they previously had prior to the injury to compensate for it.

'I have advised Ms Carroll to undertake exercise therapy and physiotherapy with greater intensity for, for example, three-month spells, where she would work very hard with me in the gym, approximately two to three visits per week. So, approximately three, three-month spells during two and a half years.'

'At that point, after those two and a half years, Dr Brady, what would you hope her condition would be?'

'People often think that prescription or that recommendation is very high and very intense. However, it is only when they start on the spine and when they realise how weak they have been will they start to understand and appreciate how hard it is to restore optimal tissue function around the spine and ribs. Very few people manage to really complete that amount and intensity of exercise. Looking at Ms Carroll's dedication to health so far, I think that she probably would be likely to manage to keep on going.'

After further detailed questioning, Denis followed with, 'Obviously, you have seen Ms Carroll on a very regular basis, you have seen her very frequently over the last three years. Have you seen her in pain during that time?'

'I have, and I have seen her very eager to return to work and even wanting to return and putting herself back into work even when she was not fit enough. I have seen this person in great distress, finding herself unable to achieve the levels of activity and work that she previously achieved.'

'In your opinion, Dr Brady, was such pain and distress as you saw in this girl, was it genuine?'

'Yes.'

'Are there fees due to you, Dr Brady, for the treatment you have given Ms Carroll over the years, or have you been paid for the treatment you have given her?'

'Up to now Ms Carroll has paid approximately £3,700 for this length of treatment.'

Mr Lynch stood up and I was intrigued about how he was going to cross-examine Dr Brady. He began by asking a number of technical questions which Dr Brady competently answered. Then suddenly, even though Dr Brady cannot prescribe medication, he could not contain himself and his remaining questions were all related to his old friend.

It struck me forcefully then that Mr Lynch appeared to have a total fixation on drugs and perhaps there was more to this than a dirty tricks campaign. They seemed to be constantly preying on his mind and they were his only input into his idea of post-surgery rehabilitation. Did I hit on something there? It reminded me of his telephone call to Michael when he said I was suffering from a psychiatric illness and I found out later that it was he, who was having problems in his personal life. And many others were suing him. His behaviour to date certainly gave me the impression he was unhinged.

He got nowhere, as usual, and Judge Johnson announced, 'Mr Lynch, I urged you this morning to take legal advice about certain things. It is not about this case, but it is about the document which does not appear to be the same as the original, the copy of which you tendered yesterday to the court and to Mr McCullough having changes in it, purporting to indicate that there was a query over one of the matters which was said here. That is a matter which I think you should take advice about, because I certainly have no option but to take certain steps about it.'

'I thank you, my Lord, for that, but all I can say is I handed…'

'Please stand when you address me.'

'I am sorry, my Lord. I handed that document over in good faith.'

'You pointed out in open court that what was a query, question mark…'

'Maybe I put a query on some document and somebody…'

'Mr Lynch, it was handed over in open court, it then was handed up to me, it has query question mark, you pointed it out to Mr McCullough, the matter will have to be further investigated, and I just say I suggest you take legal advice on it. I will rise until two o'clock.'

***

It is amazing how quickly time seems to pass when you are trying to hold it back and we could well have done with a two-hour break. Unfortunately, Dr O'Keeffe had come to court before one o'clock and advised my legal team that he had to perform an emergency operation that afternoon. He committed to testify immediately when proceedings recommenced the following morning, so Denis moved other witnesses forward. He called a vocational rehabilitation consultant I had attended who confirmed that we had gone through my general history, education and career to date. She also confirmed that I had told her about my medical history since the surgery.

Denis also asked her if we had discussed my symptoms at the time of the visit, my job responsibilities, my hobbies, most of which I had to give up and the effect it had on my piano playing. There was quite a lengthy discussion about my future prospects and Ms Smith's opinion was very guarded and pessimistic about my future work prospects.

He then asked Judge Johnson if he would permit him to recall me to the witness box to deal with special damages and announced, 'Mr Lynch feels unable to agree the matter and I have to ask her to deal with them.' *You mean, I am sure, he will not agree the matter. Nice way of putting it Denis.*

Judge Johnson replied, 'Certainly. In this case by the way, at the end of it I will be looking for written submissions, I expect, in any event, Mr McCullough. I just want to let you know that.'

If that is the case, God only knows when we will receive a verdict but, until then, I would just have to wait it out. I would not be looking forward to the slow grind of time but it was all out of my control now. And every night and every morning, I would ask my grandfather to help keep me going and make prudent decisions when I had to.

The special damages that Denis asked me to prove, when I returned to the witness box, were listed in the Book of Special Damages and included all my medical, hospital, physiotherapy, medicine, travelling expenses and monies my employers had paid me for intermittent sick leave since 1996. I also included the salary I forfeited as a result of having to take a year off to further rehabilitate myself. Because it was a legal requirement I would also have to reimburse VHI out of any monies I received if I won the case. To conclude, Denis asked me to give the book containing copies of all the vouchers and receipts to Judge Johnson.

***

Little did I predict when Denis called our next witness that it would open up a huge can of worms and give Judge Johnson even further insight into the workings of Mr Lynch's mind. What I thought was to be a brief swearing of the VHI undertaking would eventually evolve into a complete quagmire for Mr Lynch and end with such overwhelming proof of his lies that no defence was remotely possible.

Denis asked Judge Johnson, 'I do not know whether it is a matter for me, my Lord, but perhaps I should just formally ask Mr Boylan to give evidence about the undertaking which was…'

'I think it is required, yes.'

Then Michael was called to the witness box and was sworn in. I would never have guessed before Denis addressed him that it was going to be another hair-raising afternoon because Mr Lynch was by now floundering in the dirt of his crater.

'Mr Boylan, you are a solicitor with the firm of Augustus Cullen & Son, solicitors, and I think you are Ms Carroll's solicitor in this action?'

'I am a partner in the firm.'

'Were you required to give an undertaking to the Voluntary Health Insurance?'

'Yes, that is right.'

'What is the nature of that undertaking?'

'It is the standard VHI undertaking. It is dated 15th June. They require us to give it to them before they will consider continuing to pay out benefit to Ms Carroll. It was to include the items of benefit that they paid out in the claim and to reimburse them out of the proceeds of any successful claim. I can give it in to…'

'Were you obliged, therefore, as her solicitor to include these items in her claim?'

'Yes.'

'Do you know what the present sum which has been paid by the VHI and which is the subject of your undertaking?'

'They wrote to me in October to tell me – sorry, it is in the booklet there that has been handed in already…'

'Is it £15,670.17?'

'That is right, yes.'

And that was that, or so I thought. However, Mr Lynch, seemingly, could not wait to get on his feet but he did not wish to cross-examine Michael on the VHI undertaking. He was going to resurrect history and he could not contain himself. 'In all my professional life, I think I have only once ever contacted a solicitor in his practice.'

'Sorry, this isn't a question now,' interjected Judge Johnson.

'Yes.'

'That is a history.'

'Do you remember me contacting you?' he demanded of Michael.

'I do, Mr Lynch, yes.'

'When was that?'

'I believe it would be in June 1999.'

'1999 or 1997?'

'I can check it if you wish, but I believe it was 1999.'

'Would you kindly check that, please?'

Judge Johnson interrupted, 'Have you got the file there, Mr Boylan? If you would just check it, Mr Boylan? If you have it on the file, check it.'

'I believe it to be 14th June 1999.'

Then in a very angry tone, Mr Lynch asked, 'Do you recall what I said to you?'

'I took an attendance of what you said to me.'

'What do you mean by that?'

'I took a memo. After you had concluded the call with me I dictated a memorandum of what you said to me.' *Oh, I thought, I did not know that; marvellous. I was certain Mr Lynch had not expected it.*

'We all live in a community. The more we interact the better that community will be?'

Then Judge Johnson, quickly assessing what Mr Lynch was doing, interjected, 'That is philosophy. Will you ask him a question?'

'What did I say to you?' he demanded in a vitriolic tone.

'Refer to the memo, Mr Boylan, if you want to,' said the Judge.

In reply, Michael offered, 'I can provide you with a copy of it. I did not particularly want to go into all this, Mr Lynch, but…'

Oh no do not stop now, I pleaded; this is an absolute Godsend. All his lies during that conversation will come out.

'Just tell me, why not, to see what my problems are and the problems in my home.' *And what about the 'problems' you generously bestowed on me Mr Lynch and you are looking for sympathy? Remember, you did not have to put either of us through this horrible ordeal.*

Very tiredly I thought, Judge Johnson had to interject again, 'Mr Lynch…'

'Sorry, my Lord, I think he…'

'Mr Boylan does not want to open up this, but I am not quite certain what it had to do with the case. Are you saying this is something to do with the case?'

You are not aware of the contemptible untruths he told Michael in relation to the surgery, are you Judge Johnson? My heart was palpating with great anticipation for them to reveal themselves.

'I think it has.'

'Well, Mr Boylan, he wants to know what he said to you. I, myself, have difficulty following what it has to do with the case, but…'

Michael replied, 'I can read it if you wish and provide you with a copy of it.'

And so he read out:

'Attending on Vincent Lynch, cardiothoracic surgeon, the defendant. Surprised, he phoned back on 14th June 1999 in response to my recent correspondence. He acknowledged that he had received my recent letter and, indeed, the earlier letters which I had sent to him at St. Vincent's Hospital. He said he had not responded earlier as he thought this was a completely vexatious case and he was hoping it would go away.

'I cautioned him that I did not feel that he should be talking to me and he should have the benefit of legal advice rather than talking directly to me with regard to the matter. I cautioned him that I did not wish to leave myself exposed to any claim of acting unprofessionally, given that this was a contentious legal matter and we were on opposite sides, as it were.

'Despite this warning Mr Lynch was most insistent and wished to continue discussing the circumstances of the case with me. He said he had read the file thoroughly and was entirely satisfied that Ms Carroll's complaints were absolute nonsense. Initially, he advised me that his patient, Ms Carroll, was a lovely person, but she had a somewhat strange personality.'

Michael continued, 'I asked him what he meant and he said, "I will leave that for you to figure out yourself".' *Well, Mr Lynch, he did figure me out but he was far more interested in your unhinged behaviour. It was a bad move on your part, Mr Lynch, to have insisted on bringing him to account about that conversation. I think you have tripped yourself up with Michael and now your lies are being repeated as evidence in the court.*

Michael continued recounting that Mr Lynch stated my artery was wrongly sited and went on to relate what he said about the VATS procedures. 'He stated that before the instruments were introduced it was imperative that one would see what lay inside before introducing any further instruments in order to minimise mishap. I indicated that it was my understanding that the ports for the instruments would be more lateral to the side of the torso.

'I asked him which port had caused the haemorrhage. Mr Lynch was not sure and said that he would have to recheck his operation notes, but said it definitely was not the first port. He said that the damage to the vessel was caused by one of the subsequent ports and because the mammary vessel was not in its normal location adjacent to the sternum bone but was further over more lateral to the sternum bone.

'I pointed out to him that his operation notes clearly indicated the port which caused the damage to the vessel was 2.5 cm lateral to the nipple and it was our experts' contention that a port should not be inserted in such a position. Mr Lynch's immediate reaction was to dispute that the port had been inserted in such a position, that his operation notes clearly must be wrong. I pointed out that we had photographic evidence indicating a scar exactly where his operation note indicated he had put the port. Vincent Lynch countered this by stating that this could be the mark of a chest drain.'

So there we had it, his contention was now in evidence. Imagine a consultant thoracic surgeon stating his signed operation notes were incorrect. How could anyone trust a word he said and then to do an about-turn and suggest a chest drain had been pushed through my breast was the most ludicrous thing I have ever heard.

Judge Johnson interjected, 'Those photographs have been mentioned a lot. I presume they will be proved eventually. Now, Mr Lynch, next question.'

Oh no, no, no. Michael has not finished. Do something Denis, I pleaded.

Probably ecstatic now that Judge Johnson had moved on, Mr Lynch suggested Michael had a flaw in his character by pointedly asking, 'The next question is, I wonder do you feel that you could have contributed to this patient's problem?' *What a scurrilous question, I thought.*

'In what way?' demanded Judge Johnson. 'I think you'd better specify what you mean by that.'

'When I, as a doctor, use the term 'problem' my Lord, I mean if a patient comes to me with a problem, it is something that needs care. Then he addressed Michael again, 'Have you contributed to that problem and has it needed more care because of your involvement. That is what I am asking.'

'I do not believe I have contributed to the problem,' Michael calmly responded.

'What is your function as the solicitor in the case?' Judge Johnson asked.

'It is to advocate, promote the case on behalf of the plaintiff who has come to me with a complaint of significant personal injuries and I investigated that. Before I took proceedings I consulted with various experts to see whether or not she had a meritorious case, and that is what I did and that is where I see my function. I certainly was not involved in her medical treatment or care, I left that to other experts.'

'May I just consult my letters from Augustus Cullen?' Mr Lynch asked the Judge.

'Yes, certainly, you may consult your letters from Augustus Cullen.'

Denis interjected and addressed Judge Johnson, 'I do not know whether Mr Lynch is aware of it, but there is more to Mr Boylan's attendance. I do not know whether your Lordship wishes him to complete it or not.' *Oh thank goodness, Denis. There are still extremely important facts and revelations in that memorandum in relation to their telephone conversation.*

'If Mr Lynch is happy with what has already been stated, that is…'

'Indeed,' Denis replied. *This is not good, I thought.*

'I can read my first letter to you, Mr Lynch?' Michael suggested.

'That is what I want.'

'I believe it is dated 17th June 1997.'

'1997, that is correct.'

'I think I was consulted in – my first note is 13th May 1997.'

'That would be my recollection.' *You can remember Michael's first letter to you but you could not remember you went through my breast to perform VATS?*

Judge Johnson asked Michael, 'What does the letter say?'

'We act on behalf of Christine Carroll of the above address, who was treated by you and under your care. We have been asked by our client to investigate as to whether or not there are possible grounds for instituting a claim for medical negligence against you. We would emphasise that we are making absolutely no allegations of negligence at this stage, we are investigating the matter. To enable us to investigate the matter we require copies of all the relevant hospital records so that we might advise our client. The enclosed written authorisation form signed by our client will enable you to release the records to us. We look forward to hearing from you as soon as possible.'

Caught off guard and now severely flustered Mr Lynch queried, 'Have you another letter sometime that year, about July? I am sorry, I did not know this matter was coming up, so I was not prepared for it.' *But it was you who insisted on having the matter brought up, Mr Lynch, no one else. Michael warned you that he did not wish to get into it. It was a bad move on your part to bring him to account for that conversation and letters.*

'You were not prepared, I see, all right,' remarked Judge Johnson.

Michael continued, 'In August 1997: "We refer to our letter of 17th June last and your secretary's subsequent telephone call to our office. We did try and return the call and left a message that we had telephoned. To date we have not heard from you, but the records which we have requested, we would be grateful if you could send us on our client's medical records as soon as possible. If you feel able to give an explanation as to what occurred in the original operation, as to why our client has such ongoing problems, we would welcome this." I believe the context of that, now that I see it, was that your secretary had phoned up and had indicated to my secretary that you felt…'

At this, and significantly irritated and agitated, Mr Lynch blocked Michael's evidence and addressed Judge Johnson, 'First, my Lord, I did not know this was coming up.'

Then he questioned Michael in a berating manner 'I understood that I had a long telephone conversation with you at that time and you repeated much of what I said in the form of a letter. Would that be correct?'

'No, the note that I read was of the conversation in 1999.'

'No, this is earlier, it was 1997.'

'I do not believe I ever spoke to you before 1999.'

'I am sorry I have not this prepared, I did not have this prepared.'

'In 1999 I spoke to you and you…'

Judge Johnson interjected and addressed Michael, 'Have you any record of a telephone conversation prior to that?'

'No.'

'You have no recollection of it?'

'No, no, I do not believe there was any.'

Are you mixing up all the claims against you Mr Lynch? Did you, in fact, have a conversation with another solicitor contrary to what you stated earlier? And Judge Johnson being extraordinarily helpful again, gave Mr Lynch breathing space by allowing him another privilege, 'Mr Lynch, if you want to get your papers in order you can resume this cross-examination tomorrow, if you prefer to do that.'

His relief was extremely palpable. 'Thank you, my Lord.' *I was now in the depths of great disappointment because the second half of the memorandum that was crucial was not entered into evidence.*

'I will adjourn until eleven in the morning. I am not quite certain what will turn on that document, but something may and you may have observations to make on it, I am not certain, but I certainly have observations.'

Denis replied, 'May it please your Lordship.'

'Very good. I will adjourn the matter now until Dr O'Keeffe is available at eleven in the morning,' and addressing Denis asked, 'Have you many other witnesses apart from that, roughly, from a time point of view?'

'There will be the general practitioner, my Lord, and we will have to formally prove the photographs.'

'Your case should finish tomorrow?'

'I would think so, yes, unless there is some difficulty with the photographer, my Lord, but it should finish tomorrow.'

'That is all right. Very good then.'

'I wonder, my Lord, might I ask your Lordship in Mr Lynch's presence – I hope Mr Lynch will have no objection to my speaking to Mr Boylan, because I need to about the case…' *Obviously, he wanted the second half of the memorandum admitted in evidence.*

'Have you any objection…?' the Judge asked Mr Lynch.

'I have absolutely no objection,' Mr Lynch replied. *And I wondered, are you really certain, because it may add another blow to your unsustainable defence?*

'Very good then, you are given liberty to speak to Mr Boylan,' he informed Denis.

Oh bravo Denis, what a relief. I was also very eager myself to find out the remaining contents of that memorandum. Would it reveal anything I was not already aware of? I hoped so but I had to remain patient. Judge Johnson then adjourned the trial.

Following a brief discussion with Michael, I was just dying to get home as it had been a very intensive day. After taking more anonymous telephone calls, I was as exhausted as indeed was my father, that we were really grateful to retire for the night. I hoped that all the information overdrive would not keep us awake. I felt enormous relief that all my witnesses to date had performed exceptionally well and at least I would not be overly worried the following day.

Along with the crucial evidence Michael still had up his sleeve, so to speak, it would now be up to Drs O'Keeffe and Duignan to give their evidence, and I knew they would give it to the best of their abilities. I had no anxieties on that front and I fell into a deep slumber even though my chest wall was throbbing.

In my sleep, I had a very unsettling dream and perhaps it was the eerie premonition I had the previous day. However, how could one possibly top the drama since the beginning of the trial? It was possible and, definitely, highly probable.

Chapter Seventeen

As the sun rose in all its splendour and brought forth daylight on Friday the 9th, I thought perhaps it was the day when my legal team would be in a position to rest my case. My father and I set out towards our usual venue to relax and gather our thoughts but, while he became engrossed in his newspaper, I could not concentrate on reading and sat back fraught in ponderous silence.

As we approached the steps of the Four Courts I wondered whether this was the day that the contents of the holdall would be presented to us. My curiosity had peaked to the extent that I could barely wait to see what the surgical instruments were like but I could not, for the life of me, even attempt a guess as to what relevance they had, bringing them into the courtroom. What was Mr Lynch going to do with them? Intriguing to say the least.

Judge Johnson resumed the trial with an announcement in relation to my hospital file, 'After court rose yesterday, Ms Gaffney from Vincent's indicated that she wanted to remove the file and take it away as she needed it for record purposes in case of emergencies. What happened was that the file was removed, they Photostatted it and then returned it. That is all right. I think this is the complete file, very good.'

Then, appearing to want to placate Judge Johnson, Mr Lynch informed him, 'My, Lord, on your advice, I rang Karl Hayes, a solicitor with Gore & Grimes for advice concerning the Xerox copy of the operation sheet.'

'No, not the Xerox copy of the operation sheet, what appeared to me to be an alteration.'

'On the Xerox copy?'

'On the Xerox copy, yes.'

'He stated clearly…'

'I am sorry, what he said to you is of no interest to me.'

'Sorry, I have consulted him anyway.'

'That is fine. It is a matter for yourself.'

'In fact, I had been consulting him.'

'That is a matter, as far as I am concerned, Mr Lynch, you are looking after yourself. I merely felt it was my duty to warn you that some things may happen and I want to make absolutely certain that you are aware that you have got the best possible advice and that is all as long as you are happy. I have warned you I can do no more. I just wanted to make it absolutely certain that nobody could say that you were not warned, in the event of anything happening. Very good, thank you. Now, what is next?'

Denis began, 'Mr Boylan was in cross-examination.'

'Mr Boylan, yes? Any further questions, Mr Lynch?'

'No, Mr Boylan, I think everything I wanted to say, I said yesterday.'

Denis then called, 'Dr Declan O'Keeffe, please.' Dr O'Keeffe had actually cancelled a trip to London that morning so that he could appear as a witness, for which I was grateful. Mr Lynch's threats to destroy his practice had not had its intended purpose.

'Dr O'Keeffe, I think you are a consultant anaesthetist and you are also a specialist in pain management, is that correct?' Denis began.

'That is correct.'

'I think when you first saw Ms Carroll, the plaintiff in this case, she was then in hospital; is that correct?'

'That is correct.'

'When did you first see her?'

'I haven't an exact date but I think I saw her when she was in hospital in February 1997.'

'She has said in evidence again and this is not disputed, because Mr Lynch, I think has put this to her that she was in hospital undergoing a battery of tests and Mr Michael Hutchinson, a neurologist, suggested that she be seen by you and I think you saw her straight away in hospital; is that correct?'

'I can't dispute that. I would imagine that to be the case.'

'When you saw her, Dr O'Keeffe, what was her condition, what was her situation?'

'She was complaining of severe chest wall pain and she had surgery previously. I took a history of her and she gave me a history of pain.'

'Were you aware of the nature of the surgery that she had?'

'Yes, basically in her history, I understood from her that she had had a pneumothorax and then she had a chest drain put in from that. I also understood from her that she had a recurrent pneumothorax and she subsequently then had, what was planned to be a thoracoscopic blebectomy to be carried out by Mr Lynch and that intra-operatively a decision was made – and this was my understanding – that intraoperatively my understanding was made to change the surgery from a blebectomy to an open thoracotomy and my understanding was that there was bleeding or something. Then she recovered from this surgery and then she appeared to have developed a new type of pain following the surgery, where she had chest wall pain.'

'Was it pain of that type that she complained of to you when you saw her first in hospital?'

'Yes. She complained of severe chest wall pain. What she said to me was over a distribution that I have described… I formed an opinion, at the time, that it appeared to be certainly, at that stage, a post-thoracotomy syndrome, which I would characterise as a mixture of nerve damage pain and nociceptive pain from possible muscle injury.'

'Were you familiar with what you call the post-thoracotomy syndrome?'

'Yes, I am familiar with the post-thoracotomy syndrome. I would see perhaps a couple of cases a year of this syndrome.'

'What is that syndrome, can you describe it to us, Dr O'Keeffe what it is and what is its relationship to the thoracotomy?'

'In the normal course of events, after all operations, you know, it is a post-operative pain syndrome and there are a variety of operations. I mean there are chapters in books written on this, but there are a variety of operations where patients can develop pain after surgery. One of them is a thoracotomy.'

He added, 'In terms of it, what I would characterise it as, in the normal course of events, if you have any kind of surgery or any kind of a traumatic event to the body you have a period of healing and during that time there is often acute pain. But beyond three to six months if the pain persists it is then by definition chronic pain. It is both a sensory and an emotional experience. But if it goes beyond three to six months it is then, by definition, chronic. As the lady in question was beyond that period I would characterise this as a chronic pain.'

'In particular, is it of a type which you say and recognise is a post-thoracotomy syndrome?'

'Yes, I would have considered this, on the basis of what clinical signs and history that were presented to me, I would have considered it as a post-thoracotomy syndrome.'

'That is a recognised syndrome?'

'That is a well recognised syndrome.'

'I see. I think, am I correct in thinking, Dr O'Keeffe that when you are dealing with a patient who suffered from pain you attempt to get the patient to characterise the pain. Obviously pain is a subjective thing but you try to make some judgement as to what level of pain the patient is suffering?'

'Yes.'

'Did you do that in Ms Carroll's case?'

'I did that in Ms Carroll's case and it was very severe to excruciating pain.'

'Can you say what has Ms Carroll told you about the way in which this condition has affected her lifestyle, first?'

'I mean, with the greatest of respect, I have had continuing interaction with Ms Carroll for the past several years since she came into my care. I have seen the impact on her work and she has made heroic efforts to get back to work. So it has severely hampered her ability to work, you know. I can quite honestly say that she was a highly motivated patient and made serious efforts. She has informed me, and I cannot doubt her, that it certainly has had an impact on her social life.' Dr O'Keeffe continued, giving further evidence of the impact the surgery had and he also described all the scars and their location.

Then, apart from the scars, Denis asked him, 'Did you find anything else on examining her?'

'The other thing I found on examination, your Lordship, is that she had allodynia, which is a sign of nerve injury.'

'Can you just indicate where that is.'

'It is her chest wall area, here, it is her chest wall.'

Then Denis questioned him about the various treatments I had over the years.

Dr O'Keefe gave the same evidence I had already provided. He mentioned the nerve blocks, rhizotomies, physiotherapy and different kinds of medication to try and control the pain and indicated that they gave me only insignificant temporary relief. Then he added, 'I have advised her that she should consider having a spinal cord stimulator trial but she has informed me that she will not proceed with that because she is afraid of having further surgical procedures.'

'I think you went on then to say that what you think she requires and she told us about this herself, in evidence, is the spinal cord stimulator?'

'I think, certainly we have used it in other patients with post-thoracotomy syndrome and it has given them significant pain relief. Again, what I am emphasising here, I am not saying it is going to be a success but what I am saying is that the process for that technology your Lordship is that you put in the device…' Then he provided a lengthy explanation of where and how a stimulator would be placed and used and how unpleasant the surgery would be.

'Having undergone that unpleasant experience, it may not work at all?'

'As I said, there is absolutely no guarantee but I think in terms of where we are at with this young lady that it is the only option. The only therapeutic option available.' I was sitting there cringing from what Dr O'Keeffe had just described but I was not to know then that the technology was to change extremely rapidly over the coming years and was to become far less traumatic.

'Do you have anything else in your armoury to offer her apart from a spinal cord stimulator?'

'I think in the long-term, you know, despite the best efforts of these intervention modalities, I think she is going to continue to have chronic pain.'

'In the course of your treatment of Ms Carroll, I think, did you prescribe drugs and medications to her?'

'Yes.'

'What were the drugs which you prescribed?'

After Dr O'Keeffe went through the 'ladder' of analgesia he tried me on, including anti-convulsive medication he concluded, 'None of them gave her any real relief.'

'Was it you, Doctor, who was prescribing the drugs that she was taking during the period under which she has been under your care, were you the main, you were the prescribing doctor?'

'I was the initiating prescribing doctor most of the time.'

'She would have been attending you, Doctor, she said over a long period of time. How did you find her as a patient, as a person?'

'I found her a person who was, you know, who was very diligent, made serious efforts as all times to understand her illness and to help her get control of her pain. I mean, as I said, she took the medication which we gave her, she didn't respond to it.' Throughout the giving of evidence, Denis asked Dr O'Keeffe questions that the 'dogs on the street' knew Mr Lynch would be asking if his previous cross-examination of witnesses was anything to go by.

'Did she ever seem to you, and this does not normally arise in these cases, Doctor, but I ask you the question, as it has arisen in this case, did it ever seem to you that she was unreasonably demanding medication or was seeking more medication than you thought as her doctor she should have? Were the drugs that she was taking, as far as you were aware, were they the drugs that you prescribed and you thought about presumably and thought were the most appropriate for her to take?'

'At the time, yes. If I am being asked was she coming for more and more, she was up to a certain point but she was not sort of – she was somebody that I took to be with a serious pain problem but who never, for example, came back early for prescriptions and stuff. She took what she was given.'

'All of the analgesia that she was having then, Doctor, it would appear were given in the hospital environment when she was in the hospital or under your control and direction subsequently?'

'Or her general practitioner, Dr John Duignan.'

'In your view, Doctor, what effect would what you have described as Ms Carroll's chronic pain, what effect is that likely to have on her work and her lifestyle in general?'

'It varies from patient to patient, your Lordship. I mean it obviously is affecting her ability to concentrate. It obviously affects her ability to maintain concentration and go to work some days. It waxes and wanes and it flares up. Obviously from time to time it stops her working and other times she struggles to work. I think if the pain management programme helps her to cope better and she avails of technologies available she may reach a point in the future where the pain is reasonably well controlled and she can look at returning to work. But certainly with her current situation, not at the moment.'

'She has, as you know, she has taken a year off work effectively from last March. Is that a reasonable thing for her to do, in your view?'

'Certainly she was having a lot of difficulty staying at work.'

At that point I believed that Dr O'Keeffe's evidence had really portrayed the kind and extent of the suffering I had and was still enduring because of that surgery. And little did I know that there was to be a revelation that day from Dr Duignan and it came as a complete surprise and caught us all off guard.

***

I felt that Mr Lynch could not wait for his cross-examination to begin and I was waiting for the sparks to fly. Would he walk himself into another trap and ask a question that would provide Dr O'Keeffe with the opportunity to bring his threats into evidence. Oh, please, please, I implored but my gut feeling was telling me it would not come out.

Mr Lynch began by asking a strange question, 'Would you like, I think, maybe we should tell the people in the court…' *Whatever it was, I am certain it was sinister and what did he think that Dr O'Keeffe was going to join him in a theatrical farce?*

But Judge Johnson immediately interjected, 'This is not a question of deciding what is nice and good for me to hear or not. You have got to cross-examine the witness. If you wish to call evidence about things, you can tell me things, you can be sworn. But in the meantime, modest and happy fireside chats this is not. This is a cross-examination.' *Finally and about time, I sighed, Judge Johnson was losing patience with this man who would never, it appeared, follow the rules.*

For a short time then, until he reverted to his true self again, he asked Dr O'Keeffe to describe the pain, 'Dr O'Keeffe, I would like to know more about the pain. Could you describe the pain in greater detail, medically, please?'

Which he did and then Mr Lynch asked, 'You told us what made it worse and what made it better. Did this pain affect her bodily function?'

'How do you mean, Mr Lynch?'

'I mean that is a straightforward question.'

'I think you better rephrase it,' advised Judge Johnson. 'Do you mean the capacity of the body to function or her capacity to use her body?'

'Pain may affect the patient in a variety of ways and it may cause dysfunction of certain systems within a body,' explained Dr O'Keeffe.

'That is what I am asking you, has the pain caused dysfunction of her body?'

'Well, Mr Lynch, by definition she has chronic pain syndrome. By definition, certainly in terms of descriptive terms in a number of textbooks, it certainly is, it certainly would be described, certainly in terms of function it has. She certainly has difficulty working. She, apparently, by her own admission, has concentration difficulties. So it certainly appears to affect the central nervous system and has a local motor affect in terms of physical ability.' He also added, 'She may have developed post-operative fibromyalgia, which is well documented and well described.'

Then, when Dr O'Keeffe concluded his technical explanation, Mr Lynch could not wait to ask, 'I would like to bring you back to the analgesia…' *Ah, Mr Lynch, I was wondering how long it would take you to get around to your fixation.*

He began then to almost coerce Dr O'Keeffe to give him exact doses of any medication he had prescribed even though he did not have his records in front of him and like the rest of us, not knowing what medication had to do with my case, Mr Lynch's vitriolic temper came to the fore and completely inflamed he almost shouted, 'Surely to goodness, Dr O'Keeffe, you know this patient is constantly coming back to you. You must know what treatment she is on?'

'I said I cannot give you specific doses for particular days and dates.'

'Could you give me a ballpark figure, name the drugs.'

My, those sparks were indeed beginning to fly. Why cannot you just look in the book of special damages that was given to you and which contains all the prescription receipts Mr Lynch? But he was now like a bull pounding towards a red flag and when Dr O'Keeffe gave him the names of the different medication he had tried to relieve the pain with, he demanded, 'Were you ordering these yourself exclusively or I think, actually you hinted that Dr John Duignan was ordering these?'

No, Mr Lynch, he did not 'hint', he actually said he prescribed the medication, 'or her General Practitioner, Dr John Duignan' and explained why when he was giving his direct testimony. You do not listen very well do you, when Denis is examining witnesses, including me. But make no mistake about it, Judge Johnson does.

'It would be – I mean, Mr Lynch – I would say a good amount of the time I was ordering them but obviously at times, I mean she may not be able to see me. I may not have been present and Dr Duignan would have to write a prescription for her, but I would say, in general, I was writing most of her prescriptions.'

His blatant attempts to try and constantly smear my character were horribly obvious at this stage and of course backed up what Dr O'Keeffe had told me when Mr Lynch had threatened him in his office and slandered me. The more obvious it had become that Mr Lynch could not defend the surgery he performed on me the more vicious he got and gosh did he fight dirty.

He was being extremely foolish because Judge Johnson had copies of everything. It just seemed the more stories he trumped up the more we witnessed him losing control and his temper had really come to the fore because he could not get the better of my witnesses, simply because, unlike him, they were all telling the truth.

Then, suddenly, he decided to end his cross-examination. There was absolutely nothing new in it. There were no questions about the actual surgery and a very unimpressive lead-up to the analgesia.

As I sat there the thought I had the previous day really came like a bolt out of the blue. His mind still seemed totally preoccupied and fixated on medication. At every twist and turn, at every opportunity until everyone got bored to death listening to him, his complete disregard for Judge Johnson's instructions when he asked him not to ask witnesses questions they were not in a position to answer, and his continual harping on about the first pneumothorax, led me to think that there was more to this man's psyche.

He appeared so out of order that, if he was not on medication, I felt he should be. But not the kind of medication I had to take. No, on many occasions his evidence was totally irrational and bizarre and his behaviour was also frightening. And because no one was taking him seriously because the proof was on my side, it seemed to make him even more angry and frantic.

I had to take pain medication because his surgery totally debilitated me and I was in constant pain but what about Mr Lynch? Did he have so many problems in his personal life that he was on a different kind of medication? It seemed his mind was consumed by it and what would make a surgeon go as far as lunging at a half-naked woman right in front of a number of witnesses and the trial Judge? And as the case progressed so did my opinion until I was convinced I was 'barking up' the right tree.

Chapter Eighteen

As Dr O'Keeffe left the witness box and because the cross-examination by Mr Lynch was so palpably vitriolic, it felt like the air was filled with bad karma and needed to be expunged. Allowing then for a break from difficult testimony, Denis called the professional photographer who had taken pictures of my scars and had them proved. Then a consultant actuary gave detailed testimony in relation to the present value of losing my future salary.

Since Dr Duignan had arrived in court, I tentatively perused him striding to the witness box but I could never have guessed what thoughts were simmering and undulating beneath his calm and serious exterior.

Denis began his direct examination with, 'Dr Duignan, I think you are a medical doctor and you are in general practice in Stillorgan in County Dublin; is that right?'

'That is correct.'

'I think the plaintiff, Ms Christine Carroll, has been a patient of yours since, I think, 1991; is that correct?'

'That is correct.'

'Did she attend at your practice in April of 1996 in relation to a pneumothorax or a complaint of a pneumothorax?'

'Yes, she did.'

'Was she referred to hospital as a result of being seen there?'

'Yes, she was. She attended my colleague Dr Fidelma Savage with a pneumothorax, which was confirmed by chest x-ray and she was referred to the casualty department for the management of that.'

'We know that from evidence that she was admitted to St. Vincent's hospital on 30th May and she subsequently had what turned out to be a thoracotomy performed by Mr Lynch. I think you have seen her since then and you had a history of all of that; is that right?'

'Yes, indeed.'

'Did you, in fact, receive a letter or a report from Mr Lynch in early July 1996, telling you what had occurred?'

'I received a letter dated 8th July 1996, from Mr Lynch, where he described the management of the case.'

'Can you say what was in that, I think you have recorded what was in the letter?'

'I summarised it in my notes, that she was admitted under his care with a right pneumothorax and he had noted an earlier pneumothorax in April 1996. 'She had undergone a thoracoscopy on 5th of June 1996, and *that night* she had developed a massive bleed as she had an aberrant internal mammary artery in her right chest wall. I therefore had to convert to a right open thoracotomy. I dealt with the bleed and on inspection of the lung she had blebs on the apex of the right lung. The apex of the right upper lobe was excised. She was discharged home on 14th June 1996. She was to be reviewed in three weeks.'

'That is a copy of the letter, Dr Duignan, would you just look at that and see, does it appear from the records that you have that letter, that that is the letter that you received?'

'Yes, indeed.'

'Thank you. Since that time has Ms Carroll attended you on a regular basis?'

'She has.'

'What has she been complaining of?'

'Her most persistent complaint is her chest pain of a nature and intensity of which she had not suffered previously apart from when she had an acute pneumothorax.'

'I think we know that she has been treated by Dr Declan O'Keeffe. Have you, I think, from time to time prescribed drugs for her, perhaps in Dr O'Keeffe's absence or in circumstances of that sort?'

'As would be normal in cases like this, Dr O'Keeffe running a busy pain clinic, I would work in conjunction with him and would co-prescribe carefully medication when prescribed. In viewing my notes she had only required opiate type medication after this episode. There is no prior episode of opiate prescription prior to that.'

'To your knowledge or as far as you know, had she only had such drugs as had been prescribed to her by doctors?'

'Certainly, to my knowledge.'

'Would you, Doctor, speaking for yourself, would you prescribe drugs to Ms Carroll if you did not believe she required them?'

'I would not.'

'Have her complaints of pain been consistent throughout the years that you have seen her since 1996?'

'Yes, indeed.'

'How has she seemed to you as a patient in terms of her own motivation and her own ability to do what she is asked to do by yourself and other specialists?'

'I think Ms Carroll has been highly motivated and has made repeated attempts to return to her duties. I would see her as somebody with a very high work ethic.'

'Have her complaints, in your view, as far as you can judge, have they interfered with her work and her lifestyle generally?'

'Yes.'

'Is it reasonable and is it consistent with what you found that they should interfere in that way?'

'Yes.'

'She has told us that she has taken, as it were, a leave of absence from her work from last March; is that reasonable in your view?'

'I feel it is essential. She made repeated attempts to perform her duties and clearly was not able to do so. I would have seen her closely, at this time and would have witnessed the fact that she was in quite marked distress.'

Judge Johnson interjected, 'It is one o'clock now. We will have cross-examination after lunch.'

It gave me great encouragement and optimism to know that Dr Duignan's testimony was sworn into evidence and it was crucial for my case to succeed. A relieved and somewhat contented woman went to lunch that day and I was eagerly awaiting the afternoon's testaments. The trial was really peaking now and we all knew the afternoon had the propensity to enthral but, unfortunately, this case involved a real victim; it was not fictional cinema.

***

This was indeed one day when I did not mind that the lunchtime hour passed too quickly. I waited with particular anticipation for Judge Johnson to appear and resume the proceedings.

Dr Duignan took the stand again, in his same demeanour, and Mr Lynch commenced his cross-examination, 'Dr Duignan, Ms Carroll became your patient, was it 1991; would that be correct?'

'That is correct.'

'I am interested in her pre-operative condition.'

Of course you are, Mr Lynch, wouldn't you just love to find I had had some major injury or disease to blame for my condition?

He continued, 'The present situation is that she has pain, this pain has been going on since I operated on her in June of that year. I am sure you must have seen her?'

'Yes.' *Thump, thump, thump.*

'Would you as one doctor to another describe that pain?'

Judge Johnson interjected, 'I would prefer if you did not do it as one doctor to another. Do it as a witness to the court.'

Dr Duignan adamantly replied, 'I would characterise it as severe chest pain. The involvement of the limbs was not a major feature of the pain, in my understanding of it, but severe chest pain.'

'Could you be a little more precise? Could you define the site?' Mr Lynch scornfully asked.

'I am referring to my notes. In reviewing my notes, generalised right-sided chest pain.'

'What does that mean?'

'I'm sorry?' Dr Duignan asked, looking quite taken aback. *Thump, thump, thump.*

'What does that mean?'

'Do you mean in terms of?'

'What do you mean by the term generalised?'

'I am not giving it as an anatomical description other than recording what the patient referred to me as a feeling of general pain on the right side of her chest.'

'What type of pain was it?'

'I again refer to my records and other than being aware that it was a very severe pain, I would not be able to characterise it more specifically,' he emphasised. *Thump, thump, thump.*

'Was it burning, was it stinging, was it pushing, the type, what?' demanded Mr Lynch in a growing vitriolic temper.

'I would have to say severe. She was clearly in distress at the times I would have seen her with it and under the care of the pain clinic. To ask me that in five years time I would have to say the main thing that was making it better was her treatment and often not adequately so. She remained in distress.'

'Her treatment was?' Mr Lynch grilled.

'A combination of physiotherapy, the pain blocks that Dr O'Keeffe had used and medication.'

And of course it did not take him long, 'It is the medication I want to ask about.'

'Her medication, over the period after the operation, consisted of a combination of anti-inflammatory medications.'

'By that you mean, be precise,' giving Dr Duignan a blatant order. *Thump, thump, thump.*

And then, after quizzing Dr Duignan on specifics, including names and dosages, he went on to ask, in a sneaky manner, 'Doctor, is there anything else you would like to say about her medication?'

'I would like to say that it was regularly reviewed by both Dr O'Keeffe and myself. It was used in combination with other modalities to try and minimise her pain.'

Then Mr Lynch wanted to know, and I did not understand what it had to do with my case, 'Ms Carroll also has mentioned that she has had hormone therapy for a breast problem, would you tell me what that was, how much and how long?'

Denis had to interrupt. 'I am not sure, I think, my Lord, that this arose through Mr Lynch's cross-examination of Ms Carroll. I think Ms Carroll said that Mr Lynch said that she had got a phantom pregnancy, that her body had produced hormones as a result of the surgery which made her body believe that it was pregnant. I am not certain that there was any other reference.'

Again I was astonished at his remarkable memory when Judge Johnson advised, 'I have recorded her stating that she never had hormone treatment.'

'I think that is the case. She did not take it my Lord.'

'I just can't let you go without a comment,' Mr Lynch insisted to Dr Duignan. *Thump, thump, thump.*

'No, ask your question but do not preface it by saying it is a comment,' instructed Judge Johnson.

Then, Mr Lynch, as if he had any authority over the matter and unfortunately for him asked Dr Duignan a very unusual question, 'Dr Duignan, why would you not let me have access to this patient's records?'

Thump, thump, thump. The undulating thoughts came crashing onto the shore, 'I would be delighted to have the opportunity to address that question and I brought it up today when I arrived at court. In over twenty years practicing as a doctor, I have never had somebody ring me up out of the blue and say I want to see these records. I was most taken aback and most disconcerted by the approach. One, because I respect you as a physician and two, because I have a duty to my patient.'

Dr Duignan pronounced, obviously upset. 'You appeared in my surgery very soon after that and I said I would require a written request. I duly rang the Medical Protection Society for advice in this matter, never having had such an event occur before. I was advised by the Medical Protection Society that on no account was I to do so and that a request of this nature should come through the proper legal channels and would require Ms Carroll's permission. I assumed that this would follow. That is the reason that I did not.'

I sat glued to my seat with my jaw dropped and like a vast prism, unable to react. My God, I thought, he has intimidated two of my witnesses and also threatened one of them. What else has he done?

'But he took the advice of his insurance company, Mr Lynch,' interjected Judge Johnson.

Dr Duignan added, with seeming contempt, 'I found the whole manner in which I was approached quite extraordinary and one that I had never come across in over twenty years practice and therefore rang my medical protection society to see what was the thing to do. How should I respond to this matter. I further expected to hear from legal channels as to what was to be done.'

Then Mr Lynch reverted to the letter trying to convince us that he had made a genuine mistake, 'One of the letters that I sent to you obviously has an error, two errors and I am sure you picked that up, the whole thing was out of context. When I said that there was bleeding – I obviously did the procedure and I converted back at the same time. I am sorry for that error.'

Sorry because you were found out Mr Lynch, since I do not detect any authenticity in that hollow apology. So again, you are trying to cover-up. Your lies were just errors and we were all wrong because we took the information 'out of context' and I suppose the change to my operation sheet was just an unintentional jotting. Every lie you tell is put down to an innocent 'error', or 'mistake', or naivety, isn't it? I just wonder, since you told so many lies in 'a small case' like mine when it went so horribly wrong, what did you tell the families of patients who have actually died or left wheelchair-bound after one of your operations? I just dread to think.

Then Judge Johnson, obviously copping Mr Lynch's intentions interrupted him, 'Sorry, did you ever write a letter to him correcting it?'

'I was not aware of that, I am sorry, my Lord.' *You are apologising a lot now Mr Lynch, aren't you; up to your old tricks again, putting on that pleading tone of an innocent man when found out?*

'When did you become aware of this mistake, Mr Lynch?'

'When that letter was produced.' *Oh, so it is our 'mistake' that you did not withhold it from your previously appointed solicitors and signed a false affidavit?*

'Here in court. You had never read that letter before, you had never read the file in this case before you came in here to defend yourself?'

'I had, of course, I had. But frequently the copies of the letter that would go out and you would correct the first tranche. The copies underneath contained an error…'

'Sorry, are you suggesting that the print of a letter, the copy of a letter contains mistakes that the original does not?'

'When I give a letter like that, my Lord, what I do is I correct it and I hand write it.'

'Very good, right, Mr Lynch, very good.' *I am convinced Judge Johnson did not believe a word of it, it was so bizarre.*

Then the heated and revealing cross-examination concluded and Denis rounded off with, 'Just one matter, Dr Duignan, just in relation to Mr Lynch's request to you to give him access to Ms Carroll's notes. Apart from getting in contact with your medical defence union, you didn't inform Mr Boylan, Ms Carroll's solicitor, that that request that had been made, is that right?'

'I did not, no, my Medical Protection Society informed me that I should not do so until a request came through the proper channels, which I duly expected to happen. I only became aware this week that Mr Lynch was doing his own defence.'

'Was it correct that the first time you mentioned it to anybody connected with Ms Carroll's case was just as you came in the door of the court this morning?'

'Indeed, other than the Medical Protection Society.'

And as Dr Duignan left the witness box I thought, wow, that was quite a stunning surprise and discovery. Now Mr Lynch's intimidation of my general practitioner was sworn in evidence. If Judge Johnson went through all the transcripts of the case so far, he could reach only one conclusion. Coupled with all the medical records they would prove the chronic liar that Mr Lynch was and the unimaginable lengths he travelled to try to wriggle his way out of situations of his own creation. And now, in a short while, we were about to hear the conclusion of Michael's memorandum. What an incredible and exhausting day.

***

My case was now approaching its pinnacle conclusion and Denis, with his final twist up his sleeve, reminded Judge Johnson, 'That was the end of my case, my Lord. A matter has arisen. It arises, my Lord, in connection with what your Lordship is saying to Mr Lynch about that letter. It is a matter about which Mr Boylan can give evidence and it follows on from the evidence he was giving in cross-examination. I wonder would your Lordship permit me to recall him on that point?' Judge Johnson agreed. Oh thank God, I thought.

Denis addressed Michael, 'Mr Boylan, Mr Lynch was asking you in cross-examination yesterday about a telephone conversation which you had with him, I think, on 14th June 1999; is that correct?' asked Denis.

'That is correct, yes.'

'You had given evidence in relation to a substantial part of that attendance and the matter did not proceed beyond that point. But in the course of that telephone conversation did Mr Lynch read to you a letter?'

'If I could continue reading that. I am sorry I should have a copy.'

Judge Johnson asked Michael, 'This is now made immediately after the phone call?'.

'Yes, that is right. Again, I believe that as soon as I finished the conversation with Mr Lynch, I dictated this memorandum. I had read to the top of the second page in my evidence yesterday and then we changed topic.' So Michael continued, 'He read to me the contents of a letter which summarised her pre-operative clinical history, details of how the operation went and what happened in the immediate aftermath of the operation.

'It became apparent to me that he was reading a document so I asked him what document he was reading from and he indicated that it was a report he had written to Mr Joe Duignan. In this letter which he was reading quickly and which I could not make notes of verbatim he indicated that the haemorrhage was discovered that night. I queried from him therefore was it a period of hours after the surgery that the haemorrhage was first diagnosed. He appeared unclear about this fact and said that he again would have to check the notes but agreed with me that the use of the words "that night" clearly implied the passage of hours between the surgery and the detection of a haemorrhage.

'Mr Lynch then went on quickly to explain to me that they follow a protocol in the hospital for the treatment of post-operative haemorrhages, which is entitled, "cardinal treatment plan" or some other protocol which he explained meant that one waited and observed closely whether there were any signs post-operatively that would indicate haemorrhage was occurring, e.g. change in pallor, blood pressure, heart rate, evidence of fluid in the right side of the chest, etc. This is what was observed in this case, he stated and why it was necessary to convert the VATS procedure into an open procedure.' *Oh Lord, his lies know no boundaries.*

Michael continued, 'At the time I was not aware that Mr Duignan was Ms Carroll's GP. The letter he was reading from to me clearly stated that the operation proceeded uneventfully and that night she developed signs of haemorrhage. Mr Lynch explained to me that haemorrhage is often not detected or observed until after the instruments are removed. This is because it is a little bit like a boy holding his finger in the dyke. It is only when the finger is taken out that the haemorrhage occurs. Similarly when one withdraws the instrument, it is only then that the haemorrhage is detected and this is what occurred here, he said. He then went on again and suggested the real origin and reason for the ongoing pain in this case was Ms Carroll's strange personality and social history.

'I queried him as to exactly what he meant. He then went on to say that he believed Ms Carroll had a bitter matrimonial break-up and she was living and married in Canada but the marriage broke up a number of years ago and this was the explanation for her ongoing complaints.'

Gosh Mr Lynch, you are really grabbing at straws. I now knew I was right about this man. He was creating stories that would deflect from his defence of his surgery. Even though I have travelled extensively, I have never been to Canada nor have I ever had a bitter break-up with anyone. He was obviously a very unhappy and troubled man in his own personal life. In comparison, my life could hardly have been any better in 1996 when I had been looking very much forward to continuing a rich and fulfilling life in every respect.

'I said this was of complete news to me and I couldn't comment on its merit or otherwise. Mr Lynch was most insistent that if I were genuine I would check out with the client whether her social history was the explanation of her complaints. He refused to nominate solicitors to represent his interests until such time as they had taken specific instructions from the client on this to satisfy myself that there was no merit to her complaints.

'At his insistence, I indicated that I would ask my client about this. He asked that I disclose to my client that he had made this specific request and I would then revert to him. I indicated to him that regardless of this the case would be pursued against him. He said to me he had no difficulty advising the MDU to pay up in cases where he was at fault.'

Oh really, Mr Lynch? Do you not? Because sometime after that conversation did you not have to be ordered by a judge to report all your lawsuits to the MDU because you held onto them hoping that the plaintiffs, like myself, would just 'go away'?

Michael resumed, 'He said that he had a pile of other claims against him on the left-hand side of his desk. Some of them he had already instructed his defence union to settle up as he was clearly liable. Paradoxically there were some cases in which he was being sued where he felt that he had a liability and had asked his insurers to pay up but they would not sanction it. In other cases where he felt he had no culpability whatsoever his insurance company/defence union wanted to settle up. He said that lawyers were destroying and trying to destroy clinical practice.' *I laughed sardonically at that. I believe it was yourself and you alone who was responsible for your own incompetence, Mr Lynch. Not solicitors.*

'He quoted the obstetricians prohibitive insurance premiums. He said, in his case, fifty per cent of his premiums were paid for by the state and his total insurance premium was in the region of twenty-five thousand pounds of which the State paid fifty per cent.' *Mere pocket money, I thought, when one considers the income he made as a consultant. It is the ordinary taxpayers, Mr Lynch who subsidised your insurance premium and paid your public contract as well. So isn't it rather ironic that a person you damaged for life paid a part, however minute, of your salary, insurance and benefits?*

Denis confirmed with Michael, 'Is that an accurate record of the conversation, insofar as you can recall it, when you made that note?'

'I believe it to be.'

'Did you, in fact, speak to Ms Carroll about the matters that Mr Lynch complained of?'

'I did.'

'Having spoken to her were you satisfied to pursue the action?'

'I was and I actually wrote a letter to Mr Lynch after that.'

'Indicating?'

'Indicating that I had spoken to her and that there was no substance in his allegation.'

'Was that because you had said to Mr Lynch that you would speak to her and you would come back to him, as he had requested?'

'Yes and he was refusing to nominate solicitors to deal with the matter until such time as I had taken instructions on this point. That was why, to try and make some progress on the matter and try to take some of the emotion out of it that I agreed to do this.'

Judge Johnson asked, 'Are there any further questions?'

Mr Lynch took the opportunity, 'May I just ask the question. You felt that the doctor's name should have been Dr Duignan; is that correct rather than Mr Duignan?' Then the most absurd cross-examination took place between Mr Lynch and Michael about an error in Dr Duignan's name on the letter because it was typed 'Deignan'.

It was so tedious I began to get a nagging headache. I could not understand what the point of it was and Judge Johnson had to interject a number of times because I do not think that he even knew. Mr Lynch was really clutching at straws now, anything that could get him 'off the hook' so the only thing Judge Johnson could do was to offer Mr Lynch, 'Of course, you can give evidence on contradicting him.'

'Yes, all right,' Mr Lynch reluctantly replied.

'You are perfectly entitled to take the oath and give evidence contradicting him.'

'My Lord, I can just read the letter. I cannot remember back that far.'

'Sorry, whatever you do you can do in the witness box.' This last argument was so bizarre and ludicrous that all it did was to make Mr Lynch appear desperate.

But Michael's evidence was now written in stone. That telephone conversation really portrayed the make-up of the man, the lies, the cover-up and the slander. It frightened me even more to think that a doctor whose words and behaviour were that close to the edge was authorised to operate on my body. He was a consultant, a man who, in his own words defiantly dismissed the safety standards for VATS, 'I do not hold with the triangle of safety,' but did it his way and he was no Frank Sinatra.

And with that our last witness left the stand and Denis declared we had concluded our case and we would therefore sit until he would cross-examine both Mr Lynch and his witnesses. Thank goodness it was over and I gave even more thanks for the incredible way it was presented by my legal team and counsel, and the admirable and convincing testimony from all my witnesses. At this point I did not know how Mr Lynch, after losing all his credibility could gain any advantage. It had already been a long, wearisome and highly dramatic trial and who knew what was in store for me now?

But then I recoiled when I remembered his instruments were waiting to be announced. My previous premonition of frightening unease was about to play out its final trick and come home to roost in a display of the most unhinged behaviour I have ever witnessed.

Chapter Nineteen

As I sat taciturn and patient on the side bench slowly acknowledging my instinct that Denis had proved Mr Lynch negligent, I could not imagine what armour, if any, he had left with which to assuage his guilt. However, before Mr Lynch took the stand, Karen surreptitiously whispered a precautionary warning in my ear not to show any reaction whatsoever to his testimony. She instinctively suspected it was going to be very difficult for me to endure what he was liable to say. Grateful, I acknowledged and took note of her concerns. Judge Johnson addressed Mr Lynch and asked him what he would like to do.

He replied sneeringly, I thought, as if he had shown any prior consideration for my welfare, 'I would think in the interests of Ms Carroll, I think I should give evidence.' *And it was then I understood why Karen had given me fair warning. She had obviously had the measure of him.*

'It is not a question in deference to Ms Carroll. It is your right to give evidence. I wish to ask you do you wish to exercise your right now…? If you wish to give evidence now then kindly come to the witness box.'

As Mr Lynch proceeded in haste to step up to the stand, my eyes took a turn in disbelief and I felt shivers as if he was walking on my grave; he was carrying his infamous holdall. He was also lugging a large stout manual with multi-coloured tags inserted along its edge, as if he was about to give a lecture. Good grief, I mused, he was really going to be in his element. A whole courtroom of people to give him their awe-struck attention and now he has the stand to himself for as long as he wishes.

I took a few deep breaths to compose myself. However, the best outcome would be that he would repeat his spurious allegations and spout out as much absurdity and vitriol as he wished because it would only incriminate him.

After swearing the oath he began, 'My Lord, I would like to look at Ms Carroll's problem from a number of points of view. I would like to begin by dealing with pre-existing complaints prior to surgery. Seven weeks prior to her first consultation with myself she complained of a severe pain in her right chest…'

Judge Johnson noticed something odd and asked him, 'Are you reading?'

'Yes.'

'What are you reading?'

'I am reading my notes.'

'No, sorry. You are not allowed to refer to anything except notes made at the time. You cannot have a prepared script in the witness box.'

'May I look at the dates?' Mr Lynch then asked.

'You can certainly, if you want to take the hospital file or the records, you may refer to them, but you cannot read from a prepared script which you have in your hand.'

Absolutely ignoring Judge Johnson he continued, 'On the 19th of April, this lady was admitted to St. Vincent's hospital under the care of Dr John Hegarty. She had a pneumothorax diagnosed on the right side in casualty. She had complained of severe pain…' He added, 'Following that the following day she had a lot of pain with this large drain in her chest. The doctors came along and took the large drain off and they put in a much smaller drain…' *Oh, Mr Lynch, another untruth. The chest drain was removed because it had not functioned, not because it was too large.*

Then, so predictably, he began a barrage of his age-old fixation and in the end tripped himself up, 'They ordered a morphine product Cyclimorph and I think it was 10 mgs through IV.' Then he hilariously blurted out, 'I am getting mixed up now.' *I felt a guilty twinge of comeuppance. It was already sounding like content for the comedy hour. Doctor Hegarty never put me on a morphine drip. It was you who ordered me one after your brutal surgery.*

Judge Johnson interrupted, 'Sorry would you refer, if you wish to refer to the actual notes, which I am sure you have, the actual operating hospital records you can, but not to extract from scripts you have written; correct, is that not right, Mr McCullough?'

'I should say, my Lord,' Denis responded. 'I have no objection to Mr Lynch referring to the hospital notes.'

'No, but a script is wrong.'

'No, my Lord. The witness should not give evidence from a prepared script. As I say, I have no objection to his referring to this to refresh his memory.'

'If this has to be done then, rules of evidence.'

And in a plaintive and pleading tone, Mr Lynch tried to garnish as much sympathy as he could, 'This will be slow, your Honour, because I will have to constantly go from the main hospital chart back to the drug sheet and back to the main hospital chart, whereas I sat down for about ten hours providing this very accurate script to help the court.' *My God, you are only interested in the medication rather than have a defence for your surgery?*

Judge Johnson then proclaimed, 'If you wish to show it to Mr McCullough and Mr McCullough approves of it I will allow you to refer to it, but I am not going to do it otherwise. Mr McCullough, I am going to rise for five minutes. It is now seven minutes to three, I will sit again at three o'clock. If you are prepared to accept it, at that time, I will allow the doctor to use it.'

'All right, your Lordship,' Denis cooperated.

After a short adjournment Judge Johnson returned and Denis informed him, 'My Lord, I have had the opportunity of reading what Mr Lynch has prepared and I do not have any difficulty. It will save time.' *Obviously, I thought, there must have been nothing new in it and it probably rehashed previous fallacious and unsubstantiated evidence. It suddenly hit me that this was a great move. If Mr Lynch repeats all his previous lies and concocted evidence, they would now be given under oath. A brilliant stroke, Denis, I thought.*

Judge Johnson addressed Mr Lynch, 'Very well, Mr Lynch, you may do it now.' But he also stressed, 'It will speed things up but I have got to do it according to the book.'

Mr Lynch recommenced reading from his script and I listened very attentively to his words. After addressing my admission to A&E on the 19th of April 1996, he stated spuriously, 'This size of drain was inserted,' which he indicated to the court. 'That is what we call a size 32 drain. Overnight she complained of a lot of pain in the chest. They decided maybe it is the drain that is causing the pain. They reduced the large drain to this thin drain into her chest.'

Well, Mr Lynch, congratulations, perjury does not deter or frighten you, does it? Is this the reason you spent ten hours preparing the script rather than refer to the hospital records in the witness box, because you knew you would be caught out in your quagmire of lies? The records state, 'Chest x-ray carried out at 9 am and reviewed by Dr Curry, no improvement noted and chest drain not working, same was removed.' That is the reason why the tube was removed, but you already know that, do you not, Mr Lynch?

He continued to drone on then with absolute nonsense and came to, 'It is important to emphasise, my Lord, that I did not see the patient on this admission to hospital. I would also like to tell my experience of dealing with patients with pneumothorax. Some patients with pneumothorax get very severe pain others get absolutely no pain. Generally those that get severe pain, the pain will pass off after three or four hours. It is very painful to get a chest drain in.' *Interestingly Mr Lynch, you have chosen to ignore my sworn evidence that having the chest drain inserted was not too painful and why would the pain in my lung ease after a few hours when it was still collapsed? You would be a fool to forget Judge Johnson's memory and it has all been transcribed.*

He rambled on then about my admission to hospital on the 30th of May 1996 and relentlessly reiterated his assertion that I was under the care of Professor Brian Keogh until the 5th of June, so that he could spout out ludicrous statements. It was really pathetic listening to him ruthlessly trying to claw his way out. It seemed to me that he would implicate any and all of his colleagues in his quest to defend himself by whatever means necessary.

Then another lie jumped out at me, 'Professor Keogh and the registrar on that night, Dr Anne Heffernan, they decided that she did not need a chest drain.' *No, Mr Lynch, you know perfectly well you instructed the A&E doctor not to put a chest drain in because you were going to perform surgery the following day and had me fast. This regime is all documented in my admission's record.*

Continuing his testimony he lied again, 'There is one very important point about this lady's medical history. This lady had endometriosis, proven endometriosis. Perhaps you will recall that when Professor Smith was in the witness box here I asked Professor Smith how he would diagnose catamenia pneumothorax and I think he just dismissed it.'

But Judge Johnson was quick, 'I have no recollection of you ever asking the question, that question. How would you diagnose catamenia pneumothorax?'

'I clearly remember that.'

'Sorry the notes will tell it eventually but as far as I am concerned that is the first time.'

'That is particularly important in this case,' Mr Lynch emphasised.

Judge Johnson had to bring Denis into the dispute, asking him, 'Do you have any recollection of catamenia being asked?'

'I do not, my Lord.'

'Right.'

Because I had no endometriosis in the last thirty years at least.

Judge Johnson, addressing Mr Lynch again, concluded, 'You say you said that, we can check that out. Very good. Yes, carry on?'

'Ninety-eight per cent of spontaneous pneumothoraces are caused by blebs and there are about twenty or thirty other causes of spontaneous pneumothorax. I will not go over those, my Lord. But they are things from chest infections to various conditions. But one of the causes of spontaneous pneumothorax in a patient with endometriosis is this condition where you get the endometrial surface on the lung. I had to take that into consideration in the investigation and the treatment of this patient.' *Keep clocking up the lies; we have heard it all before.*

'I then go along and I push in my camera – I am sorry I have not my camera with me. What you do is you push in the camera and you see the port is in here. You push in the camera and you look around the chest. So I look around the chest and I see look there are blebs at the top. Then the next thing I say to myself is: Look, this lady has endometriosis could any endometrial tissue have come up from below.' *So now it is 'has' endometriosis and not 'had'.*

Then it struck me. The first port should have been for the camera and which he attested to. We were all assuming Mr Lynch had inserted the camera first before he placed the other instruments. What if he hadn't? This was something of paramount importance in keyhole surgery, to see if there are any obstructions present. And if I had, why did he continue with the VATS?

'Normally the next port should go in low here, but remember in this case, your honour, I had to put in a port so that I could look down, not only am I looking up, I have to look down and I am looking down for a defect in the diaphragm.' *This makes no sense because if you had inserted the camera through my side you would have seen the diaphragm if this had actually been the case. I can barely keep pace with your spins.*

He went on, 'So, now, of course, I can put ports into the patient's chest all over the chest but I have got to injure my patient as little as I can. If I can compromise by putting that in through a piece of breast tissue a little higher so that I can have her with one incision less, I think that is a very good thing.' *You call pushing a port through the substance of my breast to access my chest a piece of breast tissue?*

Judge Johnson, listening very carefully to this asked, 'Is your description of the second port: in through a little piece of breast tissue?'

'In through breast tissue.'

'Sorry, did you just say a little piece of breast tissue or straight in through the breast?'

'My Lord, I described the anatomy of the breast yesterday.'

'Sorry, I deal with the world of absolute reality. The world of absolute reality is did that port not go straight through the breast?'

'I quite honestly, my Lord, I do not understand your question. It went in through breast tissue.'

'Sorry, that is fine. If you do not understand my question…'

But Mr Lynch interjected again, 'It went through breast tissue.'

'That is fine. If you do not understand my question that is fine.' *Good grief, you may as well give up, Judge Johnson, I silently advised.*

Like a rabid terrier now, Mr Lynch surged forward with his untruths, 'I stated that it went through breast tissue and when I was speaking to Professor Smith I told him that we surgeons frequently go through breast tissue, frequently. The reason I put it in higher and more medial than usual was that I wanted to look down. I wanted to see if there was a defect in the diaphragm to see if the endometrial tissue had come up. So there is a reason why I put that port in that particular position…' *This just does not make any sense Mr Lynch. You are grabbing at straws now.*

'The next thing I did was the bleed was – I tried to control it. I couldn't control it, I put in my other small port and I put suction down to see if I could control it. I saw the situation was moving out of control. A surgeon has always got to establish control. I saw that that operation was moving out of control and I quickly did a mini-thoracotomy.' *Ah, Mr Lynch, I have just copped it. You did not immediately perform the thoracotomy; you inserted a third port under my shoulder blade after you hit my artery. Why and for how long was I bleeding?*

Then, sickeningly, his gloating came to the fore, 'I personally feel that I did a very neat mini-thoracotomy. You will very seldom see as small a thoracotomy as that in your lifetime. My Lord, just to show you how the surgery is done. Once the port…'

'Mr Lynch, you can show me how the surgery is done but I, apparently, can't tell you how cases are done.'

The most extraordinary and incredulous situation then began to unfold and I became absolutely stunned along with everyone else present in the courtroom. For a moment I really thought my eyes were deceiving me and that nothing could top the bizarre nature of the trial so far.

Mr Lynch reached down to his holdall and as he proceeded to provide a verbal explanation of how he attempted the VATS, he pulled out these two very long surgical instruments. He grabbed the large handles of a stapler in one hand and a grasper in the other and began to flail them around in an exuberant manner like some mad creature let loose in the witness box. I had to ask myself if what I was witnessing was actually real, it was so startlingly terrifying and painful to watch.

As he continued he became more and more vigorous in his movements and I gazed furtively around the large expanse of the full courtroom as if I was suspended in time; the silence was palpable and thrilling. Every face in the room appeared mesmerised and many had their mouths slack with a look of shock and utter disbelief. Mr Lynch was saying, in an urgently rising voice, 'The stapler goes in through the port. When I have it in situ I open it, I come in through my other port with my grasper. I open my grasper and I pull the tissue in here. I close it, in that I close the tissue on the blebs and then I fire it. I take off the safety guard and I fire it. When I fire it I shoot in six…' *Are we in the Wild West I wondered as I gaped?*

Judge Johnson looked clearly unsettled and anxious and gravely warned Mr Lynch, 'Be careful, it may be loaded so don't point it.'

Mr Lynch had gone over the edge and I felt nauseous thinking about my body on that theatre table and the horrific way he would have shoved the ports into and manipulated the instruments in my chest wall. I also felt at this particular time that I, as a patient, was totally lost in all of this. Mr Lynch had turned the trial into a complete circus. He was the star and in his element. He had his audience and he certainly had their captivated attention.

'I shoot in six layers of titanium staples. As I fire that, a knife slides down the middle of it…' I lost track as I cringed and put my hands over my ears.

'Now, when I was doing this procedure I ran into a bleed and I had to establish control. The way you establish control is you get in and the most important thing in surgery is to get your finger on the bleeder, because when you hit a bleeder during endoscopic surgery the blood is coming at you from two directions. It is not just going up, there are two jets going and you have to get control of that. I immediately opened the chest. I effected the repair and the repair of the bleeding artery and I also carried out the procedure on the lung.' *You did not 'repair' my artery, you sealed it off and now it cannot be used as a blood supply.*

Slowly and slowly the momentum had built up and when I believed the now packed courtroom was at breaking point, Judge Johnson suddenly fell backwards in his chair and put up his two hands to guard his face, 'Put down those things, Mr Lynch, or you will cause serious damage,' or words to that effect. Mr Lynch had almost hit him in the face with one of the instruments.

The riveted audience exploded into laughter to release the nervous, pent-up tension and I told my father I failed to understand what was funny. That was how Mr Lynch treated my body yet I knew it was not normal laughter and I doubt if anyone thought of it as humorous in the ordinary sense. My father said it all when he gasped, 'You wouldn't dose a bullock like that' and I wondered when someone was going to bring in a straightjacket.

The demonstration was utter madness and by the time Mr Lynch put his instruments away, I could well imagine how he had previously acted in the witness box when he had to be removed by the Gardaí. No wonder, after the episode in Judge Johnson's own chambers, I felt physical revulsion towards and fear of him. I have always thought he was very unstable and if I had any remaining doubts this Friday, they were well silent now.

As he finally consigned his instruments to his bag, he summed up, 'So, my Lord, I am saying that it was a matter of my judgement where those ports were placed…' *That does not mean, Mr Lynch, you were given consent to defer from safe, standard and accepted practice, placing me in mortal danger and leaving me with lifelong ill-consequences.*

Then he began to reiterate his trumped-up stories about endometriosis and the diaphragm and concluded by stating, 'Now, if I did find that she had what we call a fenestrated diaphragm, in other words, holes in the diaphragm, say I did, there is very little I can do about it surgically but the endometrial tissue has already got in. She does not have a catamenia pneumothorax. I know that now because I did a simple repair on her lung and she is perfect.'

Ah, that says it all, Mr Lynch, you know that only 'now' because you never looked for endometriosis during the surgery. Fenestrated diaphragm; holes in my diaphragm. What a convoluted mode of farce and not one mention of any of it in any of my records. And I fail to understand your logic when you say I only required a 'simple repair' and yet if you had purposely set out to destroy my physical structure I do not think you could have done a better job of it. Your entire testimony is the hallmark of an incompetent and arrogant man ultimately grabbing at any straw to vindicate yourself.

To top it all off he lauded himself, 'My Lord, we have gone over our notes in this kind of procedure and I would say, as a surgeon, I certainly have more experience in this procedure than any other surgeon in the country and considerably more.' *Is that why you were capable of succeeding in the destruction of my right chest wall, Mr Lynch, because you have so much experience? Are you not listening to what you are saying? Patting yourself on the back with this outlandish statement when you should be hanging your head.*

'I think I have done six or seven hundred open blebectomies for recurrent pneumothoraces. I have done, approximately, almost two hundred video-assisted thoracoscopies on these people. The results of the video-assisted surgery are almost as good as the open surgery. They are almost as good. They are not quite as good. You are better getting in, getting your hands on the problem and sewing the lung up. In retrospect, she has really had the best operation.' *Reneging again then?*

You call what you did to me the best operation? Dear God. If that is the case then why are you so proud of yourself for introducing VATS into the country, if indeed you did? Why did you perform two hundred VATS on patients if you thought it was not the advisable procedure? You are totally fuddling yourself.

Judge Johnson interjected, 'You did not suggest to the witnesses for the plaintiff that that was the better approach, did you?'

'My Lord, forgive me but I did.'

'I see.'

'Yes, I think…'

'Did you suggest that this was going to produce a better result than the video-assisted?'

'I did and we discussed that, yes.'

'Very good,' replied Judge Johnson.

'I think, my Lord, that is basically my presentation on that.'

But Judge Johnson was not too happy allowing Mr Lynch to think that he would not be held accountable for everything he purported under oath. This was a far cry from giving a talk at an international conference.

'Well now I wish you would get the words right, Mr Lynch. We are not in the business of making presentations here. That is your sworn evidence.'

'That is my evidence, my Lord.'

'Right. Now we will start your cross-examination now.'

It is not an easy thing to watch a person acting out of control and even though I was used to observing Mr Lynch's disturbing behaviour and was at the receiving end of his arrogance and intimidation; most people in the courtroom were not. I can imagine they all breathed a sigh of relief once he put his instruments away; I know I did.

The one thing I thought at this point was that if I lost this case after such a false litany of sworn testimony, then I would forever be afraid that anyone with wealth and power, and who is so-called 'eminent', could get away with almost anything in a court of law. As I readied myself for Mr Lynch's cross-examination, little did I know that those precarious and premonitory thoughts would eventually find a way of coming back to strike me in the most devastating and punitive way.

Chapter Twenty

Denis stood up and I braced myself for what I predicted would be the most riveting and climactic two-way struggle I would ever witness being pounded across a grass court of justice. One thing I knew, Mr Lynch was not going to like being grilled and if he had lied in his direct evidence, he was certainly going to try to cover-up under Denis's scrutiny. And thus he led Mr Lynch into his first trap, 'Mr Lynch, you told us I think in the course of cross-examining witnesses that you were the first or among the first cardiothoracic surgeons in Ireland to introduce the VATS technique?'

'That is correct. I got in touch with a US surgical firm and I had seen it in the United States and I asked them would they let me have the use of the equipment. I was very impressed by it.'

'What is it about the VATS surgery that impresses you?'

'Well the old-fashioned surgery for doing a pneumothorax used to make a huge incision about this length in the side of the chest.'

'What is the advantage of the VATS?'

'The VATS is that she had three small cosmetic incisions. Two of them are less than a centimetre in diameter and one of them is less, is only about .03 of a centimetre in diameter. So you have three small incisions.' *You are absolutely incredible, Mr Lynch, now lying about the size of my scars. Is there nothing you will not lie about? Because of your incompetence, I not only have the scars from the VATS but also the large one from the emergency thoracotomy. Your contradictions, evasions and gross over-estimation of your abilities are about to pour out over the captured audience that is already taut with suspense.*

'It is a far less invasive procedure, isn't that right?'

'Well that is debatable. You have got to get in; it is just the method of getting through the chest wall. People, enthusiasts, claim a lot for this surgery but the people who are against the video-assisted surgery say; "Look, you should just do one incision instead of doing three".'

'I assume that you must have been an enthusiast, Mr Lynch, because you brought it in. You were very impressed with it and you brought it in?'

'I was impressed with it but you can, quite honestly, get as much pain with it as you get with conventional surgery. That is the honest position.' *Honest?*

'Mr Lynch, my understanding, certainly of all of the evidence that we had from the experts on the plaintiff's side was that the advantage of having the VATS procedure was that there was far less pain likely to result from it. Both Mr Makey and Professor Smith explained why that was and I did not understand you to be disagreeing with them in point of pain and the residual effects of the thoracotomy as opposed to the VATS surgery. May I take it that you agree that an incision, whether it is a small incision or a large incision, and going in through the chest wall and moving apart the ribs and doing all that, getting your hand in, is far more likely to leave the patient in pain than the VATS procedure?'

'That is debatable and the reason why it is debatable is when you are doing the VATS procedure you are going in at different levels, you are going in through different intercostal spaces and really when you…' *So, that is your new tactic, Mr Lynch. Everything is now debatable.*

Judge Johnson interjected, 'Sorry can I just ask, do you disagree that it is necessary to jack up the ribs at times?'

'Sometimes you have to, it depends on the patient.'

'Did you suggest that that procedure might be less painful than sticking in the ports?' again referring to the open surgery.

'My Lord…'

'Did you suggest that to the witnesses for the plaintiff when you were busily cross-examining them?'

And admonishing Judge Johnson, Mr Lynch retorted, 'I think that is a moot point my Lord.'

'What is a moot point?'

'Whether…'

'Whether you put it to them or not is not a moot point, it is a point. Did you put to them or not, your view that there is no advantage from a pain point of view?'

'I think I made that point with Mr Makey, yes, I did, sir.'

'Certainly if you did it didn't come across to me.'

'I did not with Professor Smith.'

Denis continued, 'Well your evidence, Mr Lynch is that the VATS assisted surgery does not give as good a result in terms of doing the job it is intended to do and now, I understand, I may be wrong, for the first time that you are saying that it is not even better from the point of view of pain. There isn't much advantage?'

Then, in a heightened state of vitriol, Mr Lynch lashed out, 'Just listen to me. All I can do is quote facts.'

Judge Johnson again interjected, 'No, quote your own experience. You are the person who is going to give the evidence.'

'In 1996, I went to the European Thoracic Surgical Society in Heidelberg and I produced a paper on video-assisted thoracic surgery. We had followed these patients for a few years and we had done some interesting work in the laboratory that went down very well. But one of the things that was disappointing me at that time was, we seemed to be getting too many recurrences. In other words, in the long-term, when you went on in the long-term the results were not as good as the old-fashioned conventional surgery.' *So why did you choose VATS if you thought it wasn't as good?*

Denis tried to pin him down, 'I understand, Mr Lynch, you are saying, and you have said it now in evidence, that the thoracotomy, which in fact Ms Carroll got in the last analysis, normally produces a better result from the point of view of dealing with the damage to the lung. But I did not understand you to be saying, until now, that the VATS surgery was not even better from the point of view of causing less pain.

'All of the plaintiff's case, Mr Lynch, as you know, is based on the proposition that if you are going to have a VATS procedure you are not likely to have the same level of pain as will follow the thoracotomy. I didn't understand you to be challenging that point, up to now.'

Mr Lynch then proffered the most appalling explanation, 'Quite honestly, if you go along to these people who are selling this equipment, and so forth, they will tell you it is a terrific solution.'

Denis was quick, 'And you must have believed them at the time.'

Judge Johnson interjected, 'Mr Lynch, is it the situation, that you go along to certain surgeons and they will tell you this is a super operation?'

'I agree with you totally, my Lord.'

'What did you do when you were selling it? What did you do when you were recommending to patients that this was the appropriate thing to do?'

'What I told them was this is the new method and we were evaluating it carefully. We did evaluate it very carefully and one of the problems we ran into with it, initially, was that we were initially getting a terrific result, but then at a late stage, we seem to be getting more recurrences than we should so then we had to deal with that particular problem; why were we getting the recurrences? Then we went in with our sclerosant to cause a pleurodesis.'

You have got to be joking, Mr Lynch. You told me VATS was a new procedure and you were assessing it? This, I know beyond a shadow of a doubt is blatant perjury. Do you seriously believe Judge Johnson will buy that one? You only spent five minutes at my bedside before the surgery.

But Judge Johnson continued, adamantly stating, 'You did not suggest, until this point in the case, that there was no distinction in the pain levels between the video-assisted operations and the non-video-assisted operations. You made no suggestion of that until now. Is that not so?'

'I'm not sure about that, my Lord.'

'Well, I am.'

Denis interjected, 'In any event, I understand you to be saying now, and there is no dispute, that where you placed the first port was that – you heard Professor Smith and Mr Makey agreeing – that was correctly placed. I think you said in your direct evidence that normally you would not place the second port in the breast?'

'That is correct. Well, not knowingly place it in the breast.' *You mean you can place an instrument through a breast and not know it? Incredible.*

And so he went on, 'What a surgeon does in a case like that is, he says; "Look, I have got to get down here, pull that breast out of the way;" he tells the assistant to do that and he puts a small incision over it and drives in…'

Denis held tight, 'That is where I am coming to. May we take it that you do agree with Professor Smith and Mr Makey that it is not normal or accepted practice to place the second, or any other port, in the breast?'

'But with all due respect, Mr McCullough, I described the anatomy of the breast.'

'Sorry, I…'

'Just let me finish my point,' Mr Lynch vehemently demanded.

Avoiding another discourse on the anatomy of the breast, Denis went on, 'I was going to raise the anatomy and the size of the woman's breast in a moment. Do you agree this much at least, that it would not be normal or accepted practice to place the second, or any other port, in the breast itself?'

'Mr McCullough, I have been a surgeon for forty years and I have worked in the best units in the world and I know how to do surgery.'

'Mr Lynch, nobody is querying that.'

His ego came to the fore, 'I'm sorry, you are querying it. I have more experience in this operation than anybody else in the country.'

'Why, when you spoke to Mr Boylan on the telephone, why when Mr Boylan pointed out to you that your operation notes indicated that the port which caused the damage was 2.5 cm lateral to the nipple and it was the plaintiff's experts' contention that the port should not be inserted in such a position, why did you immediately dispute that the port had been entered in that position?'

'Sorry, just one second. I told you that that was a matter of my judgement where I placed that port because I felt by placing that port in that position I could work up and I could work down. If I put it in the conventional position she would have had to have a fourth incision. I felt, in my judgement, that that was not the proper thing to do for my patient.' *Yet you did make four incisions because you did not go through the triangle of safety.*

'Why did you immediately dispute that the port had been entered in that position. My question is, why did you say to Mr Boylan that you hadn't put it in the place you say…'

'I'm not sure what Mr Boylan's points are. He is making points about this and that and the other.'

Judge Johnson had to interject again, 'Mr Boylan's points are exactly the same points as the points made by the experts for the plaintiff. Why did you put the port 2.5 centimetres lateral to the nipple? Do you remember doing it?'

'I do.'

'Why were you surprised when you saw the scar?'

'That scar, my Lord, that is the scar of the thoracotomy.' *Oh dear God. No it is not, Mr Lynch, you are lying again. That is the scar on my breast. Keep clocking up the perjury.*

'Mr Lynch, what is the scar on the breast?'

'Would you have the photographs of that, please?'

'Is the scar on the breast, the scar of the mini-thoracotomy?'

'That is the thoracotomy scar.' *Are you absolutely insane and corrupt, Mr Lynch? The thoracotomy scar is around my side from front to back.*

'Well, I would like to see,' Judge Johnson demanded.

Then Denis quickly asked Mr Lynch, 'What is the enormous scar underneath the armpit?'

'Sorry, Mr McCullough, would you kindly let my Lord see that picture?'

'The photographs are somewhere there, my Lord.'

Judge Johnson replied, 'I am sure they are.'

But Denis, refusing to play into Mr Lynch's hands and allow any distraction, forcefully insisted, 'Before we come to the photographs, I want to deal with what you said to Mr Boylan. You are not answering the question I put to you. I am asking you to answer the question please. You are saying…'

But Judge Johnson interrupted, 'They are the photographs?'

And, of course delighted, Mr Lynch gratefully asked, 'My Lord, may I assist you?'

But Denis was not going to let him off the hook, 'Just for a moment, Mr Lynch, I will come to the photographs but I want to ask you this question first, and I'm cross-examining you so I am entitled to put the questions to you and you are required to answer them, with respect.

'You are telling us now, as I understand it, I think, in my belief, for the first time, that you did in fact put the second port through the breast and that you intended doing that and you say that was the best position to place it. Why, if that was the case, did you say to Mr Boylan that the note which said you did that must be wrong, and why did you go on to say to him…'

'Mr McCullough, I told you the method I used for putting in that port. I get the assistant to pull the breast out of the way, pull the skin across and then I drive in the port. I tried to minimise the damage to the breast. Mr McCullough, there has been no significant damage to that breast.' *Oh really? Now you are reneging on the fact that I had a phantom pregnancy because of it and that it was vastly swollen. Of course, we all know you lied when you were cross-examining me, insisting my breast was 'minimally enlarged' and Denis caught you out.*

'You went on then to say that Mr Boylan then said to you…'

But Mr Lynch attempted to turn the tables and become the barrister, 'Do you agree with that or do you not? Do you agree with the facts that I am stating, the anatomy of the breast that the breast stretches to the mid-axillary line?'

Judge Johnson was forced to interrupt again, 'Mr Lynch, it is Mr McCullough who asks the questions at this time, not you.'

Denis continued, 'What I'm asking you is this – I asked you that question, Mr Lynch, because for the first time I understood you to be saying that the breast was to be cleared out of the way so far as possible and you would then go in?'

'That is the key phrase – as far as possible.'

'And would it not be possible to move it further away so that the entry point would not be 2.5 centimetres from the nipple?'

'No, it would not be.' *Of course it would, Mr Lynch, if you had placed the ports through the triangle of safety.*

'When Mr Boylan said to you on the telephone that he had photographic evidence, and I will come to that now, indicating a scar exactly where your operation note indicated you had put the port, why did you say to him this could be the mark of a chest drain?'

'Let me see the photographs, please.'

'Well, first of all, why did you say to Mr Boylan the scar which he mentioned could be…'

'Mr McCullough. Mr Boylan is unreliable. In his letter he said that I mentioned a Mr…'

'The first day of this trial, you asked for that letter to be…'

'There were two words wrong in that letter…' Mr Lynch repeated.

'You asked for that letter to be withdrawn…?'

'Take "at night" out of that letter and that letter is perfect. Now, gentlemen, we are here for justice. We want the truth.'

'You said, Mr Lynch, you never wrote that letter on the first day of this trial?'

'When I saw "at night" in it but if you take out the words "at night", everything falls into context and I certainly did write that letter.'

'Did you or did you not say on the first day of the trial – did you indicate that you had not written that letter. It was not yours; you had not got it?'

'That is correct until I went back and I double-checked.'

'But you read it out to Mr Boylan over the phone?'

'Look, I double-checked and I found that that letter -- take out the words "at night" and the whole letter falls into context.'

'But, Mr Lynch, that isn't the point.'

'That is the point. That is the truth.'

'I suggest to you, Mr Lynch, you are prepared to say whatever suits you at the time and that is what passes with you for the truth.'

'That is unfair. My Lord, I would ask for that to be withdrawn.'

Judge Johnson emphatically replied, 'No, Mr Lynch.'

Denis vigorously continued, 'Mr Lynch, you said at one stage you hadn't written the letter. Then you accept…'

'Sorry, when I saw that it was "at night" and then I said to myself look at that letter, take out "at night" and everything else in that letter is perfectly correct and that is the truth, my Lord.'

Why, Mr Lynch, did you tell Michael that you had followed the cardinal treatment plan in my case? You said, and it is now in evidence, a haemorrhage was not discovered until several hours after the surgery. So how can you believe you still have any credibility with this story? And since you stated in the letter I was under your care on the 30th of May, why did you keep swearing it was not until the 5th of June?

Denis asked, now frustrated, 'Mr Lynch, surely you can…'

'Are we down here to semantics or are we down to treating a patient?'

'We are down to your understanding the truth at the moment, Mr Lynch.'

'My?'

'Your understanding of the truth.'

'Mr McCullough, I have been truthful all my life and that is a dreadful thing to say to me. I have been truthful all my life.' *Is that why you swore a false affidavit for your solicitors?*

'What about the photocopy document which arose, I think, on the second day of the trial?'

'Look, are we dealing with documents or are we dealing with this patient who has been ill?'

Judge Johnson had to intervene again, 'We are dealing with the truth.'

'They are the same thing.'

'They are not.'

Denis re-entered, 'You will recall, Mr Lynch, that you were cross-examining Professor Smith and you were dealing with him about the internal mammary vessel being in an aberrant position and you said to him in the course of cross-examination it is query aberrant position; do you remember that?'

'Well, I thought that was so and I took legal advice on that, my Lord, and I answered that at the beginning…'

Denis demanded, 'Listen to my question for a moment and then you can give whatever answer you wish. Do you remember saying that to Professor Smith – that you said it says query?'

'That is what I thought…'

Judge Johnson interrupted and solicitously advised Mr Lynch not to say anything that might land him in trouble, 'Be very careful because you may leave yourself open to criminal prosecution if you say anything so I will warn you about it.'

'Now, look, gentlemen, we are human beings. We are trying to get on with our lives. We are trying to do our best. Are we trying to tie one another in knots on a squiggle on a piece of paper?' *Well, forgive me Mr Lynch, but I would not say that you treated me like a human being either before, during or after that surgery.*

Denis intervened, 'Mr Lynch, the squiggle came from you, not from me or from anybody this side of the case.'

'I admitted to my Lord that it may have come from me.'

Judge Johnson again interjected, 'You handed it to Mr McCullough.'

'But I am talking about the squiggle…'

'That was your document from your custody. You had it and

suggested that.'

'Now, my Lord, you suggested that I seek legal advice on that.'

'I did.'

'And I sought the legal advice.'

'Answer Mr McCullough's questions now.'

But Mr Lynch insisted on continuing, 'And the legal advice…'

'We do not want to know what the legal advice was. Answer Mr McCullough.'

Denis took it up and also cautioned Mr Lynch, 'Maybe the legal advice was to answer no questions about this. If it was, you can say so in a moment but…'

'The legal advice was very simple. They told me that when you analyse this case you will go back to the original document. That is the authentic document.'

But Judge Johnson asked, 'Why did you produce an altered document to this court?'

'Well, I did not do that. Now, that is unfair, my Lord. I did not try to mislead this court and I think that is most unfair, this line of questioning. I have been a sincere, genuine, honest person all my life.'

Denis continued, 'Would you listen to my question, Mr Lynch, and let's deal with this?'

'Yes.'

'You put it to Professor Smith that the entry on the operation note was query, which…'

'That was the piece of paper that I…'

'Yes, but you put it to Professor Smith; do you remember that? Is that right?'

'That is the truth at that particular point in time.'

Denis continued, 'I then said to his Lordship, if you recall, that the copy of the note which I had had made no reference to query and I asked that you should indicate where it was. You leaned across to me and handed me this document and you pointed out that squiggle and you said that is a query?'

'Now, sir, do you really feel that that is particularly relevant to this…'

To which Judge Johnson immediately interjected, 'Yes, immensely.'

'Immensely,' Denis agreed.

And Judge Johnson emphasised, 'It is to the point of this case.'

Denis still tried to squeeze an answer out of Mr Lynch, 'I am asking the question because I submit to you it is relevant to the manner in which you have treated Ms Carroll from the time you operated on her and your approach to this case and her entitlement to bring the action. You indicated to me that that mark there meant query?'

'Look, when I was preparing for this case – I have been over it twenty, thirty, forty times trying to see that every dose of every drug is right and every comment is… I'm going round the case ticking this off and querying that and doing this and then I go back to my original copy and I see that it is not on my original copy and, my Lord, I was not trying to deceive anybody.'

Judge Johnson interjected, 'Well, this was the document produced by you in court and it has quite clearly been interfered with subsequent to it being Photostatted. It does not bear any relation to the original and you produced it – no one else.'

'This is a spontaneous thing. I mean, for God's sake, let us be reasonable.'

However, Judge Johnson clearly picked up on the word spontaneous, 'You said you prepared it twenty or thirty times, Mr Lynch.'

Mr Lynch rambled on and concluded, '…this to me is a very small kind of case…' *I thought how sickening this statement was, a 'very small kind' and yet you got it so badly wrong?*

'I am not going to ask too many more questions, Mr Lynch,' Denis advised.

'Would you like to go to the photographs, please? Could we look at them jointly?'

Can you still not remember your surgery, Mr Lynch after seeing all my scars in Judge Johnson's chambers and wading through my records up to forty times? Can you still not comprehend your own operation notes?

Denis advised, 'Well, if you take them and you can make to his Lordship whatever point you wish to make on the photographs.'

'Now, your Lordship, that cosmetically is a superb scar.' *I felt sick at his admiration.*

'Which one? The one under the arm?' asked Judge Johnson.

'This here.'

Denis refreshed Mr Lynch's memory, 'Do you see the scar on the breast itself? That is the scar you told me earlier was the thoracotomy scar?'

'Well, I don't know whether that is – I will tell you one thing, it has healed beautifully whatever it was. It is absolutely beautifully healed.'

'Your case now is that you deliberately put the port in through there so, presumably, it is your scar?'

'I put the port in to look down because the patient had endometrial tissue. Now we are indulging in armchair surgery.'

Judge Johnson again had to interject, 'Did you put the port through the breast as…'

'I put the port through breast tissue. That is correct.'

'Sorry, that photograph there, is that what you call breast tissue? That is the second scar 2.5 cm lateral to the…'

'That is where I pulled it across. The breast is being pulled across but the skin doesn't go…'

'Is that what you call breast tissue?'

'I am calling breast tissue right out to here?'

'Sorry, do you call where that…'

'Of course, I do.'

'That's all right.'

But Mr Lynch insisted on having the last word, 'But I also call that breast tissue.'

'Of course, you do, yes.'

Denis again took over, 'Why did you say a moment ago, Mr Lynch, that scar, whatever it is, has healed perfectly? If your base is right now, you know what it is if that is where you put the port deliberately?'

'Look, we are six years after the operation.'

'Ms Carroll is six years after the operation.'

'And she is in pain, she says,' responded Judge Johnson.

Denis added 'And this was an operation that you told her was a cinch.'

'No, I certainly did not use that language. She mentioned that. I certainly did not use that language. No surgeon ever tells a patient the operation is a cinch. The simplest surgery can end up a disaster.' *Well done, Mr Lynch, the one true statement you have made in this trial. How many of your surgeries have ended up disastrous?*

'You didn't challenge her on it?'

'Well, do I have to challenge everything?'

'Yes,' replied Judge Johnson.

Denis continued, 'And she said that for that reason she had no concern about it because you were so confident about it. You told her how many you had done and you said it was a cinch.'

'Mr McCullough, in my life, I have never told any patient that an operation is a cinch.' *You did, Mr Lynch and I swore to it.*

'Well, that is Ms Carroll's evidence. You certainly didn't tell her that…'

'Well, is that important?'

'That is a matter for his Lordship. You didn't tell her that fifteen per cent of your video-assisted thoracic surgery went on to open thoracotomy?'

'Oh, I certainly did because that is what happens and that is how the patient is towelled up at the beginning of the operation. The patient is made ready for an open thoracotomy and if you have to change, you just go to a different instrument and you go on with your surgery. That is standard practice.' *You malevolent liar, Mr Lynch. I never even heard of the word 'thoracotomy' until after that surgery. And, as if you would inform any patient that your conversion rate was fifteen per cent; not something to be proud of I would say.*

'Well, thirteen per cent more of your operations went on to thoracotomy than on Professor Smith's figures?'

This was like a red rag to a bull and Mr Lynch launched into a tirade of criticism of Professor Smith. Judge Johnson interjected and asked him if he had cross-examined the Professor on the issues he was criticising and he replied, 'I gave him so much criticism' and added, 'I did not know that he was going off. I did not know what his itinerary was.'

But Judge Johnson emphasised, 'Mr Smith spent an extra day here to facilitate you. Mr McCullough, it is four o'clock. If we rise, we can continue on Tuesday morning.'

'At what time, my Lord, on Tuesday?'

'Eleven o'clock. Now, Mr McCullough, I am extremely unhappy at the situation that has arisen regarding these two documents. Mr Lynch, you produced that document. It was a document which had been altered and you presented it as an unaltered document that there was a query raised on it. That was done in open court and handing it to Mr McCullough by way of correcting a statement which was made in the witness box. That is an extraordinarily serious event.'

'My Lord, I made a mistake,' Mr Lynch insisted. *Ah, another 'mistake'.*

'You certainly did, Mr Lynch.'

'My Lord, I have admitted it.'

'Who altered that piece of paper?'

'My Lord…'

'Who altered that piece of paper?'

'Just one second, my Lord, let me answer your question. I have been over this case so many times…'

'Can I have a look at that piece of paper? Mr Lynch, who altered that?'

'I can't recall altering it but I presume it must have been me. I cannot recall that my Lord. I just cannot recall that. What do you really think genuinely, my Lord, looking at that squiggle on that page? Now, be honest, be fair.'

But Mr Lynch, have you forgotten that it is not only the physical change that is the issue? You blatantly told Professor Smith during cross-examination, 'When you see in my operation notes I say a queried aberrant internal mammary artery.' That was a very coherent and emphatic statement.

'It is not a question for me to decide that, Mr Lynch. There are other people who can decide that.'

Denis then interjected, 'There is just one other question I want to ask, my Lord. Perhaps, it might shorten the matter on Tuesday.'

'Yes?'

He addressed Mr Lynch, 'If you can cast your mind back to, I think, immediately or very shortly after the examination that occurred in his

Lordship's chambers; do you remember?'

'Yes.'

'You came out here and you were in court and you said, I suggest to you, that, yes, you now accept – these may not be the precise words but you now accepted that you put the port through Ms Carroll's breast. You realised that for the first time in his Lordship's chambers; didn't you say that?'

'I have not seen Ms Carroll's chest for five years and all my life have always spoken the truth and, quite honestly, Mr McCullough, that incision is over part of Ms Carroll's breast. There is no doubt about that and I do not challenge that but what I was challenging is that the breast goes out far further than people realise. It goes out to the mid-axillary line. Would you like to consult breast anatomy on it?'

And thank God Judge Johnson intervened, 'Eleven o'clock on Tuesday morning.'

Phew, I breathed deeply. What a marathon and gruelling day. We had arrived at a landmark stage and between Mr Lynch's direct testimony and cross-examination, I felt greatly convinced that he was bereft of any credibility whatsoever. He had tried to spin a nexus of lies and failed miserably. When I believed I had seen and heard just about everything during the week nothing surpassed the frenzied way Mr Lynch and his instruments entertained us.

It transpired that my legal team were as aghast as I was at the day's events. The syndicate reporter who was present in the courtroom for most of the trial shook his head and commented to me that it was no longer funny; it had become downright tragic.

There was little to discuss with my team that late afternoon apart from trying to guess what witnesses Mr Lynch would come up with on Tuesday. I was left too exhausted to muster much enthusiasm for 'what ifs'. But what was of great consolation was knowing that no expert thoracic surgeon was going to appear in support of Mr Lynch and no one had provided a report.

My father went home to County Wexford in need of a break. I spent my time with friends and performing my usual exercises in the gym. I began to relax over the weekend with the expectation that Tuesday would be quite mundane and anti-climactic and I rid myself of some of the stress. But if I had to describe now how Tuesday was going to pan out it would detract from the comedic element of it. And it was going to offer quite remarkable humour.

Chapter Twenty-One

I had set the alarm for seven o'clock on Tuesday morning, the 13th of November, but I need not have bothered since I was awake most of the night not having succeeded in quieting my mind. This day was of monumental significance because if Mr Lynch was going to produce even one thoracic expert to support his surgery then the waters would be muddied. But having read the literature and heard the evidence, I humbly doubted whether any thoracic surgeon would support the manner in which he performed VATS.

So duly primed and eager to get the day started, with my father being my main and steadfast support, off we headed for our usual cup of coffee on that dry and unusually bright November morning. As we sauntered leisurely down the quay with the Four Courts beckoning in the distance, I was ponderously quiescent. By the time the evidence wrapped up in the late afternoon, I was going to have great hope or stark desperation.

Michael was already awaiting our arrival in the Round Hall, which was thronged with people, given it was a Tuesday and all the usual suspects were waiting to file into Court Number Two to receive mandates and decisions from Judge Johnson. It was, again, immensely captivating and enthralling but I wondered who would want to be a judge, being responsible for other peoples' fate. A great burden, I would think.

Denis informed me that they had decided not to cross-examine Mr Lynch any further. He believed they had exposed him sufficiently the previous Friday. Anything more would be the same and the transcripts would provide enough damning testimony for Judge Johnson when it came to his deliberations. Then, when the courtroom cleared, Judge Johnson got on with the business of the trial immediately. Denis informed him, 'I have no more questions for Mr Lynch in cross-examination.'

Not having the least inkling as to what was going to transpire next, I heard Judge Johnson ask, 'Mr Lynch, do you want to call any witnesses?'

My breath caught in nervous anticipation. Please God let there be none, and as I crossed my fingers I closed my eyes, and to my absolute horror Mr Lynch announced, 'My Lord, I would like to call three witnesses. I approached these people, I only approached them on Sunday evening…' I gasped and was certain my heart skipped a beat; no less than three witnesses? Who on earth are they, I wondered?

'If you want to call witnesses, call them. Are they experts?'

'They are the people who have seen this lady before she had her surgery.'

'No, sorry, are they experts?'

'I would require them as experts.' *Well they are not thoracic surgeons I thought with enormous relief.*

'Have you furnished Mr McCullough with copies of the reports of the evidence they are going to give?'

'No, I have not,' said Mr Lynch, becoming increasingly belligerent.

'That is a requirement, I am afraid, of the courts. Is that not so, Mr McCullough?'

'If these witnesses are experts and if they have furnished reports, Mr Lynch would be obliged to furnish them to me.'

'They have not furnished reports,' replied the frustrated Mr Lynch.

'Call them then, Mr Lynch.'

But Mr Lynch, now wavering, replied, 'Your Honour, I have been in touch with them again this morning and the first person that I had asked to come along was the physician that originally saw the patient, Dr John Hegarty.' *Why would you think Dr Hegarty would appear as your witness and for what reason? I had been his patient and he had, ultimately, full responsibility for my care and I had no issue with him. In my opinion, Dr Hegarty was a competent and thoroughly pleasant man.*

'Well, well, call him then.'

'Dr John Hegarty agreed to come but he stated that he would not come until he had contacted his solicitor, Arthur Cox, and he got the approval of Arthur Cox and would be accompanied by a senior counsel designated by Arthur Cox.'

'Mr Lynch, do you want to call a witness or do you not?'

'I want to call…'

'Then call them. It is your case, you have chosen to appear for yourself, now call the witness you want to call.'

'My Lord, what do you actually mean by that? What time frame have I?'

'Now. The case has been going for a week. It is now your time to call your witnesses.'

'My Lord, I was on to Professor Keogh this morning twice or three times, I was on to him three or four times last night…' *This was a terrible waste of the court's valuable time.*

'Mr Lynch, I am not interested in your problems…'

'… and he tells me that he cannot appear in this court until 3:00 p.m. today.'

'Did you subpoena him?'

'I did not…'

'Did you ask him before this morning?'

'I asked him on Sunday evening.' *I wondered what relevance the apparently reluctant Professor Keogh had to these proceedings. But who was the nebulous third witness?*

Judge Johnson then, understandably annoyed, rebuked Mr Lynch, 'That is no way to conduct a case of this magnitude. Mr Lynch, you have chosen to run your own case. Now, you may run your life in accordance with your rules, and it is quite clear to me you have, but this court is run in accordance with the law. Have you got a witness to call?'

'I have three, but I just cannot call them…'

'Have you any witness in court to call?'

'My Lord, I have no witnesses in court to…'

'So, what are we to do?' Judge Johnson asked, greatly concerned and frustrated.

The case was fast becoming the most peculiar and oddly entertaining drama one could wish for, if an onlooker. It was like a clip from *Live at the Apollo* rather than a high court trial. I could not resist its entertainment factor even though I was a reluctant participant. As if he was purposely antagonising Judge Johnson he reverted to Dr Hegarty.

'My Lord, the first person I went to was Dr John Hegarty and he has a lot of experience of court, I have none, that is obvious.' *Ah, Mr Lynch, but have you forgotten you informed Judge Johnson you have been in court 'frequently'?*

Judge Johnson drew the line, 'Mr Lynch, sorry, I do not want to hear what he had to say. You are here, it is your opportunity to call witnesses. Either you have a witness to call or you have not.'

'My Lord, they tell me that they will come…'

'You did not prepare your case, did you?'

Here I was, with my life held in abeyance, while Mr Lynch thought fit to stand there and frustrate us all. And with so many people waiting for both criminal and civil cases to get to trial and with the number of judges so limited, here he was, holding up the entire process with his wanton intentions.

'I certainly did not subpoena them,' Mr Lynch returned in an aggravated tone.

'Why not?'

'…I requested them.'

'When did you request them?'

'I requested them on Sunday night.'

'I see. You did not think of doing it before the weekend?'

'I requested them on the advice of medical colleagues.'

'As far as I am concerned, Mr Lynch, I am going to rise for five minutes. If you do not have your witnesses here, then I am going to consider the case closed, unless Mr McCullough has another submission to make. But it seems to me you come here, you haven't an application to make, you haven't got witnesses and you do not appear to have taken the correct steps to get them here.'

'My Lord, I contacted Gordon Grimes in this matter…'

'Sorry, please, I deal with the solicitor on record. If you want Messrs. Gordon Grimes to come on record for you, fine.'

'I think they should, my Lord.'

Then Judge Johnson advised Mr Lynch that if he could get a representative from Gore & Grimes to court immediately to come on record then they could deal with the matter and he asked, 'How long will it take you to do that?'

'I will phone up Gordon Grimes. They are nearby. I have already asked…'

'I will now rise and I will sit again in ten minutes and, Mr Lynch, I will then hear what you have got to say…'

'My Lord, under the constitution have I right to do what I am doing?' Mr Lynch asked in a truculent manner.

I wondered when you were going to bring that up Mr Lynch, but remember, I have equal rights to have my case heard and in a manner that is also fair to me. Forgotten that, have you? I believe you have been afforded far too many privileges because of your decision to represent yourself.

'Of course you have, but, Mr Lynch, I have the right to conduct the case in accordance with law. I am not going to hang around here until you decide what to do. Do you follow me?'

'Very clearly, I follow you, my Lord,' he retorted in a sardonic undertone.

Judge Johnson, obviously understanding and fearful of how all this nonsense was affecting my rights, finally brought me back into the picture, 'Mr McCullough has a client, as well. You have been here for a week. You have chosen not to bother getting witnesses until this weekend. That was your decision.'

'That is correct, my Lord.'

'Yes, well, now, I will rise for ten minutes to see what you want to do next.'

The case was again temporarily suspended while Mr Lynch scampered off to track down his solicitor. *This was the stuff of Monty Python.*

Judge Johnson duly reappeared and asked, 'Mr Lynch, what do you want to do?'

'My Lord, I feel I should go that route, because I need help in this case. My Lord, you asked me to bring my solicitor to court – well, he is here in the court…'

'No, I did not ask you to bring your solicitor to court, I asked you to get advice from him. If he wants to come on record, he is welcome in court. If he does not want to come on record, he is of no interest to me.'

Then all of a sudden, absolute bedlam broke out on the floor of the courtroom. Mr Karl Hayes of Gore Grimes & Co. entered the courtroom and stealthily appeared right behind Mr Lynch and I was watching this comedy of errors with much amusement. He was of shorter stature and necessarily had to raise himself up on the balls of his feet to whisper over Mr Lynch's right shoulder, close to his ear, telling him what to say, like an amateur ventriloquist.

Mr Hayes had failed to come on record as Mr Lynch's legal representative and this mayhem carried on for some time. I should have been extremely angry but instead it was the absolute hallmark of comedy. Once again the audience was enthralled in the grip of suspense.

Mr Lynch asked Judge Johnson, 'I wonder if Mr Hayes would reply to that. Mr Hayes says that I have to deal with that.'

But the Judge was adamant, 'He has no right of audience except as a solicitor on record. If he is not on record, that is it. You are not getting legal advice, in other words. Mr Lynch, you are not getting legal advice. Legal advice is a solicitor on record, not someone whispering over your shoulder and letting you talk.'

At this point the entire courtroom erupted with laughter and we were yet again, riveted in our seats, staring with incredulity at this circus act causing ructions in the high court, blatantly disregarding Judge Johnson's instructions. It was so horribly absurd and uproarious concurrently. The deadlocked situation continued without Mr Lynch bringing Mr Hayes on record. If that was not enough and not for the first time, Mr Lynch almost caused me to react with an outburst of laughter by coming out with another of his hilarious observations, *'I am confused my Lord.'*

I almost choked in an attempt to stop hiccupping and I could feel my father having tremendous difficulty containing himself. I had to take deep slow breaths to calm my composure and ensure I had my poker face intact. I did not wish to add to Judge Johnson's woes.

Denis interjected, 'If Mr Lynch's application, my Lord, is to have the matter put back to three o'clock, if your Lordship…'

Judge Johnson, without further ado, decided to extricate himself from the stalemate and announced, 'I will take up another matter in the meantime and I will resume this case at three o'clock.'

In the end, while the buffoonery in the courtroom continued, it seemed it was the most prudent way Judge Johnson could regain some control because the double act would not respect court procedures. As I had initially predicted, Mr Lynch had finally taken over the court. Judge Johnson, before he turned to go, advised Mr Lynch to regularise his position and he would resume the trial to hear Professor Keogh's evidence. At least, I thought, we could all indulge in a long break.

As we filed back into the courtroom just before three, Michael approached me and asked if I knew who had accompanied Mr Lynch in. I told him I had never seen him before, or at least I could not recall ever seeing him. It transpired, however, that it was indeed Professor Keogh.

Judge Johnson resumed the trial and asked, 'Now, Mr Lynch, have you got witnesses?

'My Lord, I have a witness here at the moment.'

'Right, very good. Then call your witnesses.'

'I would like to call Professor Brian Keogh.'

As Professor Keogh, who is not a thoracic surgeon, strode up to the witness box I, for the life of me, could not understand, after so much time and water had gone under the bridge and the copious hundreds of patients who would have passed through St. Vincent's hospital since the surgery, how he could possibly have remembered me, unless Mr Lynch had substantially primed him.

It transpired, true to form, Mr Lynch's obviously callous intention was to bring him into the fold of his dirty tricks campaign. The majority of his few absurd questions were in relation to medication that had been administered to me and which I had absolutely no control over. I thought it made the Professor look like a fool.

There I had been, on the morning of May the 31st 1996, with a collapsed lung and pneumonia on an intravenous drip of antibiotics and in pain, totally at the mercy of doctors. By the time, however, Denis had done with him he had pulled back from the brink and testified he had only seen me one time, the morning after I was admitted, when I would have told him I was Mr Lynch's patient and was fasting for surgery. In addition, my treatment regime had already been written up in the admissions notes. No wonder I had not remembered him.

When he was dismissed by Judge Johnson I would have placed a large wager that he regretted having been caught up in Mr Lynch's malevolent capers. Since he had seemingly been pressurised by Mr Lynch with his copious telephone calls, I did not know to what extent, if any, he felt compelled to appear as a witness. I did not know him and he certainly did not know me.

The testimony was a squandered waste of time and Professor Keogh, I thought, had a sheepish look on his face as he left the stand. Mr Lynch had got nowhere except to add to his own irreparably damaged credibility.

'Now, your next witness,' said Judge Johnson.

'My Lord, my next witness has not arrived in court. I phoned his wife when I left court this morning and she tried to get the information…'

'Honestly, Mr Lynch,' replied a, by now, seriously frustrated Judge, 'there are ways and means in court other than phoning people's wives. I will rise and I will wait until such time as the witness arrives, as long as the witness comes before four o'clock today.'

'My Lord, I am prepared to forego my other witnesses.'

But Judge Johnson, apparently understanding Mr Lynch's, I believed, sinister modus operandi, insisted, 'No, no, I am not going to cut you short under any circumstances, Mr Lynch. I will wait until four o'clock to see whether the witness comes, or any other witness comes, as the case may be.' *So here we go, left twiddling our thumbs again. There is no thoracic expert pounding on your door, eager to defend your surgery. Says a lot, I think, and we all continued waiting for him to pull a rabbit out of a hat.*

Once the clock struck four, Judge Johnson reappeared and Mr Lynch addressed him, 'My Lord, my two witnesses have not turned up. I have been consulting with my colleagues, they are eminent men and I feel I have to listen to them, and they suggested that perhaps I should ask you for an adjournment.'

'It is not a question of what they suggested, are you asking me for an adjournment? It is you who must make up your mind, do not be relying on what other people say. I am sure you feel that way inclined. I want to know are you asking for an adjournment?'

Then finally, 'I am asking for an adjournment.' This is a nightmare I almost cried out. What would Judge Johnson decide? I anxiously awaited his decision.

'Until when and for what purpose?'

'The main reason I am asking for an adjournment is my advice that I am not going to succeed unless I get specialised legal advice and I have got to act on that.' As he was saying this, Professor Keogh, who was seated behind Mr Lynch, grabbed my attention and I could swear, as he was putting his forehead down into the palms of his hands, he mouthed the words, 'Oh, no.' He appeared visibly distressed.

What makes you think, Mr Lynch, you will succeed even if you bring in legal representation? The reason you are in this state is not because you represented yourself; it is because you did not perform the surgery properly and because you told an unbelievable number of untruths and spurious stories to the court. Now you have realised what you have done and you are trying to find a way to get out of the mess you created for yourself and at my expense. You are trying to have it every way, I thought, as I waited anxious and distraught at this superimposed trauma and I felt enough was enough.

'What I will do is this, Mr Lynch – and, Mr McCullough, what have you got to say to this?'

'I appreciate Mr Lynch's position, my Lord. I would say, my Lord that it is a pity that he did not listen to this advice or it was not given at an earlier point in time. I am concerned about the plaintiff's position…' *I was seriously angry at this point because I could see Mr Lynch dragging me through more years of this treatment.*

'Of course,' replied the Judge.

'I am concerned about that if your Lordship gives judgement in favour of the plaintiff there may be difficulties in recovering or executing that judgement, my Lord, and the more time goes on, the more concern I have about that. I do not know what period of adjournment Mr Lynch is seeking, but if he now seeks, my Lord, to bring in at the end of the case legal advice, it seems to me that whatever adjournment he is going to require is going to be longer rather than shorter, my Lord, and I am concerned about the plaintiff's position.'

Then Judge Johnson announced his decision, 'The situation is it is now Tuesday. I have got to go to the special criminal court next week and I will be there possibly until Christmas.' *This could not be worse, I thought, now completely and utterly dismayed.*

'Mr Lynch, I will give you an adjournment from now until next Friday morning at eleven o'clock. In any event, it is my intention – the evidence in the case now having closed…'

Denis interjected, 'I wonder if your Lordship would ask Mr Lynch whether he has, in fact, closed his case.'

'Mr Lynch, I take it the evidence in the case is now finished, you are not calling any more evidence?'

'My Lord, I will not call more evidence.'

'All right then, the evidence in the case is now closed and under those circumstances I was going, in any event, because of Mr Lynch's position, to invite and require the parties to make written submissions on the facts as proved and on the law in this case before I give judgement.' *Oh thank God, I silently and gratefully acknowledged.*

'May it please your Lordship,' said Denis.

'I will adjourn the matter until Friday at eleven o'clock. I do not want the written submissions before Friday, obviously. I will adjourn the matter until Friday and, Mr Lynch, we will see what the situation regarding any advice you may decide to take in the meantime on that day is. I am very glad that you have decided to follow this course, I think it is the prudent thing to do.

'I will adjourn the matter until Friday at eleven o'clock, and whatever applications may have to be dealt with then I will deal with at that time, in the light of any advice Mr Lynch may have got. I am just putting you on alert I will then be requesting, irrespective of with or without legal advice, written submissions both on the facts and the law.'

Denis added, 'Perhaps I should just say, my Lord, in the plaintiff's interest, obviously, as your Lordship might anticipate, we would regard the case as closed and would not be prepared to countenance any reopening of the case to any extent. The plaintiff, I think, has gone through enough.'

'Yes, that is reasonable.' My body slouched with great relief. 'The case has been conducted as the case was conducted and it is my intention to return the file which we obtained from St. Vincent's Hospital to St. Vincent's Hospital. I am getting the registrar to retain the document which was produced by Mr Lynch, that is to be retained with the file. The main file can go back, that is to be retained with the papers in the case.'

Then, alluding to Mr Lynch's letter to my general practitioner, Dr Duignan, after the surgery, he asked Denis, 'The only other letter was the letter which was read out at the very beginning – was that handed in to court?'

'It is in the book before your Lordship.'

I knew it would take a considerable amount of time for submissions to be presented but at least I would rest in that no other evidence could be introduced. The trial was not over but the testimonies were. However, I would not know until Friday what Mr Lynch would come up with having taken legal advice. And so, as far as I was involved, the case was closed and the fact that Mr Lynch had not one shred of support for his disastrous surgery left me with the hope I so longed for. Michael, Denis and Karen did not falter in protecting my interests. It is at times like this when one is grateful to have competent and professional representation.

I was under no illusion, however, that a verdict would be given in this case anytime soon. I had to wait until Friday to find out the next step and after a round-up discussion with my legal team it was time to go home, put my feet up after another absurd day and try not to dwell on the future. Easier said than done, however, because I knew the next few days of waiting would be torturous unless I found ways to totally distract myself. The slow grind of time was now to become my worst enemy.

Chapter Twenty-Two

Friday the 1st crept up on me more quickly than I anticipated because I wanted to stave off possible bad news of more adjournments to facilitate Mr Lynch. I was beginning to think that we might as well place him in the role of judge as well as barrister since he was practically running the show. Then he could be my executioner and have done with it.

It was with some trepidation that my father and I entered the Four Courts that morning, after our usual frequenting of our favourite café. I was ready to get the ordeal of the trial over with but, when one wishes for something that desperately, invariably things turn out the opposite way. Michael gave me an update on what he thought was going to happen and, as usual, it was to benefit Mr Lynch. Why did I even entertain the thought that anything would be different?

As Judge Johnson opened the proceedings, it transpired that Mr Lynch had, indeed, made the decision to bring in legal representation. The hearing turned out to be very brief because his senior counsel, Mr James Nugent, requested sufficient time to produce the written submissions. In conclusion, Judge Johnson granted yet another adjournment until the 15th of December. That was that, hardly worth putting in an appearance but important, I felt, to show that I had not wavered in my determination. However, my patience with this entire process of the trial was now waning fast. The day when Judge Johnson would deliver his verdict in the case seemed aeons away and in another 'Big Bang'.

Christmas and New Year passed again before Michael informed me that Judge Johnson would hear the written submissions on Friday, the 22nd of February 2002. So into the Four Courts with a refreshed state of mind, somewhat renewed vitality, boosts of expresso and familial and friendly support, I, again, cautiously stepped into court and began the process of reacquainting myself with the judiciary.

Judge Johnson had worked his way through the entirety of the submissions, I was delighted to hear and by the end of the proceedings that day, the stenographer had transcribed almost thirty-five pages of evidence. He was certainly leaving no stone unturned, as they say.

Again I waited, continuously trying to toughen my nerves, when I received a letter from Michael announcing that the barristers would present their final submissions on the 20th of March. The day turned out much like the last hearing but with one exceptional difference: Judge Johnson advised the trial was over but since it would take him some time to go through all and sundry, he gave a reserved judgement. I had begun to think I would never see the end.

***

The future quality of my remaining life was now literally in Judge Johnson's hands. I was either going to win the case and recover some semblance of security or lose and have to sell my home, having used up all my savings for expenses connected with both the surgery and the trial. And what then?

The big question now was how long Judge Johnson would take to reach a verdict. Anxiety, fear, and hope were some of the emotions I felt; all jumbled up together. I was in an indolent mood during that moratorium, apart from keeping my rehabilitation regime going. I was unwavering in my quest to readjust my physical structure but I was ultimately in denial of the true prognosis of my future. It was all wishful thinking on my part. There was a myriad of questions I could have tormented myself with but the obvious one was that if I did, indeed, win the case how was I going to get Mr Lynch to pay the award? However, I would be dragged through the supreme court appeal first so I focused on the immediate torment.

During this time of expectation and waiting every night, before I attempted to sleep, I pleaded for a higher power to help Judge Johnson see the truth. Doubts about winning the case kept trying to intercept and play tricks with my mind. After the craziness of the trial, I knew anything could happen.

Every day I trod a step closer and every morning I renewed my vigour. Whenever the telephone rang I answered it hesitantly while holding my breath, thinking it might be Michael. March turned into April and then into May and when I least expected it, I was caught off guard, Judge Johnson had reached a verdict and would deliver it on Tuesday, the 16th of May. As it was only four days after my birthday, I decided to celebrate it well since my life could change again forever.

I can remember the eve of the 16th with clear recollection. Well before I retired to bed, I lit a small stout vanilla-scented candle and placed it in front of a large photograph of my grandfather. Since the verdict was already reached I knew nothing more could be done but I asked him to support me through the sleeplessness of the dark hours ahead and the following morning's nerve-racking suspense. I had no map to steer me.

Six hours after midnight I could no longer lie without twisting and turning and in the process hurting my chest wall. Therefore, I slowly arose and made preparations for a hearty breakfast for when my father got up. I turned on the BBC world news and tried to place myself in the footsteps of people who were suffering around the globe and to put my predicament in perspective. My ordeal seemed so insignificant in comparison but it did nothing to allay my dread. However, the news and analyses did help to distract me. As daylight slowly made its appearance, I dressed extra carefully and put on my best business attire and accessories. I predicted that one or two cameras would be flashing that day and, whatever the outcome, I was not going to be able to avoid them. I would hold my head up high because if I lost the case I could well imagine the extent Mr Lynch would go to, to gloat. I believed there would be no end to his callousness.

As we meandered towards the Four Courts and approached the side entrance, I thought the sky seemed very depressingly grey and cloying. By walking slowly I felt I was putting off the inevitable and every step was a step towards my fate. As we entered the Round Hall through the well-travelled corridors I felt I was entering a dream. Was this really me here? It was something I only read in newspapers, saw on television or in films. How did I get to this stage, where had the confidence come from and how on earth did I get enough stamina to see it through? I had no answers.

Everyone was apprehensive that morning and not given to the usual loquacious chatter. No one could second-guess Judge Johnson and no one tried to. As we filed into Court Number Two for the last time I hoped, my instinct pulled me towards the benches at the back of the courtroom. Because of the fear I had developed of Mr Lynch, I sat as far from him as possible and centred myself between my father and one of my closest friends. Even if I won the case I did not wish to look at the man.

Then suddenly the court rose and Judge Johnson entered. I grasped my friend's hand and leaned against my father. This was it, the moment of truth. I held my breath, closed my eyes and bowed my head as Judge Johnson began to speak. The guillotine was poised.

In a coherent, lucid and serious voice, Judge Johnson began to read from his judgement by summing up the facts of the case, identifying me as the plaintiff and Mr Lynch as, 'The defendant is a retired cardiothoracic surgeon who carries on practice at the Blackrock Clinic and in St. Vincent's Hospital. Whereas it is a medical negligence claim it is somewhat unfortunate that though the plaintiff was represented by counsel and solicitors the defendant's solicitor came off record some weeks before the trial. The defendant in these circumstances chose to represent himself. The plaintiff's claim is for damages for personal injuries arising out of what the plaintiff says is the negligence of the defendant in the execution of a thoracotomy on the 5th of June 1996.'

Judge Johnson continued, beginning with the facts after my first pneumothorax, explaining what a bleb is on the lung and how VATS should be performed. He concluded with: 'No complications had been described to her and no alternative was suggested to her nor was it suggested that the possibility of having to switch to an open thoracotomy, or that there was any possibility of long-lasting pain. Video-assisted thoracic surgery, as above stated, is conducted by the insertion of three ports in what is described as the triangle of safety that is under the armpit to give access to the chest.' *No clue yet. Gosh, I thought, I had better breathe. This was sheer torture.*

He continued with technical explanations of why and how the camera is used and inserted and the placing of the other instruments. 'The older method of doing this operation is an open thoracotomy which involves making a much larger incision along the ribcage to enable the surgeon to place his hands inside the ribcage of the chest and carry out the operation visually. This operation is well known and well established and involves usually the jacking up of the ribs which enables the insertion of the hand between them.

'The advantage of the VATS procedure over the older form of surgery is clearly stated by Professor Smith, an expert on behalf of the plaintiff, as follows: "The amount of surgical damage inflicted on the chest wall in dealing with the problems is much less. This gives rise to three benefits one of which is a series of wounds which heal much more quickly and are much more immediately controlled by analgesics. The second one is the metabolic effect of an operation to the effect on the general body system of having a big muscle-slicing operation is profound. You lose nitrogen, you lose body weight. The third is that many patients, and it depends on the literature you read some are between ten and thirty per cent of the patients having a lateral thoracotomy, end up with persistent pain.'

So far I was following every word hoping that the next would give me some indication of where Judge Johnson was leading us. I thought he would have mentioned what the extra pressure of the emergency would have placed on my chest wall. As I glanced at my friend I realised just how hard I was squeezing her hand but she had not winced even once.

Judge Johnson continued with further facts and then got to the nub of the case, 'In this case criticism of the defendant by the plaintiff is that the second port which was placed by the defendant through the main portion of the plaintiff's breast caused a bleed which was perfectly foreseeable. This resulted in the conversion to an ordinary or open thoracotomy as a result of which the plaintiff was exposed to post-thoracotomy pain syndrome and from which she now suffers.'

Then, after presenting further evidence from Mr Arthur Makey and Professor Smith he added, in relation to the question of liability, 'Having regard to the fact that the negligence claimed in this case relates solely to the positioning of the ports I am quite satisfied that Professor Smith is well qualified to give evidence in this regard. In this regard the first port according, to the medical notes, was inserted in a manner which caused no difficulty whatsoever. The insertion of the second port 2.5 cm lateral to the right nipple was the one that caused the difficulty.

'The medical notes indicate that in the course of the insertion of the second port the defendant struck the internal mammary vessel which caused a bleed as a result of which the defendant had to convert from VATS to the open thoracic surgery procedure. The defendant indicated that this mammary vessel was out of position.

'Both Mr Smith and Mr Mackey, another expert on behalf of the plaintiff who had done many operations on the chest, were astonished to find that the internal mammary vessel was in the position which the defendant says it was but was not in the least bit surprised to find that there was another vessel which would have caused a bleed having regard to the extremely vascular structure which is the breast.

'They both held that, and swore that, under no circumstances should this port have been placed where it was, namely, right in the middle of the breast. The experts were quite clear that the defendant was perfectly correct once the bleed occurred it was correct to switch to open thoracic surgery. However, it is quite clear from the evidence of Mr Smith and Mr Makey that, had the port not been placed in that position, there would have been no need to switch over and it was the sworn evidence of the experts that the present plaintiff's condition is caused by the open thoracotomy and the necessity to switch to it.

'It is quite clear from their evidence that under no circumstances whatsoever should a port have been placed in the breast in the position in which it was and no justification whatsoever could be made for placing it in that position.

'In dealing with the defendant's response to this evidence it is necessary to look at a number of documents and other matters which were produced during the case. The first item is the operating sheet filled in at the time of the operation which indicated that the second port was put in 2.5 cm lateral to the nipple and it went on to say that this port hit the interior mammary vessels which were in an aberrant position and there was a loss of blood.

'When confronted with this fact initially by Mr Boylan, that is the solicitor for the plaintiff, when the defendant phoned him, and when Mr Boylan pointed out the operation notes indicating that the damage from the second port was caused through the vessel, was 2.5 cm lateral to the nipple the defendant's immediate reaction was to dispute that the port had been inserted in such a position and that the operation notes must be wrong. When it was pointed out to him that the photographic evidence indicating a scar exactly where his operation notes indicated he had put the port, the defendant accounted for this by stating that this could have been the mark of a chest drain.'

I keenly remember Mr Lynch also stating, under oath, during Denis's cross-examination, that it was the main thoracotomy scar.

'The document which indicated in what apparently is the defendant's own script that he had struck the mammary vessel which was in an inappropriate place figured in the case, when the defendant attempted to suggest to Mr McCullough, counsel for the plaintiff, that in fact the document read "query mammary vessel".

'It is quite clear that at this point the defendant attempted to introduce a false or fabricated document by having it altered to include a squiggle which he said was a query. That squiggle did not appear on the original nor on the copies which had been provided to Mr McCullough or to the court. The defendant then attempted to brush off this matter as irrelevant.

However, it is quite clear that the documents in the main had been Photostatted, whereas the document produced by the defendant, which was retained on the court file had clearly been altered by what appeared to be a biro as the indentation of the squiggle is visible to the naked eye.

'It was most unusual to have the defendant conduct his own case and initially I thought many aspects of the defendant's attitude to the court might be put down to naivety. However, as a result of a number of incidents which took place in the course of the case which I will detail my views have changed.'

Oh thank God, I almost burst out; Judge Johnson has seen the truth. Can I dare believe it? It was incredible, and suddenly and involuntarily my body visibly relaxed as tension was released and slowly effused. I eventually let go of the vice-like grip I had of my friend's hand only to see that her knuckles were white. Can I dare hope that Mr Lynch will not only be found negligent but that his negligence caused the extremely serious injuries I have been suffering since his incompetent surgery?

'It was only in my own presence and in the presence of the two experts for the plaintiff, when the defendant was actually presented with the plaintiff's breast and the scar, he finally admitted that it was where the second port had been put.

'On the 3rd of July 1996 the defendant wrote a letter to Dr Duignan the plaintiff's general practitioner indicating in the third paragraph thereof: "A video-assisted thoracoscopy was done on the 5th of June 1996. That night she developed a massive bleed as she had an aberrant internal mammary artery in the right chest wall." Quite clearly, this letter was in contradiction to the notes of the operation. The defendant initially said he had never written it and then, when it was quite clear that he had written it, he indicated that there were only two words wrong with it and namely where it said "that night".

'All through the case the defendant continually referred to the level of the intake of drugs of the plaintiff. He appeared to ignore the fact that the drugs which the plaintiff got were prescribed by doctors. The defendant then relied great emphasis on the fact that the plaintiff had been suffering pain before the operation.

'He appeared to be completely unaware of the fact that it was for the purpose of the removal of the pain which she was suffering that the plaintiff was undergoing the operation. Then in the course of his conversation with Mr Boylan he indicated that the plaintiff's problems may have come from some other source namely her personality.

'Then, in the course of giving his own defence, the defendant indicated that the second port was inserted for the purposes of looking up and down the chest cavity. This was a completely new suggestion which had never been put or made under any circumstances to the plaintiff's experts and in my view demonstrated nothing short of dishonesty on behalf of the defendant.

'The defendant then went on to say that in reality the VATS operation was not as good as the old-fashioned open thoracotomy and in a bizarre piece of evidence towards the end of this evidence he indicated that the people who sell the equipment will tell you anything for the purposes of selling.

'This particular turn of events where the defendant was now, so to speak, reneging on the effectiveness of the VATS procedure which he himself had introduced into Ireland, he said that it was not as good as the old operation, demonstrated to me that, what I had thought initially had been naivety was far from it.

'I had the opportunity of watching the defendant (a) conduct his own case and (b) give evidence and (c) be subject to cross-examination and at the end of the case I came to the conclusion and I am satisfied that when it came to a dispute on questions of fact I would not accept the defendant's evidence on any of the facts which were in dispute between the parties.

'The words which may be displayed on the transcript are only part of the case, and the body language which emanated from the defendant demonstrated to my mind, with absolute clarity, where the truth of this case lay. Therefore I am satisfied that in accordance with the plaintiff's case that the defendant was negligent in placing the second port in the breast where he did, caused the transfer to the emergency thoracotomy. This exposed the plaintiff to a danger of pain to which she should not have been exposed and she has suffered that pain. I am satisfied that this pain was suffered as the result of the negligence of the defendant.'

Had I heard correctly? Judge Johnson did not believe 'any' of Mr Lynch's evidence? None of his lies, contradictions and fabricated stories saved him. I never quite believed that I could get justice in a court of law but unless my mental capacity had diminished completely, Judge Johnson had just delivered it. He had heard everything, he had witnessed everything and now he had spoken it. My, my. The clarity of his understanding of the entire make-up of Mr Lynch was quite extraordinary in my opinion; he had got it so right.

Negligent. That word, so powerful and so damning and to hear it from the mouth of the President of the High Court meant that no matter what happened in the future it would be written down for posterity. Mr Lynch was tried and convicted in a court of law.

I knew, from having heard about other awards having been granted to patients, that I would be lucky to even recover what I had paid out since June of 1996. Because Mr Lynch would have to pay the award out of his own pocket, I wondered whether Judge Johnson would take that into consideration, regardless of what wealth he had amassed.

Even at that moment I was vividly conscious of the fact that I had only won the first battle. Mr Lynch, if he had not been out for retribution before, was certainly going to go on a rampage after this and I was going to have to now face the supreme court.

From sheer and overwhelming relief, I almost burst out sobbing. Instead, I closed my eyes again while Judge Johnson read further from his statement in relation to the case law he had referred to in determining the award of liability.

He stated that I had, indeed, suffered greatly as a result of that negligent operation and said that, 'After the operation the plaintiff woke in great pain and discomfort and has continued to be in pain and discomfort ever since. Despite a number of treatments for this pain, none have been effective to date. She has been treated by Dr Declan O'Keeffe a pain specialist who has conducted two rhizotomies on her and also she has undergone a long and sustained course of physiotherapy to cope with the disability from which she now suffers.'

He summarised the effect it had on my career and all the social and sporting interests I had no choice but to relinquish and the most important thing of all was my inability 'to continue her piano playing at which she was a very proficient performer.'

At that moment I felt a surge of tremendous satisfaction knowing that Judge Johnson had accepted what I had sworn in the witness box and, in addition, the witnesses who appeared for me. Nearing the end of his judgement he summed up, 'the effects of the pain from which she now suffers as a result of the negligence of the defendant have totally altered and changed her life.

'The evidence is uncontradicted from Dr O'Keeffe that she will continue to have right-sided chest wall pain for the rest of her life. It has been suggested that a spinal cord stimulator might be inserted but the plaintiff is reluctant to have any further surgery and I quite understand that. With regard to the future I think on the balance of probabilities the evidence indicated the plaintiff is never going to be pain free and is highly unlikely to get back to the level of earnings which she was at prior to this incident.'

Judge Johnson concluded, 'She will continue in the future to have permanent consequences of a disabling nature.' And with that he announced the award. While I was absolutely delighted I had won the case, after adding up all the expenses of my medical and physiotherapy care and the trial, net loss of earnings for the period of my rehabilitation and the sum I would have to return to the VHI, I was left with a fraction of what I would have earned to sustain me for the remainder of my life.

If I did not recover I would lose up to one and a half million euro gross salary to age sixty-five, all else being equal, and I had no pension to speak of. I wondered what Mr Lynch's annual pension was now paying him in comparison.

I was so grateful we had won the case and I came out of it with some security and having recouped my losses that I did not dwell on the rightness or wrongness of the actual award. If I had dared allow myself to think about it, I could have been sitting in that courtroom, on that day, having lost everything I had clung onto and could have ended up putting my head into my hands, as I remember Professor Keogh doing, and seemingly mouthing the words, 'Oh, no.' I could have been left financially bereft with no funds to spend on my future healthcare. It was over, the end of the first leg of the crooked road with its bends and twists and turns. I could not see around the corner and I did not want to go there that day.

Mr Lynch's counsel, Mr Nugent, rose and asked Judge Johnson to grant a stay on the award pending the outcome of the appeal. It was sanctioned on the condition that Mr Lynch pay a sum of one hundred thousand euro to me immediately. Nothing surprising there, I thought. Given that Mr Lynch now faced a personal bill of not only my award but legal fees in addition, an amount I could not even begin to imagine, so much time and energy had been put into my case, I felt he would do just about anything to avoid paying one cent.

I had not been out for revenge nor felt any hate, although I cannot deny that I felt justice had been well served, but it was so tenuous given that I faced the appeal and I could not allow myself to close the book on it. Judge Johnson had given his verdict, we all stood up and my knees buckled. I did not have the least desire to even glance to see if Mr Lynch was in the courtroom but I felt if he had been he had probably scampered off, not wishing to show his face. It was not for the first time I thought that, ultimately, a bully is usually a coward.

As we filed out of Court Number Two, I was in a daze. People kept congratulating me and yet I could see no reason for celebrating. This was not the national lottery. I was not cured and I had no idea what I faced in the future. My only emotion was pure and unmitigated relief and I was deathly tired. When we all gathered in the Round Hall I did not know what to say to Michael, Denis and Karen. 'Thank you' just did not convey enough.

They had been through so much themselves and had probably never experienced such a case before. I will always remember Michael telling me that I did not seem excited at the verdict and I felt terrible about that. I tried to explain to him that I was so drained from it all and knowing that Mr Lynch would appeal it, I could not seem to muster up any energy to adequately portray just how grateful I was for all their unyielding support. Unusually, words had failed me.

As we were leaving the Round Hall, Eileen Whelan, a presenter with Raidió Teilifís Éireann (RTE), approached me and introduced herself. She asked me if I would be willing to give her an interview and TV3 followed suit. I had always been an admirer of Eileen and I would have given just about anything to relay the whole horrid saga if its release would help put a system in place so that patients who are injured through negligence could obtain answers to their questions without having to go through such a terrible and aggressive litigious route.

Even having gone through such a route I still failed to know what had happened to me in that theatre. So, with great regret, it being difficult to hold my tongue, I told her that it would not be prudent to give an interview since an appeal was forthcoming and I did not wish to give Mr Lynch any ammunition for it. If he were to lose his appeal I would be more than happy to give the interview. Who knew in which direction the gale force wind would now blow?

Much to my amazement, Eileen warned me that it would not be possible to escape the media attention as the photographers were on the roof. Good grief, I thought, this was not something I had had time to consider. Having been cloistered in the courtroom in my own little niche, I had forgotten the outside world and how important and unprecedented my case was because of Mr Lynch. I told her that we were going to the basement café as we badly needed coffee and scones and I would notify her several minutes before I was due to leave; that was the least I could do.

Since now there was no avoiding the media, I thought I might as well go out the main doors and because I was going to be filmed I felt I had better check to ensure I had no smudges on my face. I was used to doing my own hair and make-up and I felt great that I still had a measure of vanity left. But, again, as I took a superficial backward glance in the mirror I looked as if I had not a care in the world and was in full health. But, again, I dismissed the observation.

An hour or so had passed before I informed Eileen that I was prepared to leave in five minutes, to allow her time to pass the word. I took several deep breaths and managed to convince myself that it was just like another piano performance or business presentation and I was about to face an audience. So now, without one look backwards, I put on a relaxed front and as broad a smile as I could.

I had this strange feeling as if I was walking in slow motion, towards the double doors, not knowing what was on the other side. My left hand went up and I pulled the handle to open the door. As a gap appeared I walked out and was immediately and intensely blinded by flashlights. There were so many I was startled and almost stumbled backwards having to brace myself before I attempted to walk down the steps with composure. I had had no idea of the enormity of the situation. It was like a sea of photographers and then the cameras began rolling. Another experience to add to my curriculum vitae, I mused; all in a day's work.

Finally, having been photographed and filmed, we went for lunch up the quays completely unaware that the outcome of the case was already on the one o'clock news. My phone began to ring signalling the first of many calls. It was going to take considerable time for the verdict to sink in and it was absolute relief knowing that whatever transpired next and no matter how much and how well Mr Lynch denied the facts, Judge Johnson's words were indelibly written down in his judgement and I would have them forever.

When my father and I arrived home all the news channels were reporting the outcome of the case, Mr Lynch's solicitors coming off record and that he had represented himself. It was also broadcast that he had altered the evidential copy of my operation record. RTE went into it a little further and, of course, all the national papers carried the story the following day.

All I could think of at the end of that day, having taken my phone off the hook, was to get down to our family home in County Wexford for a peaceful break. As my bedroom is on the entire top floor of the back wing of the house, whenever I close the door absolutely no one can hear me nor I anyone else; all one can hear is complete and comforting silence. As soon as I arrived, I collapsed into my bed with a cup of tea on my side table, put on an Andrea Bocelli disc, and my parents were completely unaware that I was crying in private with gut wrenching force, finally pouring out all the emotion I had been carrying. I did not want to upset them.

The last time I had sobbed like that was when I left the hospital in June 1996 on my brother's shoulder. Now, for the first time, I allowed myself to indulge in self-pity, not only for everything I had lost in my life but for the next battle I was going to have to face, in only a fraction of my health. There was no way out; I was well and truly trapped.

Chapter Twenty-Three

The most important antecedence I had on my mind upon my return to Dublin, having had plenty of rest, regular walks in the open countryside and a reprieve from the ongoing stress, was to write to Michael. I wanted to properly convey my appreciation and to thank him adequately for his unquestionable competence, professionalism and the dedication he, Denis and Karen had shown to win my case. Regardless of the outcome of the appeal and what the future held in store for me now, I would never rescind a word I wrote in my letter. If the unthinkable supervened, I certainly would not be laying the blame at their door.

My greatest and most immediate concern in relation to the appeal was that Mr Lynch would try to resolutely delay and drag it out as long as possible with retarding force, especially since Judge Johnson had approved the stay on a large portion of the award. Almost immediately, Mr Lynch's solicitor, the same Mr Hayes, informed Michael that he was serving a notice of appeal to the supreme court against the 'entire' order and judgement of the first trial. An agreement was reached between them that we would not contest it if the supreme court would fix the earliest possible date to hear the appeal, hopefully in September of that year, an overly sanguine expectation I believed. The entreaty was sanctioned on June the 28th, which meant I was not to receive a cent pending its outcome.

For me haste and urgency at this stage were far more importantly prominent in my mind than monitory considerations. I was enormously concerned it would be the distant future before the appeal was heard, however, because Mr Lynch's counsel had not represented him throughout the trial, they had no transcripts. Yet again, I was to endure further postponement while Mr Lynch's needs were met.

I mulled over how his legal team was going to prepare and construct his appeal given that the transcripts were mine and had cost me a staggering sum of two and a half thousand euro. Then much to my chagrin, Mr Hayes requested a full set of the transcripts from Michael without having to pay for them. It is apparently professional courtesy for this to be done and because I trusted Michael, I just had to accede to it. I must say, however, I found this particularly plaguy, galling and acutely ironic. I could well be providing the rope to the hangman for my own execution. But what else could I do except swallow it? Mr Lynch was really having it every way. If I had not been angry before, now I was furious.

In mid-September, Michael forwarded me a copy of the submitted appeal document and my counsel's response to it. Mr Lynch, not surprisingly, propounded no less than ten basis of appeal including, 'That the trial was conducted by the Learned Trial Judge in such a manner as made it impossible for the defendant to conduct his defence properly (and ultimately at all); That the Learned Trial Judge did not give the defendant a fair trial; That the Learned Trial Judge misdirected himself in law in concluding that there was evidence upon which he could conclude that the defendant was negligent; That the Learned Trial Judge was wrong in law in holding that the ill effects alleged to be suffered by the plaintiff were the consequence of any negligence of the defendant.' And so on and so forth.

It seemed to me they just tossed every conceivable argument into the melting pot hoping to make soup out of it. Mr Lynch, I was adamant, would give tongue to and enounce a caboodle of hypercriticisms to secure a retrial and efface the judgement of medical negligence, saving himself a fortune in the process.

I perused my own counsel's response and I must declare they presented such a cogent and convincing refutation of every citation in the appeal and provided so many examples that I failed to even consider that Mr Lynch could succeed. While Michael is not one to give false hope, I got the impression that he did not think the appeal would be fruitful either. None of us was arrogantly confident and one could not even risk prognosticating what the supreme court judges would do. I prepared myself for another extended wait.

***

Having prolonged my year off work for rehabilitation another two months to the 4th of June 2002, I disquietly and with unease put myself back into my role wondering if all the rehabilitation had made a substantial difference. However, gradually the whole weakness of my entire chest wall began to betray me and the strain and tension only exacerbated the intercostal nerve pain. My stamina began to wax and wane and I found myself regressing, and I finally collapsed. I discerned and understood very well then that 'the writing was on the wall', but facing it was extremely difficult as it was the last vestige of my former life I had yet to lose.

I had been far too optimistic during the trial that I would eventually overcome my physical disabilities but underplaying things was my nature and I was also still suspended in a kind of disbelief. Come January 2003, I finally succumbed and had to relinquish my long and hard fought-for career and substantial salary. I was terribly sad and with that, the remaining piece of cliff finally broke away along with the houses and they smashed onto the rocks far below, scattering their ruins.

I strived to hang on to the belief, however, that one day, with the rapid advances in technology, and allowing a little more time to ease my grave apprehension of placing my life in someone else's hands, something would be effective in giving me some reprieve from the constant and debilitating neuropathic pain. I had succeeded in rebuilding my physical structure to a certain extent but the nerve damage kept driving me demented. Never having a break from it was such gruelling going.

Unfortunately my right hand still did not function properly and would gnarl up frequently and, of course, I would never be rid of the awful and unnecessary scarring. I was going to try and rebuild those houses into a different style rather than allow the strong, uncaring waters drag the remnants out to sea.

In the meantime, for distraction, I decided to immerse myself in academia; it would keep my mind occupied and focused. My body may have been terribly damaged but I still hoped I had a few 'little grey cells' left functioning. And with that, I decided to update my master of business administration courses for the contemporary business world. Availing of that opportunity was going to be the smartest thing I could have done at that stage. I could work it around my continued rehabilitation programme and keep my mind and body moving ardently forward.

Since I always had a predilection towards academia and its related necessity to study, that love was something I could now fall back on to keep me going. Regardless of the outcome of the appeal, I still had a life to live and I could not function unless my brain was working positively on something productive and worthwhile. Even if I could never use it again to produce an income, any further education, I believed, would never be a waste.

***

The New Year 2003 turned a new page in another stage of my life but there was still no sign of a date for the appeal hearing. January turned into February and then into March and as I was about to make contact, Michael telephoned me to let me know that the trial was finally fixed for the 25th, barring any application for an adjournment by Mr Lynch. I could not foretell on what grounds he could stall or postpone it but then, I would never have suspected he would have said his own operation sheet must be wrong either.

A week before the hearing, I stayed with my parents in order to distract my mind and not ponder on a possible negative outcome of the appeal. My father, for the first and only time could not come that day so my mother was going to accompany me in lieu. I was rather apprehensive about her being in the courtroom because one has to listen to all sorts of unpleasant questions and comments and she was unused to it. So there I was, on the 25th of March 2003, having to go back into the Four Courts and it felt like 'Groundhog Day'.

When we all arrived at the Four Courts, and after introductions, we were directed to a modern courtroom. To my utter disappointment, it had a stuffy and claustrophobic feel to it. It had lower ceilings, none of the ornate ambience of the original courtroom and was much smaller. I was glad I was not going to have to spend two weeks in it. I did not see Mr Lynch that morning but just in case he arrived, we sat in the back pew.

For some unknown reason, I had assumed three judges would hear the appeal but as the court rose in session five appeared and immediately my instinct told me, I do not know why, it was a very bad omen. Before that day, I had time to consider the consequences for the medical profession of a surgeon being found guilty of altering or adding to a hospital record. That was my only fear as I faced the Supreme Court Justices. Thus I sat back and braced myself as Chief Justice Keane opened the proceedings. I cannot remember exactly how long the hearing lasted but from the way the grilling of the barristers was going it appeared to me the issue the judges concentrated on more than any other was the alteration to Mr Lynch's evidential copy of my operation sheet. I was not surprised as it would have had huge implications for the medical profession and, therefore, I felt certain that no investigation would be conducted in relation to whether a surgeon made a premeditated change to a hospital record.

Whatever else was asked was only sporadic, as I recall, and I knew that Mr Lynch was going to get away somehow with the judgement made against him being overturned. I paid particular attention to Chief Justice Keane's questions and I inherently knew my immediate fate was sealed.

My mother was restless beside me and I knew she had become very anxious. I remember having to whisper to her, in order to calm her, that Mr Lynch was going to get a retrial and that it was all right; there was no need to worry. I cannot say it was a fait accompli, since it was only speculation on my part, but that was how I felt. As I listened, my mind thought back to my counsel's response to the appeal document. I recalled some very important references Denis and Karen had included in relation to the advantage the trial judge has over the appellate court if he has been able to hear, see and witness so much more than what had been transcribed. It seemed so apt and appropriate in my case:

'It is clear from the Judgement of the Trial Judge that he did not accept the credibility of the Defendant' [Unreported Judgement, page 8, 1st paragraph]. It was not just the demeanour of the witness which resulted in this but also the inconsistencies in his explanations which are outlined in the Judgement, O'Higgins C.J. in Northern Bank Finance .v. Charlton [1979] IR 149 reiterated the traditional difficulty which an Appellate Court finds in estimating the credibility of witnesses from written depositions he cited with approval Lindley MR in the Court of Appeal Coughlan .v. Coughlan [1898] I CH 704 as follows:

"When as often happens, much turns on the relative credibility of witnesses who have been examined and cross-examined before the judge, the court is sensitive of the great advantage he has in seeing and hearing them. It is often difficult to estimate correctly the relative credibility of witnesses from written depositions and when the question arises which witness is to be believed rather than another and that question turns on manner and demeanour, the Court of Appeal always is and must be guided by the impression made on the judge who saw the witnesses."

Further, "[a] Judge's findings on fact can and will be reviewed on appeal. Such findings will be subjected to the normal tests as to whether they are supported by the evidence given at the trial. If such findings are firmly based on the sworn testimony of witnesses seen and heard and accepted by the judge, then the Court of Appeal, recognising this to be an area of credibility, they will not interfere." (O'Higgins CJ in Northern Bank Finance .v. Charlton [1979] IR 149 at Page 180) .

I remember Judge Johnson himself specifically stating in his judgement, 'The words which may be displayed on the transcript are only part of the case, and the body language which emanated from the defendant demonstrated to my mind, with absolute clarity, where the truth of this case lay.' I wondered what the supreme court judges would have made of Mr Lynch's attempted assault on my person, sequestered under their own roof so to speak, if they had witnessed him lunging at me and his startling attempts to cover-up the fact that he had operated through my breast. I had been right when thinking going to court guarantees no justice.

When the hearing concluded, I joined my legal team at the back of the courtroom and we discussed what we had gleaned from it. While Michael, Denis and Karen used words of encouragement, I did not believe any of them felt confident that Mr Lynch would lose the appeal and I remember vividly my opinion regarding Chief Justice Keane.

I felt dejected but resigned leaving the Four Courts that day but there was nothing anyone could do now; I had to accept the inevitable. I would be extremely surprised if it were to go my way. I only hoped that the supreme court judges would deliver their verdict with some urgency and surprisingly it was rather quick; the 15th of May was set for judgement day.

Still another birthday passed but this time I paid no attention to it. I wondered how many more were to come before the ultimate conclusion of my case. All I could do at this stage was to keep faith with my grandfather that he would help me through the day and keep my chin up after the supreme court's decision was announced.

As sunrise loomed close on the 15th, the last thing I wanted to do was venture near the courts but, of course, I did. I do not believe I have ever been a coward and I would face the worst in the same way as I faced the best. It was very important for me to be there with my legal team and to show them that no matter how hard it got, I would not falter in my determination. My father was back in situ by my side and, again, we revisited our usual haunt for our usual pick-me-up. The time came, however, when we could not put off getting to the Four Courts any longer.

We took our seats in the courtroom and I was not in the least nervous or downhearted because I was resigned to the inevitable. The judges appeared, Chief Justice Keane delivered the judgement and I heard the expected nails being driven into my coffin, 'I would allow the appeal, set aside the judgement and order of the high court and order a retrial.'

When we exited the courtroom it was with purposeful intention that Karen, my father and I walked leisurely down one of the myriad of corridors to discuss our armoury for the third battle of wills. Then startlingly, Mr Lynch appeared out of nowhere and what he did was so reprehensible, undignified and vicious that I could only gape at him stupefied.

He had surreptitiously tracked me down and began to walk back and forth past me, within whispering distance, gloating with the ugliest smirk I had ever seen on anyone's face. The only thing he achieved was to act out his contempt. He was obviously exultant and getting vengeful satisfaction from it.

Every time I had thought Mr Lynch had done his worst I was constantly amazed again. As he continued to perform his grotesque antics with great gusto, unfortunately for him he absolutely failed to get any reaction or satisfaction from me. I kept looking at him aghast and incredulous, thinking he was very unstable and my only emotion was one of disgust. He was acting as if my case had been struck out and he was free to go.

Not for the first time did he miss the point: he had to face another trial and all his previous lies and intimidating behaviour would catch up with him and come crashing down with the full force of a ton of bricks. Now I had absolutely nothing to fear about the case itself and I was very confident I would win the retrial. Not only that but I was going to have another opportunity to testify. I do not know how many times I had found that he lacked intelligence and foresight; he seemed to be only interested in immediate gratification. What did he think, that I was still going to 'go away'?

Yes, the supreme court used its authority to stamp out the verdict of medical negligence. Yes, you have saved a fortune and yes, you will not now face a possible investigation into your alteration of one of the key facts of my case. However, Mr Lynch, the supreme court has not said you are innocent of negligence either. All I have to do now is start again with a new blank slate but there will be substantially more damning evidence added to it this time.

As all this was pounding and racing through my mind, Mr Lynch disappeared and when I thought he had become exhausted by his juvenile posturing, he returned sprightly in front of us but this time almost dragging the photographer, who I despised, with him and began pointing me out. *I sardonically chuckled, you need not have bothered, Mr Lynch; he already knows me.* All I could think of was that he was devoid of any decency whatsoever and, unfortunately for him, he had just given me fair warning of his sinister intentions.

When the duo in arms finally put down their swords and left, Michael's assistant joined us and we devised a plan to foil Mr Lynch's attempts to have me harassed. He went off to bring his car through the perimeter of the Four Courts and before my father and I left, Michael joined us and we advised him of Mr Lynch's despicable behaviour.

As I sat in the car I stared straight ahead with a blank expression on my face and out of the corner of my eye, I saw the shocked look on the photographer's face when he realised I had thwarted his obvious intentions. I could well imagine he was probably livid. Mr Lynch had failed but was he not the coward who would not show his face after Judge Johnson had delivered his verdict? As the car distanced itself from the photographer, I allowed myself a guilty little giggle; I felt I owed myself that at least.

Not long after the supreme court's decision, Michael forwarded a copy of the judgement document and when I read the rationales for invoking a retrial I was dumbfounded. As I thought, the main reason was that Judge Johnson should have given Mr Lynch the benefit of the doubt regarding the altering of his evidential copy of the operation notes.

The Chief Justice made his summation, 'The conclusion is unavoidable, in my view, that this trial was unsatisfactory and that there must be a retrial. In the circumstances, it is unnecessary to come to any conclusion on the other grounds of appeal in relation to both liability and damages relied upon the defendant. I am conscious of the difficulty that a new trial will create for the plaintiff in circumstances which are none of her making. However, it is essential that in any case, but particularly in a case of such importance to both the plaintiff and the defendant, that the trial is conducted in a manner which, objectively viewed, can be regarded as fair to both parties. That did not happen here.'

It certainly did not. If anyone received a fair trial, it was Mr Lynch. He lied throughout the trial and I told the truth yet I endured all the negative consequences of Mr Lynch's litany of trumped-up stories, lies and absolutely no reverence for the rules of the court.

While I could do nothing but accept the supreme court's verdict, I felt extremely disappointed not only for myself but also for my legal team and counsel in addition. As for Judge Johnson, I was particularly dismayed. He had initially put down Mr Lynch's behaviour to naivety and gave him every assistance. It was only as the trial progressed did he change his mind. I actually felt great sympathy for him as he saw the whole truth.

I wondered just how exactly my rights had been protected in all this sordid quagmire of litigation and having to face a retrial. Then, just as I was thinking I could never be shocked again, I was to be in the frame of a terrible and devastating announcement from the supreme court that would test the nerves and mental capacity of the strongest person. On the morning of the 21st of May, Murphy's Law reared its ugly head again. Michael telephoned me and, when I answered, I knew immediately something dreadful had happened. I sat down quickly in anticipation of bad news; I knew by his voice it was ominous. He proceeded to tell me that the supreme court had made a decision in relation to the costs of the appeal and then the bombshell: they landed me with Mr Lynch's costs and, of course, my own.

I sat there astonished with nervous tension, as I could not understand the logic of it. Michael did not appear to have a rational explanation for it either. It had far-reaching consequences because even if I were to win the retrial I would still have to pay that bill. I could not take it in that on the one hand the supreme court totally blamed Judge Johnson for the circumstances leading to the retrial yet I was the one who suffered all the dastardly consequences, and I felt my hands had been severely slapped. As I thought back to everything I had been subjected to by Mr Lynch and now this, I was reeling with nausea and despair.

An awful black cloud congealed around me and once I overcame the terrible shock of Michael's pronouncement, I gathered up the courage to ask him what, in his estimation, Mr Lynch's costs would be. Then I gasped, approximately fifty thousand euro. I panicked as there was one thing that I was very frightened and certain of: if I was forced to pay the costs immediately, I would have to put my home up for sale.

When I told everyone this latest account of events not one person could understand it or the fairness of it; every person thought I had misunderstood. So here I was, already down a personal fortune and how having to pay Mr Lynch's appeal costs and all my witnesses and other expenses a second time. If Judge Johnson's award was a benchmark and I won again, I would probably come out of it with very little or at a loss since I owed the legal fees for the first trial and the appeal. However, my brain refused to contemplate losing the next trial; it was seemingly protecting itself. I had to keep going just to pay my bills and the heavy serrated trap was now well secured and began to tighten its stranglehold.

Chapter Twenty-Four

I was so appreciatively glad it was summertime after the fallout. Problems seem to be more bearable when the sun is shining and, since August was soon approaching, the courts would be closing down for a recess. Once I had a reprieve from all the turmoil, my situation appeared more tolerable. I had to continue to keep faith with my legal team to let it all work out for me in the end. Everyone who supported me during the first trial would help see me through the next and as long as I kept my intensive rehabilitation going, I hoped to be able to maintain my stamina.

Events took a new turn. Mr Hayes asked Michael to postpone making an application for a court date for the retrial because he was attempting to lobby Mr Lynch's insurers to come back on board and insure him. Apparently, Mr Lynch had certain senior consultants trying to persuade the MDU to do this. I knew then I could be waiting well into 2004 for my case to get to trial. How much older was I going to get? Michael acceded to the request as long as there was no question of Mr Lynch pursuing his legal costs immediately, which now I did not have to pay before November at the earliest, which was at least something.

While Mr Lynch's needs were being indulged again and I was waiting anxiously, I wondered how I could continue to assist Michael with the retrial. There had to be something and I was suddenly struck with a brainwave. Of course. Why had I not thought of it before?' Mr Lynch must have published articles in medical journals on the subject of VATS and I decided to search the internet.

In his sworn testimony and cross-examination, he reneged on both the effectiveness and much reduced trauma and level of pain of VATS over open surgery. I wanted to focus on finding discrepancies and conflicting statements between his sworn evidence in the witness box and any published articles. If there was anything, surely that, in my opinion would be perjurous.

It did not take me very long to find the first article which was co-authored by M Loubani and V Lynch of the Thoracic Surgery Unit, St.

Vincent's Hospital, Elm Park, Dublin 4, by *The Journal of Respiratory Medicine* (2000) 94, 888-890. The title of the article read, 'Video-assisted thoracoscopic bullectomy and acromycin pleurodesis: an effective treatment for spontaneous pneumothorax.' This was significantly opportune and ideal given that it was published even before the first trial commenced.

As I read through the article, the first contradiction to Mr Lynch's sworn testimony struck me forcefully, 'VATS has become the more acceptable method of the treatment of spontaneous pneumothorax since it avoids many of the complications and morbidity associated with thoracotomy while achieving the same results in terms of recurrence. It is well tolerated by patients and results in less respiratory dysfunction and trauma than a thoracotomy. VATS is also more cost-effective in treating patients with first time or recurrent spontaneous pneumothorax with less morbidity.' *My gosh, I thought, this is high carat gold dust and is completely different from his sworn testimony.*

I was perturbed and confused when I discovered the following, 'The great advantage of VATS is the fact that frequently it is easy to visualise blebs that cannot be seen on a chest x-ray or CT scan of the chest.' *So how could he not detect my artery and steer clear of it?*

Then the clincher presented itself. In relation to the placement of the ports Mr Lynch stated, for a study of forty-nine patients, 'The lung was collapsed and a 12 mm port was introduced in the sixth intercostal space at the mid-axillary line. Two other ports (5 mm and 12 mm) were introduced in the fourth intercostal space and the anterior and posterior axillary lines.'

Oh dear God, Mr Lynch, that is the 'triangle of safety' you told Professor Smith during the trial you did not hold with. What were you doing, putting a port through my breast? Even your third port was placed incorrectly, right up under my scapula. I wonder how you are going to get out of this enormous predicament in the next trial. I felt as if the article had assailed me. What a discovery.

I soon discovered a second article published in the 2002 April-June edition of the *Irish Journal of Medical Science*, titled, 'Thoracoscopic Management of Primary Spontaneous Pneumothorax' co-authored by SS Connolly, C Hurson and V Lynch, again from the Thoracic Surgery Unit, St. Vincent's University Hospital, Dublin. At the end of the article it says, 'All correspondence to Mr V Lynch.' I was absolutely gagging to read it and I was not disappointed.

'VATS is the preferred option for the surgical management of primary spontaneous pneumothorax (PSP).' And as I read on, I was completely astonished, 'Thoracotomy, however, is associated with morbidity. Almost all of this morbidity is associated with the incision and rib spreading producing post-operative pain and scarring. VATS avoids major muscle division, rib spreading and neurovascular damage. Thoracoscopy has less post-thoracotomy pain and post-operative respiratory dysfunction,' *another major sworn contradiction.*

No wonder I was left in such a mess after the emergency thoracotomy. *How could you sit there Mr Lynch, in that witness box, knowing you published one article and you were going to publish another totally refuting your sworn testimony and your answers to Denis's questions during cross-examination? You had no fear, whatsoever, did you, of the consequences of perjurious lies?*

As I had been reading the second article something I thought that was very peculiar caught and grabbed my attention. It stated, 'A review was undertaken of one hundred and thirteen consecutive cases of PSP involving one hundred and eight patients, all managed with a VATS approach in a single thoracic unit by a single surgeon between 1992 and 1997. All the information was retrieved from the medical records department.' This must include my surgery, I thought, because it was performed in 1996 and I had exactly that: a PSP.

The article continued, 'The indication for conversion to open surgery was severe adhesions precluding a clear view in six cases' (which I did not have), 'adhesional bleeding in two patients' (which I did not have) and 'equipment failure in a further two patients' (which did not apply to me). Where was my case included in this study?

I read on, 'Post-operative haemorrhage occurred in two patients, both managed with blebectomy alone, necessitating an open procedure on day one in each.' That did not refer to me either because my artery was lacerated during the VATS procedure not post-operatively. So where was I included in the study? And then I wondered… was it a possibility? My mind was racing.

Was it conceivable that he falsely included my case as one of the two that had 'post-operative' haemorrhage as he had stated in his letter to my GP? Otherwise, I was not included in the statistics at all. The more I thought about it the more I feared this was the case. Good grief, if that was the case, surely both the publishing of an inaccurate study and an inaccurate report to a patient's GP, have to be fraud. Unless, he committed perjury under oath, which I believed to be the case.

I thought these articles were very compelling and with great excitement, I sent them to Michael who believed they would be very useful for the retrial. I chuckled to myself; little does Mr Lynch know what I have just discovered and I hoped that they would prove that he had committed perjury in the first trial.

***

The retrial was finally fixed for the 2nd of December but Mr Hayes objected strenuously to it and was given leave to apply in October to make his objections regarding the trial date. Then, out of the blue, Michael informed me that the elusive powers that be had persuaded Mr Lynch's insurers to reinstate his indemnification and they appointed, again, Arthur Cox & Co. to represent him. If he had only cooperated with them in the first place and not signed a false affidavit, I may have been spared well over two years of the trauma of a horrid litigation case that went horribly wrong.

I had mixed feelings about this of course. The case would be tried in a normal fashion, although by this stage I had forgotten exactly what normality meant. If I won I would not have to pursue Mr Lynch for payment of the award. On the other hand, it would let him off scot-free financially and I thought it very ironic that the solicitors who knew he had sworn a false affidavit were going to represent him again. What confidence did they have in believing anything he told them?

Then, one day, many months after the supreme court appeal, I went out for a stroll in the afternoon and arrived home at around 6 p.m. I retrieved a large brown envelope from my post box from Michael. I made the enormous mistake of not following my own rule: not to open possible contentious post until the following morning so I would not worry all night long and could make relevant telephones calls. I slowly and tentatively opened the envelope and when I read the contents I flopped down onto one of my cream leather sofas in terrible shock.

The bill for Mr Lynch's appeal costs amounted to almost a staggering one hundred and nine thousand euro. Fifty thousand was terrible; one hundred and nine was obscene. I was struck down with a vastly foreboding attack of despondency and sat there in total bewilderment. I was so glad Michael had made the agreement that I would not have to pay the bill until at least November. What was I going to do after that if the retrial was delayed again? And it still stuck in my craw that I was liable for Mr Lynch's costs even if I won the second trial.

Proceedings began to unfold then in full swing and even if I had no choice but to pass yet another Christmas at least the case was not at a standstill. Michael informed me that he had arranged for the reappearance of Professor Smith and Mr Makey along with all my other witnesses for the retrial and decided, to be sure to be sure, and to put an end to this case forever, to obtain another opinion from a third consultant thoracic surgeon in England. Now for the upcoming retrial I was facing even higher costs than the first.

What was really absurd to me was the fact that Mr Lynch's solicitors wanted me reviewed by their own appointed consultant pain specialist and consultant psychiatrist. I found this unmercifully comic because it was definitely putting the horse after the cart. It seemed to me it was all an unpleasant and ludicrous game. I had no choice but to attend them but when I studied their reports nothing contained therein gave me any concerns for the trial; they were very predictable.

In the meantime, I carried on as usual with the various rehabilitation programmes and Dr O'Keeffe, on one of my visits, updated me on the technology that had advanced so much that now the spinal cord stimulator did not have to be placed along the spinal column. I told him I was still too apprehensive about surgery but that I would consider it in about another year when I felt able to cope with it. I knew eventually I would have it inserted since I now began to finally believe that the nerve pain would never burn itself out.

Arthur Cox & Co. informed Michael that they would be seeking discovery of my medical records from Dr Duignan going back *ten* years prior to the surgery. He felt that this was probably at Mr Lynch's insistence and I could imagine he could not wait to pick through all my personal details. The thought of it made me nauseous because of his, in my opinion, excessively aggressive and malevolent personality. What my previous medical history had got to do with the case was irrelevant. I had nothing to worry about in the records but I felt a creepy sensation seep through me.

Michael asked Arthur Cox & Co. to specify the reasons why they were seeking the records and what relevance they had to the issues in the case. In his letter to them he emphasised, 'We make this point to you not trying to be in any way obstructive or uncooperative but you must appreciate that your client, during the currency of these proceedings both before and during the trial has proffered several conflicting and contradictory explanations for the plaintiff's injuries and complaints.

'In the light of this and having regard for the fact that your firm represented the defendant until shortly before the first trial, without ever making a request for voluntary discovery of general practitioner's records, we are somewhat surprised at this request now. Furthermore, we would point out that seeking the records for a ten-year period prior to the surgery, in our view, is excessive.'

He also stressed, 'We would emphasise, however, that the plaintiff under no circumstances will agree to adjourn the action on the grounds that the defendant is now seeking discovery of general practitioner's records at the eleventh hour.' In the end, however, in order to give them absolutely no cause to delay the trial date further, I signed the release form.

***

In October, I received the report from our third expert witness, Mr PB Rajesh, Consultant Thoracic Surgeon of the Birmingham Heartlands Hospital. His report was one of the most detailed and comprehensive I have ever read and it was entirely critical of Mr Lynch's treatment. I knew it would blow his credibility apart.

As I scrutinised Mr Rajesh's opinions in fine detail, certain ones jumped out at me that totally refuted Mr Lynch's sworn evidence. 'She was operated on, on 5.6.96 after what appears to be a sketchy explanation of the operative procedure without any documentation in any of the notes by Mr Lynch himself or any of his team discussing the risks, the benefits and the remote chance of having to convert a video-assisted thoracic procedure to an open thoracotomy. The letter to Dr John Duignan dated 3rd July 1996 was rather scanty.

'The details of her transfer, the procedure and the complication, which she had, are not explicitly described. I am surprised that he states that she had blebs at the apex of the right upper lung instead of calling it the apex of the right upper lobe. He also mentions in his defence regarding catamenia pneumothorax and he does not make any mention of inspecting the diaphragm in either the operation notes or any subsequent letters.' *Yes,*

yes, exactly what Judge Johnson stated in his judgement, that Mr Lynch was dishonest in introducing this newly concocted reason for going through my breast.

The next statement was going to rob Mr Lynch of any credible defence, 'I would like to further comment that I have not personally read or heard during my extensive discussions with various video-assisted thoracoscopic surgeons that to look at the diaphragm one has to pierce the breast tissue and insert a rather medial port for that purpose.'

But the most damning statement of all was that not only was the second port incorrectly inserted through my breast but also the other two ports were put through sites different to Mr Rajesh's practice at the Heartlands Hospital. He went into significant explanation of exactly where all three ports should have been placed, the visualising of the chest, the positioning of the TV monitors, the type of ports used and so on.

As to Mr Lynch's assertion that my artery was aberrant he commented, 'In my own experience of having been a cardiothoracic surgeon for the last twenty years, I have not come across an aberrant internal mammary artery on the chest wall far away from the para-sternal area. Having performed over 700 coronary artery operations, I have never come across this situation. I do believe that it was an error of judgement to place a port 2.5 cm lateral to the nipple, through breast tissue as this has got a major impact on breast pain, as the incision heals with fibrous tissue as well as the further thoracotomy incision, which has resulted in both breast pain and chest wall pain. It is clear from the follow-up notes and notes of various specialists including the neurologist and the pain specialist that she has now got post-thoracotomy pain syndrome.'

There was so much more in his report that portrayed to me how deficient Mr Lynch's skills were and there he had been, lauding himself in the witness box, asserting he was the most experienced VATS surgeon in the country and sickeningly admiring his scars. I could not imagine how he was going to backtrack from the first trial, how he would deal with the subsequent articles I had discovered, three highly experienced consultant cardiothoracic surgeons and all my other witnesses in addition.

We were going to be well armed for the battle but I had already been stung and I was very apprehensive facing the judiciary again. But it was the only way to try to get out of the, if not deadly, strangling trap I was in and the debt had piled high.

Chapter Twenty-Five

As I predicted, 2003 became relegated to the past with this continuing absurdity dangling over me. Mr Lynch's representatives had been scurrying around trying to find an expert thoracic witness to support his surgery. I took courage from it, however, because I did not believe they would have any success.

I had to face, yet again, another deferment to February the 17th 2004. This interim period dragged on monotonously and just when I began to believe that the trial would indeed commence on the 17th, Arthur Cox & Co. tried yet again to secure another extension because they had still failed in their attempts to find an expert witness. This was now becoming an endless pantomime and a very bad one at that. However, due to Michael's continuing pressure, he succeeded in preventing any further delay, much to everyone's relief on my side at least.

Before the retrial, Michael asked me, just to be prepared even though it was irrelevant to my case, if I would give him a list of people who would testify as to my character and could portray the kind of person I was physically before the surgery and the subsequent pain and suffering I experienced. I contacted my closest friends since they were the ones who constantly assisted me afterwards. Of course, my family would have also testified since I had gone from a completely independent person to a dependent one.

However, the one person who knew most about my suffering first hand from the day of the surgery of course, was Edward. He had contacted me sporadically over the years. After talking it over with Michael, I decided to telephone him. I, therefore, rang him and explained the situation. He came to Dublin immediately to discuss the issue of testifying. He said he would be more than willing to do it. I told him it was very unlikely that anyone would be called as the case had nothing to do with my character but at least it was a backup. I asked him if he had ever missed me and his reply was that when he was with me he did not realise just what pressure meant.

In addition, I asked him if he had received my message wishing him a happy Christmas. He told me his fiancé had picked up his messages and went berserk. I responded that if he had let me know he had become engaged I would never have left a message. Before he left that day, I told him if I needed him in court, I would contact him.

***

On the eve of the 17th, my night was filled with fretful sleep disturbance and I was so exhausted the next morning that only pure adrenaline gave me a lift. Again, my father and I stuck rigidly to the routine we had established since the very beginning of the first trial, now over two years and three months. I do not know how I mustered the courage and ability to drag myself to the Four Courts facing another gruelling nightmare and my body was protesting in the only way it knew how; my pain levels were demanding me not to. All I wanted was to see the day out with as much dignity as I could manage.

When we arrived in the Round Hall we were to discover a new phenomenon; there was no judge available to hear my case. I gave my father an incredulous look and we both shook our heads. It became then a matter of frustratingly hanging idly around with time passing slowly through our fingers; there was no sign of movement. My patience began to wane with pain and boredom. Eventually Michael found us a consultation room to wait in and when my father and I were alone it suddenly dawned on me that perhaps there were manoeuvrings going on behind the scenes and the insurers wanted to settle the case.

After I conveyed my suspicions to my father, Denis entered the room, sat down, and informed me that the MDU offered me a sum that was farcical. This had to be the biggest and most insulting jest of all and I began to laugh scornfully at this horrible game of wits. Denis informed me that he did not wish to come in and offer me this absurd figure but the MDU had insisted. The sum would have just about covered my expenses to date for the direct consequences of the surgery and the trial and, needless to say, I declined the offer.

When Denis left the room I commented to my father, 'They have got to be kidding if they think I had won a high court trial, been dragged through the Supreme Court of Appeal, now facing a second trial and settle for less than Judge Johnson had awarded me in the first place. Especially now that I had had to forfeit my career and owed Mr Lynch's costs of one hundred and nine thousand euro.'

I waited again in uneasy anticipation when Denis returned with another offer of double the original offer. The MDU, I felt certain, must have believed I had a meritorious case against Mr Lynch. I had calculated that given my now realistic view of my health, having lost my career and with the monies I would have to fork out in the future for continuing physiotherapy and surgery, even that amount was insufficient and totally unrealistic. Since I still had a mortgage and all household bills to pay, cleaners to hire, taxis when I could not drive and many more outlays because I could not lift anything heavy and strain my chest wall, I turned down their latest offer.

Around 3 p.m. a judge became available to begin the retrial immediately and the case was being heard in another of the many modern courtrooms in which I knew I would feel very uncomfortable; I would not be as far away from Mr Lynch as I would have liked. I steeled myself for it because no matter how I felt physically I was going to hold my head up high in front of him and his representatives if it was the last thing I was capable of doing on this earth.

It transpired that the trial judge turned out to be none other than Mr Justice Kearns, the judge who had Mr Lynch previously removed from court by the Gardaí. One might say having him as the trial judge was an advantage to me but I did not believe so. In fact, I felt a frisson of apprehension pass through my mind and it began to gather momentum and run away with itself. What if Judge Kearns now had to show not only was he not biased against Mr Lynch but also that he had to be seen not to be so? What if I won and the same thing happened all over again?

I did not think my rights had been protected during this litigation process and I suffered grave consequences. How on earth could I trust the judiciary now? I knew going through another trial with these fears would cause great havoc with my health and I had no funds left if history repeated itself.

I knew my legal team had the preponderance of evidence stacked against Mr Lynch and he, in the end, was unable to find support. If this had been a case about any other issue, I knew my mind would hold strong but it wasn't; it was for severe personal injuries and the last thing I wanted was for my health to relapse.

Now that I had no faith in the judiciary I ran scared; the stress of it all could set me back. Judge Kearns opened the proceedings but there was only sufficient time, thankfully, for the barristers to present their opening arguments. I was so relieved I did not have to testify that late afternoon. In the morning I would be fresh, able and willing and I needed the evening to prepare.

Once my father and I left the Four Courts that afternoon, we walked up the quays and partook of a very leisurely and substantial meal and discussed the day's events. The one thing we agreed on was that the insurers definitely wanted to settle. When we arrived home, I asked my friends not to come to see me that evening because I was by then physically and emotionally drained and needed to do some serious thinking. Also, I wanted to retire to bed early to take the pressure off my upper body. I estimated that the following day would be the most important and crucial since the supreme court hearing.

As dawn approached the following morning, I had my mind almost made up. I arose to give myself enough time to get specially groomed because I wanted to show Mr Lynch and his team I was ready, confident and undeterred even though I felt like I was about to collapse. After consuming our breakfast, my father and I were both atypically silent going for our coffee.

When we arrived in the Round Hall we were ushered again into the same consultation room, waiting for the trial to recommence. After some considerable time Michael joined us and we walked up the stairs into the passageway where the courtroom was situated. Inside the double doors was a long bench facing down the length of the corridor on which we seated ourselves. At the far end of the corridor, beside more double doors, people I had not seen before were in serious discussion and I assumed they were representatives of Arthur Cox & Co. and the MDU. There was no sign of Mr Lynch and if negotiations were going on I imagine he wanted to keep a low profile. I had reached a decision and I advised my team I would try and settle.

It soon became very clear to me, however, that the word 'negotiation' was a complete misnomer and the MDU were not going to budge one cent. There were more patients suing Mr Lynch, I knew, as he had 'stacks' of claims against him. I tried to up the award to another fifty thousand and even twenty but to no avail. I could have tried bluffing but I was not a poker player and what if it backfired? My health was too important to me.

I was as certain as anyone could be, having gone through a trial knowing all the lies and spurious stories Mr Lynch had concocted and given in evidence, that he would be proved negligent again. How could I possibly lose? But I never expected either that he would secure a retrial in his appeal and yet that is exactly what happened. Since I do not know the workings of the supreme court and had to bow to their decision, on a personal level I believe Judge Johnson did hear and see the truth of it all and I was constantly astonished and awed by his remarkable memory and by the clarity of his understanding of Mr Lynch and the surgery he performed.

Even though the supreme court hung the blame for the retrial securely around his neck and punished me severely with the consequences, I could not then and I cannot now lay the blame at his door from my own personal perspective. I had to accept my fate but logically I could not understand why I was being punished. I could not again place my life in the hands of the judiciary; I could not risk it.

Before I made my final decision, I double-checked with Michael if Mr Lynch's representatives had approached him about my signing a 'gagging' clause. If they insisted on it I would absolutely refuse to sign anything that would prevent me from speaking out about the whole sordid saga. But they had not even mentioned it to him; who knows why? Perhaps because the case had already been in the public domain? However, there was one major thing I had to worry about; I could not afford to pay Mr Lynch's one hundred and nine thousand euro and it really rankled me. In addition, that I had to pay the man who destroyed my life without displaying one ounce of regret or empathy.

As I was mulling over my options I was suddenly struck with another brainwave and I immediately made my decision. I informed Michael I would accept the settlement offer on the condition that Mr Lynch paid his own appeal costs. He hurried off to give my ultimatum and as I was staring down the corridor at Mr Lynch's representatives, he suddenly appeared and they became entrenched in serious discussion.

I knew if Mr Lynch agreed to pay his appeal costs out of his own pocket, it would be the most definitive proof and acknowledgement of his negligence in my view. In the end, it did not take long and Michael returned to tell me the news that he had agreed and I was not in the least surprised. I knew I was letting him off the hook with no official count of medical negligence against him but I also knew he had retired and could injure no one else.

At the time, I really should have asked that Mr Lynch personally pay me for, at least, my non-reimbursable expenses for the first trial, almost thirty thousand euro, and all my out-of-pocket expenses due to his dastardly surgery. Not to mention my loss of earnings to date I thought in hindsight, rather a little too late.

Unfortunately for Mr Lynch, the next thing that happened could never have been planned and since I received no justice in the courts of law, I felt at this point I was bestowed with a kind of natural justice. What no one realised was that the double doors at the far end of the corridor were locked, preventing Mr Lynch from sneaking out. Even though I was some distance away, my eyesight was good enough to watch him frantically making attempts to open them and then the shock when he realised he could not escape that way. At the most crucial and unexpected time fate can intervene and that old adage 'you reap what you sow' certainly proved true.

Hurriedly, knowing he would have to pass me at the opposite end of the corridor, he began to walk 'The Green Mile' and this time with his head bowed. All I could do was sit there and stare at him with no expression on my face. No, unlike Mr Lynch, I did not smirk or gloat; I was going to maintain my dignity.

But I do remember thinking how high his head was and his appalling behaviour after the supreme court ruling and if I had been very mean of spirit I could have gone out and found the same photographer he had pointed me out to. But I was not even tempted to. I was just glad that I had never stooped as low as him and all that prancing and viciousness after the appeal came back to haunt him. That old cliché, 'Do not count your chickens…' was certainly apt.

As he came further towards me I felt he was now embarrassed by his ugly display of rancour on that fateful day when the supreme court gave him a retrial. But then again, perhaps it did not bother him in the slightest. As he reached me he bowed his head even further with his chin close to his chest and he was afraid to look up to see if he had reached the end of the corridor. My eyes followed him as he passed me but it was not over yet; he still had my father and others who were sitting a little further up near the doors to pass by. It was during those minutes I felt, for the first time, great contentment.

After he had bolted through the double doors of the corridor everyone filed into the courtroom and when Judge Kearns reconvened the trial he was informed by Mr Lynch's barrister, Mr Nugent, that the case had been settled and the terms of the settlement. He approved the agreements and announced that he was happy that it was finally over.

Well, I thought, all the shenanigans should never have happened in the first place but I wonder could Mr Lynch ever be controlled. As we left the courtroom the strangest feeling overcame me. There I was, having practically lived in the court system since November 2001 and then in a split second it was all over. It was a great shock to the system and I did not know how to handle it; I was battle weary. This was finality; I never had to come here again and I could not quite believe that I had survived it.

All I could think of doing was to give all my legal team, Michael, Denis and Karen grateful and sincere hugs because I was speechless. It is difficult to comprehend or convey how I felt because throughout the months and years the wheels had turned slowly and then in the flick of an eyelash they ground to a halt.

Something Denis said to me then will remain with me for the remainder of my life and made it all seem worthwhile. As I was giving him a hug I said, 'Thank you for being so nice to me,' and he replied, 'Well, it was easy to be nice to you, Christine.' And it was then that I really believed I had kept my dignity throughout the entire litigious process, even when things turned nasty, eerie and ugly.

It was during those occasions that I was so thankful I had such a professional and competent legal team and counsel. I was very fortunate I had had a trial judge, Mr Richard Johnson, who was meticulous in his understanding of the case and his observations were completely objective. In addition, he had to put up with the whims of Mr Lynch who refused to follow instructions and basically ignored him. He was the surgeon, the barrister and, in my opinion, he probably thought he was the judge as well.

Unfortunately very few people knew the retrial had commenced and was settled. That day, because we were away from the Round Hall and everything happened so quickly in the end, there were no photographers or people to film its conclusion. I was very disappointed because I wanted to publicly acknowledge my team's efforts on my behalf and also stress the horrific, and for many patients who are severely injured through medical negligence, and unendurable court procedures as there is no other avenue for them.

There was only a very brief paragraph in the papers the following day stating that the case had been settled. It had felt really strange extending my goodbyes to Denis and Karen on that final day. After Michael told me he would be in contact and left, we all went to lunch and lingered for some time. For a while I had to relish the thought that it is only when people take risks and speak up that systems get changed and rogues are weeded out. But it means supernumerary suffering.

Then, on the 10th of March 2004, Michael told me the MDU had paid the award but he had to send approximately nineteen thousand euro to the VHI and retain over eight thousand euro more for additional legal disbursements for the retrial. And even to the end all Mr Lynch had done was to laud himself, in his opinion, as being the most experienced VATS surgeon in the country and admired the scars he had inflicted on my body.

I could not believe how quickly Michael forwarded the cheque to me having become so used to delays and at that point I really needed some funds. I had no clue as to the fees I owed to Michael and counsel but I am certain it would have left me worse off than before the litigation commenced. Then, to my astonishment when I read his letter with shaking hands, they had decided to waive the fees. 'In the circumstances that have arisen in this case, which are practically unique, both myself and counsel were happy to make this gesture in an effort to secure a just settlement for you.' It was unbelievable that he called what he, Denis and Karen forfeited, a 'gesture'. The most understated word in the English language attributed to my case. This was no 'gesture', it was my life.

There were just no words to describe how I felt at that moment; there are no words I could ever think of to adequately and properly describe what was done for me on my behalf. I knew my team was very competent, professional and compassionate towards their clients but this 'gesture', as Michael called it was uniquely honourable. How incredible it was. And all my witnesses and people who know me, including my own doctors have been impressed by not only their competence but also struck by their humanity.

At the other end of the spectrum, when I thought I knew every aspect of Mr Lynch's character, his threatening behaviour and after hearing his spurious defence, I was in store for a further startling revelation that finally infuriated me.

Chapter Twenty-Six

I knew something was dreadfully wrong. I was confused and bewildered in a semi-conscious state. And then it came to me. Of course, I am in a hospital bed and what I had been petrified about had not happened. That was it; I was not screaming. I felt very sore but that was normal post-operative discomfort. No one can quite understand the enormous relief I felt.

It was the 8th of December 2006 more than a decade since the trauma, pain and fearful challenge changed my life forever and almost three years since the end of the litigation process. I had finally found the courage to have the spinal cord stimulator implanted. Having exhausted my will power, no further rehabilitation exercises or wishful thinking could cure my condition. That dreadful surgery had cast a very long shadow.

Once the litigation process was over and my mind began to recover from the onslaught of the trials, I had to begin thinking about what the future had in store for me. This was reality, given the beastly damage to the nerves in my chest wall, along with my other symptoms. I kept to my physiotherapy regime and I was still at the stage when I thought mind could overcome matter and I was going to keep on that course for another while longer.

I caught up again with the world of academia to try to switch my mind off the constant stinging and throbbing pain to somehow trick my brain. I kept on hoping that if somehow a cure could be found I would at least be up-to-date with the business world and return to my previous wonderful career.

On the 26th of July 2006, I went to see Dr O'Keeffe and put my forehead down on his desk. As I finally looked up at him, I confessed that without intervention I had accepted that the fear of not being able to cope with the pain any longer had far surpassed the fear of having the spinal cord stimulator inserted. He had been right all along; I was never going to be 'cured'. But who knows what scientific developments may occur in the future? I was getting older and had less resilience.

I sincerely believe Dr O'Keeffe was very happy and relieved for my sake that I had finally overcome my dread of further surgery and he immediately sprang into action. Obviously, there was no guarantee the technology would ease my symptoms but it was the only scientific method available at the time that might give me some chance.

While I was in his office, we briefly referred to the trial and I told him that not only had Mr Lynch threatened to destroy his practice but that Dr Duignan had been at the receiving end of his intimidation in addition and about which he had testified in court. I was completely unprepared yet again for another appalling revelation. It transpired that Mr Lynch had returned to Dr O'Keeffe a second time and tried to persuade him to change his evidence. I was stunned and shook my head in disgust. I was now seething with anger that a person as incorrigible as Mr Lynch could get away with what I can only consider perpetrating illegal actions. In addition, while I was waiting for approval to have the surgery, I was in trepidation at the thought of going back into the same hospital to revisit the scene of the crime that held such horrific memories for me.

When I was finally admitted for the surgery, I remember I was wheeled down to the theatre and I was barely through the doors when I was anaesthetised. Dr O'Keeffe had said to me afterwards that I had been through enough traumas without adding to them and I can honestly say he did everything to ease my mind. He knew my anxiety was genuine.

The procedure involved using keyhole methods of surgery, implanting a protected battery under the skin in my abdomen, running leads up internally to my chest wall and suturing the wires connected to the leads at the exact sites of the nerve damage. These wires create a magnetic field that convert nerve pain into a different kind of sensation.

Two days after coming round from the surgery the company technician came to see me and gave me the equipment. I began to think of myself as the bionic woman. I remained in hospital for five nights so Dr O'Keeffe could monitor the effect of the stimulator, even though I was up and walking around the day following the surgery. I thought back to 1996 when I should have ended up intact and suffering only from normal post-operative soreness. Then, when the padding was eventually removed, I stood rigid and stared in the mirror. I had additional scars in my ribs and old wounds had been opened up. If the scars were joined up I would have looked like a patchwork quilt, I mused.

Once Dr O'Keeffe was satisfied I could manage the complicated equipment over the Christmas holiday season, I was discharged. I immediately managed to achieve a lower level of pain and reduce the number of massive flare-ups I often had to endure. I devoured the thick instruction manual in order to achieve the maximum efficiency out of the system. Although the tingling sensation was very strange, I adjusted to it eventually. When the pain increased from time to time, I could only manage to turn up the intensity of the stimulator to a certain level because I would experience a stinging feeling. It did take some effort to become comfortable with its use but as time moved on I became confident that I was using it properly.

Chronic pain seems to be one of the most common and debilitating conditions there is. During the years after the surgery when I was sitting in Dr O'Keeffe's waiting room, scores of people would be waiting hours to see him; many of them were in agony and some angry, others seriously depressed and despondent and everyone hoping that even one of the various treatments available would ease their suffering. I sat with them, not engaging in the various conversations because, rather than talk about my own condition, I wanted to keep my mind off of it. However, I could not help hearing what patients were saying and it always depressed me knowing about the surgical mishaps and negligence, car accidents, and the various other diseases and injuries people are afflicted with. Those in wheelchairs, on walking sticks with pain lines etched on their faces and many with a need to talk, to get some comfort from others in the same condition.

The effects on patients' and their families' lives are devastating. Lives left broken and dreams never to be realised. And no one expects a cure because those who suffer from chronic pain, whatever the cause, know that if they have suffered for a number of years, it is highly likely they will continue to do so. This kind of pain can cause severe and irreparable damage, both physically and mentally. The latest statistics I received from Dr O'Keeffe in relation to chronic pain were baffling. It is estimated that 1.5 billion people in the world suffer from it; 115 million in the US; 200 million in Europe and 1.5 million in Ireland; staggering numbers. The cost in the US has reached up to 3 trillion dollars and in Ireland 6½ billion euro. This chronic pain syndrome should be urgently highlighted.

Unfortunately for me, in early 2008, one of the wires that was sutured to the site of my worst pain migrated and it put me back into my previous situation, one I had never wished to and could not revisit. I had been warned prior to the operation that there was a thirty per cent chance this could occur and I had to wait until October the 31st to have the wire repositioned.

I was over my fear, however, of further surgery and had again no ill effects from the operation. Because Dr O'Keeffe was my surgeon I overcame the terror of putting my life in someone else's hands. Even the minutest of improvement is worth an entire fortune; to get a break in constant, crucifying pain is incalculable. Unless one suffers from it, it is extremely difficult to explain to others its torment and agony. It is rather like raw, absolute and permanent grief one has to endure to understand its devastation.

To my utter disappointment the entire system failed after another six months and so I was knocked back again into a misery that I could not now tolerate. Having known what it was like to get some relief from a constant stretching of the nerves, it was intolerable to accept that it was taken away from me. Dr O'Keeffe decided he would remove the old system and implant a state of the art one from Medtronics.

I was well over a year waiting for the surgery and he advised me I could have it done on Christmas Eve. I felt it would be the most remarkable, treasured and irreplaceable gift I had ever or would ever receive at Christmas but alas it was not to happen and I was really despondent. Due to a winter vomiting bug, all elective surgeries were cancelled, and when April of 2010 arrived, when I was exhausted and could endure the pain no longer, I finally collapsed and spent two nights on a trolley in the A&E department, it was so crowded, and I went from there straight to theatre.

Dr O'Keeffe spent considerable time checking and rechecking the sites of entry with me. The leads and wires had to be placed and sutured with considerable precision. I was anaesthetised then and when I woke up, apart from being extremely sore and could barely move, again nothing untoward had happened to me. More entries had been made through my ribs and old wounds had to be reused and old scars were opened up again.

Although I was in hospital for five days and initially found it difficult to move, it was absolute paradise compared to what I suffered in 1996. Following some adjustment to the programming of the system after I was discharged, and having studied the accompanying manual in minute detail again, I got it working to its maximum efficiency. It takes five hours every third day to give the battery a total recharge because the system has to be working continuously, without interruption. Some people with chronic pain experience it with intermittent breaks but mine was absolute.

My chest wall still seizes up from time to time because my physical structure had been so damaged that I could never, with the greatest will in the world, reconstruct it like it had been prior to 1996. My hand still does not function properly and continues to gnarl up. I never regained the ability to play my precious piano to the same level again and I slowly let it fade from my life.

When I was slowly recovering from the operation at home, a good friend picked me up in her car one day and brought me to lunch in a restaurant on the main street of Sandycove, a seaside village southeast of Dublin city. After a sumptuous and indolent meal, we left the restaurant and began strolling down towards the side street where her car was parked. I was wearing black knee-high boots and a black belted woollen coat that had a high ruche collar up to my chin. My hair had grown considerably longer since the trial, with waves framing my face so only my features were visible. I had my arms folded across my chest wall and used my handbag to support it. I was still extremely sore and weak but I knew it was only temporary.

Then, much to my astonishment, who turned the corner, walking briskly in our direction? None other than Mr Lynch. I was completely taken aback and anxious as it was the first time I had set eyes on him since the day of the legal settlement. I put my hand furtively to my forehead and exclaimed to my friend, 'Oh dear Lord, look who is coming.' I was very startled to say the least. She did not remember him but I certainly did; how would I ever forget that face looming over me in the hospital bed and those terrifying eyes.

As he came closer I noticed he was dressed in casual clothing and the only change I detected was that his white hair was longer. I did not know whether he would recognise me I was so well covered. Just in case, however, I moved to the inside of the footpath. As he was about to pass by I took a furtive glance at him and he locked eyes with mine; there was not a hint of recognition in them.

What was difficult to stomach was that there was I having had further surgery after fourteen years, holding up my chest wall and connected to a system I would have to use for the remainder of my life. I would continue to face surgery to change the battery and the insertion of new systems as technology developed.

And there was Mr Lynch, seemingly in the best of health and fitness and probably living out his retirement with very comfortable means. I, however, had lost everything and was a substantial way from retirement age having to fork out constant sums from my award to keep going and it was not going to last long.

I was obviously very concerned and always wondered if Mr Lynch had lied to other patients and their families and how many of his patients were left seriously debilitated or even died during or after his operations. As he testified himself, he had two stacks of claims against him. If his conversion rate, for my 'small kind of case' that only required a 'simple repair' from VATS to open thoracic surgery was thirteen per cent higher than the international average, what was his failure rate for more serious conditions?

After a high court trial, a Supreme Court Appeal and the commencement of another, I still have no definitive answers for what happened to me on that theatre table. Between Mr Lynch's lies, spurious stories, threats, intimidation and tampering with my witnesses, his attempted assault on my person and perjury, he weaved a complicated web and I will never know the truth. Mine is not the only case. The high court has now developed a website, www.courts.ie, that contains litigious information and there are copious cases against Mr Lynch.

What really bothered and upset me, when reviewing the cases against Mr Lynch, the CEO of St. Vincent's Hospital, Mr Nicholas Jermyn was listed as co-defender in every case except mine because I had not sued the hospital. Since he knew of all these cases, why and how could the hospital not have taken steps to prevent Mr Lynch from injuring more people? After all, there are grievance and disciplinary procedures in place in the consultants' contract to deal with these issues.

If they had tried and obviously did not succeed, my overwhelming opinion is that I should have the right to have any operation performed on me both video- and audio-recorded. I may not wish to see it but if anything untoward ever happened again, it is there for an independent body to review.

As all these thoughts were racing through my mind, my friend and I reached the corner and, as I was about to take a step forward into the next stage of my precarious future, I turned around for a last glimpse, I hoped, of Mr Lynch. As he purposely and sprightly entered a nearby shop, the only thing I could feel, as if it were true, was that long-time used cliché, 'You got away with murder.'

Mr Lynch died on the 22nd of March 2018, 'peacefully'. I believe he was in his eighties. Many people asked me what my reaction to his death had been and I only felt numbness. I believe that sometime after all the litigation ended, he began to lecture in Dublin City University while I was continuously struggling to improve the quality of my life. I can only imagine afterwards that he left behind all his broken promises, lifelong injuries and perhaps even deaths without any remorse whatsoever and continued to live a lifestyle he was used to.

However, aside from the brutal damage to my body and Mr Lynch's sometimes-outrageous behaviour during the entire long drawn-out litigation process, the one life-enhancing trait he never succeeded in destroying was my spirit. In the year 2013, three years since the last spinal cord stimulator was implanted, I regained some quality of life and breaks in unbearable pain.

No, I could never work again. No, I could never perform all the active pursuits I so enjoyed before that surgery. No, my hand never regained its full function and no, none of my personal aspirations were ever fulfilled. But I always strongly, and consistently hoped that one day, even though I will never be cured, a fact that took a considerable number of years for me to accept, I would experience regular breaks in agonising pain, even though I have to constantly live with all the electronic paraphernalia on a daily basis. I have that insatiable belief that my spirit will win out in the end.

Those remarkable scientists are developing technology at such a speedy and creative pace that one day I may be selected as a candidate for an even more effective stimulator and one that is easier to use. Whether and when it will happen is unknown but when one's life has been stripped bare, the only inherently positive attributes to cling on to are hope and willpower.

Chapter Twenty-Seven

I was very happy after Mr Lynch retired from the public hospital when the trial was in progress because he could do no further damage to patients. But even though he had retired from the public hospital and began to work for DCU, I was really worried and feared for any influential negatives his input may have had on students. Who else would get away with it? I have so many regrets that my physical condition had prevented me from pursuing the second trial but, alas, there was nothing I could do except write about the horrid and tragic saga and perhaps assist in changing the law in Ireland that would require doctors and hospitals to own up when there is either a mistake or medical negligence.

I am a member of an organisation called the Medical Injuries Alliance (MIA) that is trying, in conjunction with the UK, to accomplish exactly that. However, given how long that would take, in the meantime countless patients may suffer and/or die. I would be very surprised even after all these years, if there were no more rogue surgeons in the hospital system.

I remember after the trials had concluded I met a friend of a friend and he exclaimed to me, 'The last time I saw you, Christine, you were on television.'

'Oh that,' I replied, downplaying it. I should not have been surprised but then he told me his mother was very grateful to me and I could not understand why. I had never met her. Then he announced, referring to Mr Lynch, 'He butchered my father and then he died.' I had had no idea the effect of taking Mr Lynch to trial had on those who had suffered at his hands.

During the years after the stimulator had been replaced, although I had to forfeit a large salary, I came to the realisation that for many years I had been working far too hard. I was always one, along with my career friends, who put far too much pressure on ourselves. People might say that we had a great work ethic or were very diligent and conscientious, working long hours and taking work home became a regular habit.

Yet, what were we losing out on? I have discovered that there are copious pastimes that do not require physical strain but enhance my life and it is now the opportunity to know what time flexibility actually means. I began to savour small things. I can take day by day, whatever way I choose and I have total control over my own life apart from when pain dictates it. More time to spend with friends, time to create a garden, not by myself of course but I selected the flowering shrubs and watch them grow and no murder was committed in the process of its creation, much to my surprise.

I can maintain my structure and flexibility by attending the gym to keep strong at my own pace. Time spent in hospital having had so many procedures and constant visits to Drs O'Keeffe and Duignan were minimised. All those clichés such as, 'smell the roses', 'take it step by step', 'the past is gone and the future will take care of itself' and 'what matters is the present' have now influenced the way I live. The big change came in my vocabulary. I altered the words, 'I have to' to 'I want to'.

Throughout the years, my birthday and Christmas never passed without contact from Edward; he had remained a bachelor but I had moved on and the trust was gone.

Besides my health, there was a more important issue that was deeply troubling me. While I regularly and frequently went home to see my parents, I became very worried and concerned about my father's deterioration as he was frequently passing out. For about five years beforehand, I became very fearful about what my life would be like without him. All my life I loved him unconditionally.

When his hip gave way and he was in dreadful, chronic pain and then became depressed because he could not get out of his bed; it was almost as if I was feeling it too. He told me that until then he never realised what I had gone through for so many years but now he definitely understood. I pulled out all the stops and he had a new hip and rehabilitation within six months.

He could hardly believe he was no longer in excruciating pain. Moreover, contrary to what Mr Lynch said in court, that there is no such thing as a 'perfect' operation, he was, as usual, wrong. My father's surgeon performed what he had promised to deliver in Cappagh Hospital and he was quite brilliant.

I decided then to move from Dublin to within a stone's throw from my parents in case they needed assistance and to be close at hand if they became ill and/or had to go to hospital. When I was deciding this, I realised that the funds I received from the award were dwindling as the bottom fell out of interest rates so the move would also benefit me financially. I could rent out my apartment for income.

It was May 2014 when I made the move, joined the gym and developed many further interests. I did not have the fear of wondering how I would fill my time and I realised I had a keen interest in going to auctions and developing an interest in antiques. Anything that would not put a strain on my chest wall.

As time passed, it would not be long before I had to cope with my father's death and I knew I would be utterly devastated as we were so close. I was really looking forward to seeing more of him. Unfortunately, I did not get as much time as I thought. Towards the end of December 2015, I spent four hours in the kitchen with him and he was speaking, as if it was his last confession and he poured his heart out.

My instincts were going berserk as they warned me that he was nearing the end. He was too calm, he looked too well and there was a serenity about him I had never seen before. He had much to get off his chest and he and I could always have a proper conversation as well as banter. I was his only daughter.

After four hours, when he became tired, I said I would leave and he appeared content as he walked me to my car. I was always rather tactile but this time I threw my arms around him for ages not wanting to let go and gave him a big kiss on his forehead and said 'goodnight pops'. Strange, I had never called him that before.

He gave me his usual wide smile and his eyes were glowing. I knew this was the last time I would ever again be able to speak with him and my heart lurched but I remained calm so he would not suspect anything.

A few days later, he had his final collapse at home and was unconscious; I knew he was dying. When I reached the hospital, his breathing was dreadful but I grasped his hand as he often held mine when I was very ill and I kept speaking to him in his right ear. I told him who was at his bedside and after a long while he tried to move the hand I was holding towards my mother. Then it stopped and it was his final sign of life.

A room became available, and he was transferred. I remained sitting on a chair being vigilant beside him, still holding his hand and stroking his arm, still speaking to him in his ear. When the rest of the family went home to get some rest, I could not move, I just could not leave him on his own as he could have gone at any moment. I told him I always loved him and I know that he loved me and I begged him to let go, that everything was all right and not to suffer any longer.

When I became very sleepy, I placed a pillow against his chest and still holding onto him, I fell into oblivion and when I woke up I realised it had been the best sleep I had ever had. Just my father and I. Around 7 a.m., the nurse came in and asked me if I was alone. She said that I should not have to cope on my own. I said 'Oh Lisa, this is wonderful, so peaceful, and silent,' (apart from his laboured breathing) and I could keep talking to him with no one else listening. It could not have been better; it could not have been planned.

He died that day, 28th of December 2015 and, as I looked at him, I could hear him drawing his last breath. As his muscles settled, his whole head and face had become thinner and it was as if I was looking at my grandfather. After his death I was raw with grief. I was relieved when I could cry bucket loads but sometimes I would curl up and never wanted to move or see people, but I eventually did.

Little did I know that at this period of grief, I would receive enormous and constant support. Even if I was distraught, friends would get me up and out and there was always someone who would just listen and be a presence. My friends were there throughout all of the stages of the grief I endured.

Even after everything that had devastated me physically and the supernumerary traumas of having to go through adversarial court situations, nothing, but nothing fazed me emotionally as the passing of my beloved father. I dwelt on the fact that he no longer suffered but I was broken.

However, I like to think that he had a hand in sending me this gorgeous one-year-old cat that had been cruelly abandoned and had become feral. He kept appearing at my window and one day when he showed up, he had bitten off more than he could chew. A rat had taught him a harsh lesson. Half his face had an abscess and his mouth was cut so I put him in the car and took him to the vet for surgery.

Although he knows the territory, I did not have the heart not to adopt him. Even though I have looked after him, he gave me much more. A live and undemanding presence when I curled up and laughter when he got up to his old tricks. He was ever so polite and neighbours told me he certainly came to the right house but I was by far the lucky one. I had never ever thought of owning a cat but at least he is independent. The timing of his arrival and my father's passing even if coincidental, I like to think he is still looking out for me.

I never tried to mask the grief; I knew I would have to deal with it in its entirety and all the different stages head on but now I love to think about my father and remember all the great times we had together and his compassion for a long time after that surgery. I can only now listen to the CDs of his sonorous voice and at last I am able to place his photograph next to my grandfather's on my piano.

I had been seeing Dr O'Keeffe every six months since the last system was implanted but then at the beginning of 2017 the battery began to fail. I had to recharge it all the time although I did get a good seven years out of it. As he always did, he sent a letter to the VHI promptly to get approval for changing the battery and when the letter arrived, I was subdued to note that there was a different doctor's name in the letter who would be performing the surgery. It informed me that the operation would take place in St. Francis Hospital in Mullingar in October 2018.

I was very puzzled about this so when I contacted Dr O'Keeffe's secretary, she informed me that he would be performing the surgery but he was also training a new colleague in his special techniques. That was such a relief. After I was admitted, I met Dr O'Keeffe first and he advised me that he was training some pain specialists but he always had it in mind that when he completely retired, I would be looked after. Although I never relayed my fears to him about what would happen to me once he retired or if anything untoward happened to him but I need not have worried because he was already a step in front.

When his colleague came to see me to ask some questions, I think he was taken aback. He said I looked so well. Obviously, I informed him I am not an ill person, that I suffer from unnatural causes and always keep myself healthy. He explained the surgery properly and told me that sometimes the leads become permanently stuck to the battery and in that case the entire system would have to be removed and another inserted. I had never thought of this side effect but, to be truthful, I was not nervous once I knew Dr O'Keeffe would be performing it with his colleague's assistance.

I thought the operation would be painless but it was much more sore than I thought. I remained in the hospital until the following day and Dr

O'Keeffe informed me that I would be very uncomfortable for a while and not to do anything physical, e.g. gym exercises. After I recovered, the pain subsided and a very neat and thorough job had been performed. I am hoping I can get ten years out of this new battery.

So now, I live on with minute worries subconsciously and who knows what the scientists will have developed by the time I require another battery or, for that matter, a new system. I do not know how many surgeons are out there with the mentality of Mr Lynch with inadequate skills. The system seems to have allowed them to continue unabated. I hope it has improved because everyone has a health problem or knows someone who has suffered at the hands of some doctors. I will never understand, when doctors have well-covered insurance, why they cannot just own up and not put patients like me through such supernumerary hell with the courts.

In the end, I did not get any answers. Mr Lynch lied in court, the supreme court landed me with his costs and my own, and I received no justice unless one calls a meagre sum of money justice. The meticulous Judge Johnson's verdict was undone.

However, I do not dwell on the past; self-pity does no good. I have rearranged my present and future to gain as much out of life as I can. It may not be what I had aspired to before that surgery but there are so many things one can replace them with. In addition, with the rapid advances in technology I believe that it can have a beneficial effect on all those who suffer incessantly. I know I was extremely fortunate to have attracted the right professionals who did everything they could to restore a quality of life I can live with.

All my friends stuck with me through thick and thin. They always said to me, 'Christine, no matter what happens to you, you always land on your feet.' That is true as I was always a survivor. The surgery in 1996 certainly proved that and after all these years, when all is said and done, I still believe 'I was born under a lucky star'. But just in case I desperately need a back up, perhaps Brutus, my special cat, can be persuaded to donate a few of his precious nine lives.

Available worldwide from
Amazon and all good bookstores

A True Jeopardy Press Publication

Printed in Poland
by Amazon Fulfillment
Poland Sp. z o.o., Wrocław

59037395R00155